Lawyer
Manley

FIRST
TIME UP

Manley — the legal lion. He put the same energy, concentration and application into every case he handled, regardless of its importance or who was involved

Lawyer Manley

FIRST TIME UP

Jackie Ranston

The Press University of the West Indies

Barbados • Jamaica • Trinidad and Tobago

The Press University of the West Indies
1A Aqueduct Flats Mona
Kingston 7 Jamaica

ISBN 976-640-081-4
ISBN 976-640-082-2 (pbk.)

03 02 01 00 99   5 4 3 2 01
CATALOGUING IN PUBLICATION DATA

Ranston, Jackie.
   Lawyer Manley / Jackie Ranston

   p. cm.

   Contents: v. 1. First time up
   Includes bibliographical references and index.

   ISBN 976-640-081-4
   ISBN 976-640-082-2 (pbk.)

   1. Manley, Norman Washington, 1893–1969
   2. Lawyers – Jamaica – Biography.
   3. Politicians – Jamaica – Biography.
   4. Jamaica – Biography. I. Title.

   F1886. M34 R36 1998   972.92

Cover illustration an adaptation of 'At the Bar – Mr N.W. Manley' as seen through the eyes of *Gleaner* cartoonist, Cliff Tyrell, 11 December 1926.

Text and cover design by Dennis Ranston
Text set in Classic Garmond 10.5 pt

To Wayne Brown

CONTENTS

LIST OF ILLUSTRATIONS

TABLE OF CASES

FOREWORD

Norman Manley's career in the law was distinguished from the start. His painstaking and thorough research into every aspect of his cases, his meticulous analysis of all the relevant factors, his knowledge of human nature and his passion for the idea of the law all combined to make him a most complete and formidable advocate.

This book deals with the beginning of Manley's career, as a junior, accepting cases which many other lawyers might consider hopeless. As this book makes clear, Manley was not content to simply accept assignments, he embraced the causes of his clients with passion and dedication, becoming as it were, a detective himself, to ferret out the facts and to reconstruct as best he could, the real stories behind the bald facts of the tragedies in which his clients were involved.

It was this passion for the truth and the determination to arrive at it which lent so much drama to the cases in which he was involved. This was so, whether he was assigned by the Crown to defend a poor person, or whether he had been engaged to represent the interests of wealthy clients. Whoever his clients were, rich or poor, they could have no more able defender than N. W. Manley. Within three years of his entering into practice the *Gleaner* wrote: "Mr Manley must be congratulated as a barrister on the persistent and brilliant fight he has made for the liberty as well as the life of Louise Walker . . . in this instance we must remember that he was employed by the Crown itself to defend the woman and the fees attached to such a function are fixed. In a private case his remuneration would probably have been three or four times as much . . . but if his remuneration has been ten times as much he could not have worked harder, more conscientiously, more brilliantly . . ."

And again: "He won the confidence and admiration of the solicitors . . . because they recognized in him a lawyer learned in the law, a man honest in his presentation of a case and an effective but eminently courteous cross-examiner."

If Manley's stature was high outside the courtroom, it was at least as high inside. Mr Justice Adrian Clarke told the accused in the Alexander murder case: "If genius is an infinite capacity for taking pains, you have been defended by a genius." Later, Mr Justice Sellars told Manley in an English court in 1946: "I would express the pleasure it has been in the court and the satisfaction the prisoner must have experienced, to have you appear in this case."

Manley's learning and versatility were epitomized in the Vicks trade mark case in 1951, when the Lord Chancellor described his submissions as ". . . the best argument I have ever heard in a trade mark case".

For more than half his legal career, Manley was concurrently engaged on the case of Jamaica — leading the country's struggle to be independent and master of its own affairs. In the decade of the Thirties he had convinced the United Fruit Company to pay a voluntary cess to a Jamaican non-governmental organization, Jamaica Welfare. Under Manley's direction, Jamaica Welfare began the groundbreaking and vital work of community development in Jamaica. Manley's legal work was to be subordinated — at great personal sacrifice — to the major effort of his life, securing the independence of Jamaica and earning for him the popular title, 'Father of the Nation'.

Manley is in every sense, monumental. His achievements were so far-reaching and so various that it is no doubt a little intimidating to attempt the task of placing him and his work in their proper historical perspective. For this reason, very little has so far been done. But it is work that must be done. Manley is too important to the law, to the politics and culture of Jamaica and the Caribbean, to remain mainly a figure of myth and legend. This book is important in that it is the first attempt to document his legal career. After documentation will come analysis and it is to be hoped that this work, of which this volume is only the first part, will provoke more interest in attempting to define Manley's role more clearly in the great history he did so much to create.

Vivian O. Blake, OJ, QC

PREFACE

In 1962, Norman Manley himself had the idea of writing a book on his court cases. From the notes he left behind, it is interesting to see that of all the cases he conducted during thirty-three years of active practice, he chose to start with the Spalding murder trial: a case which had tormented him from start to finish as a fledgling lawyer in 1924 (see Vol. One, p. 103). Manley wrote a few sample pages, but never quite settled down to it. The attempt was thrown aside, never to be taken up again.[1]

For my part, I began researching Manley's law career as back-up material for Edna Manley's biography.[2] In 1972, I met Wayne Brown, the Trinidadian poet and writer who was in Jamaica working, initially, on a survey of the post-1938 development of the arts in Jamaica and Edna Manley's relationship to it. His perspective changed when Edna turned over to him a number of filing cabinets and cardboard boxes filled with letters, diaries and other memorabilia. The letters, of which there were nearly 2,000, introduced to a far greater extent than Wayne had envisaged, the figure of her husband, Norman. As Wayne's emphasis shifted towards a biography, he asked if I would assist him with researching background material. It resulted in my ploughing through some 17,000 copies of the *Gleaner* from 1922 to 1970, in addition to numerous other references which included both Norman and Edna Manley's diaries, letters, and Basil McFarlane's tape recorded interviews with Manley before his death.

As Wayne pruned and pulled apart my notes and reminded me that research was often a thankless task, I gathered the scattered remains and filed my notes on Manley's legal life — basically one-liners, viz., *N in Court* followed by the date. Why? I was intrigued. Everyone knew Manley the politician; few knew Manley the lawyer.

During the Norman Manley era, the *Gleaner* published verbatim accounts of the proceedings in both the upper and lower courts on a daily basis. These were recorded by certain *Gleaner* journalists who were exceptionally skilled in shorthand and operated independently from the court stenographers. From September 1922, until he closed his practice in 1955, there is scarcely a day when the courts were in session, that the name N.W. Manley does not appear in the *Gleaner*'s court reports, and these formed the basis of my initial research.

The publication of a book devoted to Manley's legal career was often mooted over the years. Sir Philip Sherlock, for instance, dealt briefly with the subject in his biography of Manley saying the cases "properly belong to a longer book".[3] In 1986, the Hon. Vivian Blake, OJ, QC, one of Manley's former colleagues both in politics and law, noted in his Norman Manley Memorial Lecture[4] that apart from the *Gleaner*'s court reports, no permanent public record of Manley's cases had been preserved. "Unfortunately", Blake observed, "we are, as a people, yet to develop a heightened sense of the importance of our own history." It was Blake's hope that "one day in the not-too-distant future, some diligent and enterprising young lawyer will do the necessary research and undertake the publication of a book". While such comments rekindled my interest, they also urged caution: law was not my discipline. On the other hand, I was minded of G.K. Chesterton, the English author, who summed up the value of the jury system by noting that when it came to such a vital matter, the administrators of justice asked men who knew no more law than he did. I began to go through each case individually from the microfilmed copies of the *Gleaner* stored at the National Library; thousands of them. This is no collective term used for effect; I stopped counting when I reached 3,000. The one-liners now became summaries with notes of special interest relating to each case, but still falling far short of the stuff books are made of. Lack of funds placed photocopying out of the question, but every now and then a little could be wrested from personal funds to duplicate the longer, more complex cases. Later, through the kindness of Aaron Matalon, then of the ICD Group, and Twin Guinep Publishers, I was able to copy the bulk of the trials which I had initially selected for publication.

Next, I got permission from Douglas Manley to research his father's private papers to which I had been privy during my work with Wayne Brown. These had now been deposited as a private collection at the Jamaica Archives in Spanish Town. The material had been catalogued since I had seen it last and there were several new and exciting additions, including over 800-odd copies of Opinions, one bundle mindfully labelled *Opinions of Importance* in his own hand. There were boxes, too, laden with notes relating to specific cases, but most were incomplete. One box, for example, on the Beard murder trial (1946) contained only photographs and depositions, no trial notes or court report. The original transcript of the trial had been destroyed in England and the court reports I had researched in the *Manchester Guardian* were totally inadequate. Further investigations, however, revealed that the solicitor, Noel Nethersole, had been in court with Manley and left his own written account of the proceedings. This, together with an interview with Michael Manley and a Jamaican RAF navigator, both of whom had been present at the trial, produced enough material to piece the case together. This piecemeal approach proved to be the fate of many cases. Surprisingly, Norman Manley was not so precise and proper in his paperwork as I had imagined. I was not prepared to find so many of his Opinions undated and no mention of the solicitor for whom they were written. True, these are obviously *his* copies but still, they are typewritten with his handwritten amendments. I just assumed that he would have automatically headed and dated them, regardless, but then, I presumed too much and was faced with yet another task of placing them in some sort of time frame. The Garvey Opinion (see Vol. One, p. 141) is a prime example. Beginning in 1920, Amy Ashwood brought a series of legal actions against Marcus Garvey. This Opinion could have been written any time within a fifteen-year period. It was important to date it as accurately as possible because this was not the only time that Manley's path crossed with Garvey's. (In fact, one aspect of Manley's law work is the number of times the same character crops up, though not always in the same guise. Clients turn up as witnesses, or jurors and vice versa. Elias Alexander had the dubious role of being Manley's client on two occasions before he became the victim in the case which became a *cause célèbre*: the Alexander murder trial!)

Manley's trial notes are another story altogether. The surviving notebooks of the young lawyer of the 1920s are pristine, lean, demy volumes; the handwriting neat, precise, almost manufactured.[5] By 1931 he'd switched to unwieldy foolscap ledgers, over an inch thick, the initial orderly handwriting graduating to lumbering scrawls with grotesque caricatures of dogs gnawing into the margins. Interesting, psychologically, but not half as fascinating as the bits of algebra and geometry that pop up throughout these pages.[6]

Manley was an adept mathematician. Maths, he said, was the only subject in which he had shown any promise as a youth.[7] As a lawyer, he used it to help him work out knotty legal problems or test the validity of a theory. This was especially true of the McPhail murder trial (1940) where Michael Manley confirmed that his father had "worked out geometrically on paper" *how* the victim could have been shot, then promptly sent Michael off to put his theory to the test. In due course, Michael returned to his father: "Dad, it works." And using an unloaded revolver, Michael demonstrated how it was done. Manley subsequently

A page from one of Manley's early trial notes, Hawthorne v. Barclay (1923) is neat and precise, unlike the scrawl and doodles (opposite) which characterized later trial notes

The Markings of Lands & Grooves were
present in the test bullets & the
fatal bullets.

(a) 6 Grooves & 6 Lands each and _ he[ff]
ha[

(b) Hair lines or definite scratches in
the grooves

(c) ~~Definite scratches in~~

(c·) Flattening of the Lands —⎫ 2
    or Rounding off   c   ⎬ of
                           ⎭ the
                             Land[

Same applies to the fatal bullets.

• Scratches refer to the raised portion
on the bullet.

Even to the naked eye there is
a nick in the muzzle of revolver
which would account for the
~~............................~~ on the
bullet ~~...~~

~~...~~ Same type & size of revolver bullet used on
the 12th Dec. & on 4 Jan. 31 — but not same
mark. By mark I mean a very slight variation
in any & method of retention in this case —
4 on 1·31 was more suitable probably — longer fi[
the that fired on 12 Dec. Drumelli...
very slightly greater ~~than that~~ of the 12th altho[
clean reproduction of barrel after revolver gun. after

practised it, and practised it, then went into court and did it in front of the jury.[8]

Another primary source for research was Manley's diaries, but he was not a faithful recorder of the daily events in his life. "I will never keep an intelligent diary," he wrote on 3 July 1937. "I will never be able to write my intimate thoughts, if any, for myself alone." When he did, the results were revealing: "A sort of animal wisdom beat me," he acknowledged on losing a murder trial[9]. He took the following day off: "I needed it", he conceded, "after coming so close to breaking point."

The letters that Norman and Edna Manley exchanged over the years were also another source for getting behind the scenes on some of Manley's cases. "I have just come in from Port Maria having finished this week's travels — & as I won a nice touch & go murder case there I suppose I should feel satisfied." Or, "One may as well be resigned to there being a v. small field in Criminal work unless you adopt unprofessional tactics."[10]

Edna Manley was a more faithful diarist than her husband, but she penned precious little about his legal life.[11] One reason was that early in his law career, Manley decided that he would "keep out, really keep out, talk about law and cases".[12] And he did. The legal minds I tapped over the years all confirmed that Manley was not given to discussion of his court appearances. All, however, were anxious to share memories of their victories over the legal lion or reminisce about those cases in which they personally appeared or assisted Manley, but these memories sprang mainly from the late forties and fifties.

Where possible, all these primary data were married to the relevant court reports, with back-up material provided by Law Reports and Supreme Court Judgments. An earlier, and sad, discovery was that transcripts of trials, certainly in the case of an acquittal, are not normally kept by the courts, and those that are, have suffered from neglect. As early as 1929, the governor complained to the Legislative Council about the unsatisfactory condition of the records housed at the Supreme Court. "These documents have become food for cockroaches and moths," he said, and suggested that the records be removed to the Institute of Jamaica.[13] Certain documents were later deposited with the Jamaica Archives, but the majority were left to slowly crumble into dust.

The court reports themselves also presented some anxious moments. Not infrequently, the *Gleaner's* coverage of a trial omitted critical parts of the defence or prosecution. One reason was the wretched acoustic properties of the Supreme Court which reporters said prevented them from "fully drinking in the words of eloquence and

Manley resorts to algebra during a trial to help him test the validity of a theory. In this instance, the direction of the fatal bullet which killed Elias Alexander wisdom which flow from the Bench and the Bar".[14] And if a barrister cited an authority, the details were hardly ever reported. This is to be regretted since Manley was quick to cite authorities and the references would have been valuable. The criteria for selecting cases for publication, then, rested not entirely on Manley's presentation, the personalities involved, or whether the case established a precedent, reflected the social, racial and ethnic mix of Jamaica or simply represented the more spectacular aspects of Manley's court work, but on the availability of information to document a case.

Those cases which were selected for publication in Volume One alone, amounted to thousands of pages of court reports which were keyed into the computer and edited numberless times until they acquired what was considered a more readable form. A good many trials, in their raw state, comfortably ran over 100 letter-size pages; single-spaced. The most pressing problem was repetition. The verbatim accounts of numerous witnesses, sandwiched between opening and closing addresses from both the prosecution and the defence, were subtle variations on a common theme which had to be scrupulously edited. Depending on the intricacy of the subject, two or three days of trial were manageable, but trials which lasted anything up to seventeen days, comprising five to seven hours of testimony at any one session, were a nightmare. More often than not, I worked back from the closing addresses. In this way, I could dispense with what hindsight had designated superficial witnesses, and then proceed to condense the remaining material by summing up chunks of dialogue as narrative: not an easy task when it came to cross-examination. It is only in works of fiction that counsel demolishes a witness with a few well-chosen questions. The process can go on for hours, days even. There are exceptions, when the questioning is brief and lethal. But, generally, Manley would slowly and purposefully roll out a succession of well planned questions which would carry him through to the intended conclusion. In one diary entry, for example, he tells us, "XXed all day and made progress . . ."[15] Obviously, in such instances, one was hard put to cut and paste reams of dialogue without disturbing the flow of an artfully devised climax.

The language used throughout the trials presented its own problems. One gets the impression that most persons on entering the witness box were mindful of their language but we are at the mercy of the court reporters here and have to rely on their interpretation of a person's pattern of speech. Some reporters would faithfully record dialect, others would use reported speech, unless the actual words used, such as a conversation overheard by a witness, were critical to the case. In some instances, Chinese and Syrian immigrants were not fluent enough in English to speak for themselves and an interpreter would be brought into court to assist them.

Some cases needed an introduction in order to set the scene and better understand the circumstances. Manley's opening address during the Chinese arson case, for example — "Wherever there's a fire, there's a Chinaman," — would be lost on the reader unless one understood the attitude regarding the Chinese community at that time (see Vol. One, p. 30). This brings us to the use of such derogatory terms as "Chinaman" and "Coolie". They were in common usage in Jamaica, by all classes, especially during the 1920s, and it was decided to leave them as they were reported, as a reflection of the times. By the same token, it was interesting to note that even mild four-letter words such as *damn* and *hell* were taboo and never quoted in full. Additionally, an expression such as *infernal lie* would be met with rebuke, with one judge threatening to send a witness to jail for using "such language" in court (see Vol. One, p. 63).

Court style of address, too, changed over the years. Judges of the High Court were addressed as "Your Honour" until 1951, when King George VI approved a uniform mode of addressing judges in colonial territories. As of 10 July that month, judges were addressed as "My Lord" or "Your Lordships" and it fell first to Norman Manley to so address a judge, his good friend the Hon. J.E.D. Carberry, Acting Chief Justice, as "M'Lud".[16] Overall, the words as spoken by the participants, and recorded by the reporters, have been used as far as possible, the language allowing the characters to reveal themselves in their own inimitable way.

Still on the subject of language, there is one element in this work which is both contrived and yet true to historical fact. Manley's conversations with the late Leslie Clerk, are imagined (see for example Vol. One, p. 5) but the words or views expressed by Manley are essentially his own, rendered either in letters to his wife, his diaries, private papers, unfinished autobiography or in interviews with Basil McFarlane and recorded on tape. This suppositional reconstruction was provoked by the need for narrative to connect events and convey information. Additionally, Edna Manley noted that Clerk was the only person with whom Manley would discuss his work and that they "would have talked law and its problems endlessly".[17]

When it came to participating barristers and judges, I found pitifully little has been researched or written about our Bench and Bar, and was hard pressed to produce even a basic biographical sketch for some of them. But in the courtroom, appearing against Manley or moderating him from the Bench, we see them all in action. At this point, one should note that the majority of High Court judges serving in Jamaica were selected by the secretary of state for the colonies and sent here from England or other colonial territories for specific terms. Henry Isaac Close Brown was the first Jamaican to be appointed a Supreme Court judge in 1919.

The presentation of the cases was cause for some thought. Initially, one or two volumes concentrating on individual case studies was uppermost in the mind. An alternative was to present a series of cases under topics, but neither approach gave a balanced view of Manley's legal career. When the cases were placed in chronological order, however, a fascinating social history of Jamaica emerged and it was decided to opt for a loose arrangement of cases in narrative style from 1922 to 1955 covering several volumes. Such an arrangement had the merit of satisfying the aim of the work which was to illustrate Manley's legal skills and acumen through a sampling of the colourful and varied procession of clients and cases over the years, in addition to reflecting Jamaica's changing social and political climate.

ACKNOWLEDGEMENTS

I wish to express my gratitude to Dr Douglas Manley for granting me access to the Manley Papers and to the Rt Hon. Michael Manley, the Hon. Vivian Blake, OJ, QC, the Hon. Leacroft Robinson, OJ, QC, Anna Maria Hendriks and Richard Ashenheim for sharing their memories and thoughts.

The Hon. Douglas Fletcher, OJ, CBE, PC, not only provided some illuminating remembrances but kindly offered the use of the library at Myers Fletcher & Gordon.

I am grateful to Basil McFarlane for allowing me to quote from the (unpublished) transcripts of the interviews he conducted with Norman Manley in 1968/9; Wayne Brown for the quote from his tape recorded interview with Mona Swithenbank and Vivien Carrington, Desmond Henry and the Hon. Hector Wynter, OJ, for commenting on parts of the manuscript at various stages.

Special thanks to Aaron Matalon of the ICD Group (now Mechala) and Twin Guinep Publishers for assisting with the photocopying of several lengthy trials.

The staff of the institutions in which the research was carried out were consistently helpful over the years, particularly John Aarons Director, National Library of Jamaica; the Government Archivist, Elizabeth Williams and Yvonne Lawrence of the Supreme Court Library.

Valerie Facey extended her friendship and faith throughout while my husband, Dennis, not only listened but cheered me on and was responsible for the layout, cover design and the illustrations on pp. 3, 133 and the photograph on p. 180. All of which brings me to my final thanks, to Olive Senior, not only for her editing skills but her unflagging spirit which helped immeasurably to sustain my own. Ultimately, however, any oversights are entirely my responsibility.

For permission to use photographs, we are grateful to the following: Estate of Edna Manley, p. 94; Garvey Centenary Official Souvenir, Jamaica Cultural Development Corporation, pp. 143-44; Mr Gilbert Griffith, p. 71; The Gleaner Co., pp. xiv, 6, 10, 16, 24, 41, 43, 54, 58, 60, 80, 87, 103, 106, 124, 148, 149, 150, 156 and 161; Anna Maria Hendriks, p. 5; Jamaica Archives, pp. xx, xxvi, xxvii, xxix; Jamaica Information Service, p.14; National Library of Jamaica, frontispiece, facing p. 1 and pp. xxiii, xxxii, 15, 20, 34, 35, 79, 140; *Planters' Punch*, p. 22 and the *Red Book of the West Indies*, p. 90.

SERIES INTRODUCTION

On 2 February 1955, Norman Washington Manley, QC, MM, gave up his lucrative law practice to become Chief Minister of Jamaica. "I have spent my life on many cases", he said, "and now I turn my back for good and all on that life and take into my hands the case of the people of Jamaica."[1] He was sixty-one years old. In the thirty-three years from 1922 to 1955, he had become, in the words of his legal colleagues, "the doyen of the local Bar"; a "legend" whose memory would "remain a benediction".[2]

By now the road that led to his fame is well known. Born on 4 July 1893 at Roxburgh, Manchester, where his father was a produce dealer, Manley attended Jamaica College and became a notable schoolboy athlete. In 1914 he won the Rhodes Scholarship and left Jamaica later that year for England and Oxford to study law and read for the Bar. His studies were interrupted by the war where he saw active service at Ypres and the Somme and was awarded the Military Medal. His younger brother, Roy, was killed in action. Manley returned to Oxford in 1919 where he took second class honours in the Bachelor of Civil Law (BCL) at Jesus College, and delivered a "brilliant" paper on Samuel Butler which provoked a heated argument about evolution despite some days when he thought he and his peers "all very foolish" and wondered why "we didn't clear out and do something sensible" such as "till the soil or breed chickens".[3]

Manley was the Prizeman (Essay) at Gray's Inn and was called to the Bar on 20 April 1921. In June that year he married his cousin, Edna Swithenbank, in London. Come August 1922, Manley, along with his bride and infant son Douglas, returned to Jamaica after spending some time in London reading in Chambers as a pupil of S.C.N. Goodman, and observing the practice of the English courts. Then began his formidable and illustrious career at the Bar. By his own account, "it started slowly, but two very exciting cases caught public attention".[4] Both involved murder between intimates: *Rex* v. *Spalding* in September 1924 (see Vol. One, p. 103) saw Luther Spalding charged with the murder of his paramour, Miriam Ross, whose body was discovered buried in his banana field. Two years later, a young woman, Louise Walker, hit the headlines when she was accused of murdering her lover, Stedman Case (see Vol. One, p. 149). The majority of murders committed in Jamaica from the late nineteenth century to 1926 were 'crimes of passion'[5] but, until Louise Walker was charged, the accused were mostly men. Manley was assigned by the Crown to defend both Luther Spalding and Louise Walker. "From then", Manley observed, "the speed of the growth of my practice was almost legendary."[6]

A career at the Bar in Jamaica at that time was one of the few professions open to the independent middle class. "But the way the profession was organized", Manley explained, "five men only earned a decent living as barristers."[7] Until 1972, the legal profession in Jamaica was divided between barristers and solicitors. Solicitors qualified by serving as articled clerks in solicitors' offices. Although they could appear in the lower courts, their work was primarily concerned with advising clients and drafting documents. When a client's case was to be heard in the High Court, the solicitor would brief a barrister, since he (and later, she)[8] alone had the right of audience in this and higher tribunals.

Barristers were trained in England; after they were called to the Bar they were able to practise in Jamaica, usually being retained by a solicitor. Barristers with good connections among solicitors of heavy calendars consequently received more briefs and made more money. Solicitors and articled clerks made it a point of duty to attend court on a regular basis to observe the barristers in action. Manley forged to the front almost at once. "He won the confidence and the admiration of the solicitors", ran a *Gleaner* editorial, as early as 1925, because they recognized in him "a lawyer learned in the law, a man honest in his presentation of a case, and an effective but eminently courteous cross-examiner."[9] As a result, Manley was rewarded by a deluge of briefs.

The Jamaican Bar at that time was not lacking in other brilliant individuals. Henry Milne Radcliffe, for example, took silk[10] in 1924, was appointed Assistant to the Attorney-General in 1926 and presided over the local law examinations taken by the articled clerks who said they found in him "a true ideal".[11] J.A.G. Smith, described as the "lean, black aristocrat"[12] of the legal profession, was a fearless advocate who straddled the Bar a dozen years prior to Manley. He was strong on legalities but lacking in technique, his long-winded eloquence often robbed his utterances of a magnetic quality. Hector Josephs, was also slow of delivery but a brilliant lawyer. He annoyed solicitors by skimming over briefs, ignoring instructions and relying on his own inherent brilliance to win a case.[13] A Jamaica Scholar, Josephs entered Trinity Hall, Cambridge in 1891 to become First Prizeman in Law the following year and Law Tripos 1893/4. He was called to the Bar, Lincoln's Inn, in 1896 and returned home to appear in many prominent cases. Josephs took silk in 1911 and was the first black to be appointed a colonial attorney-general (of British Guiana) in 1925. At the time and for many years later, he was the highest ranking Jamaican in the colonial civil service. John St John Yates was called to the Bar, Inner Temple, in May 1903 and acted as Attorney-General and Chief Justice of Jamaica before leaving the island in October 1926 on being appointed Puisne Judge of the Gold Coast. Other young barristers admitted at the same time as Manley were also to attain the first rank. Among them was Colin (later Sir Colin) McGregor. A Munro man, McGregor was stern, strong and dedicated to details. In 1925 he entered the Judicial Services as Clerk of the Courts; by 1957 he had become Chief Justice of Jamaica. Then there was Alfred (later Sir Alfred) Baillie Rennie. In early 1923, the *Gleaner* noted "the addition to the Bar of two promising barristers in Messrs. Manley and Rennie".[14]

What gave Manley the edge over his peers? Manley himself offers a likely answer: "An absolutely egotistic determination to win every case I was engaged in, which I regard as the most important attribute of an advocate . . . a total will to win, so that you stop at nothing but deal with maximum concentration, maximum personal observation, maximum study, maximum everything . . ."[15]

As was the custom in those days, noteworthy trials got long reports in the Press and soon the name N.W. Manley was appearing regularly in the *Gleaner*. "After the excellent cross-examination by Mr Manley", ran one report, "the witnesses for the prosecution were completely annihilated."[16] By June 1930, we find Mr K.J. Wylie, the Oxford Secretary to the Rhodes Trustees, writing to Manley: "Everybody tells me that you are a great swell and practically leader of the Bar."[17]

As 1931 got into its stride, there was talk of making Manley a King's Counsel,[18] not only in the legal community but from the public at large. "I could sit for days and listen to the arguments of Mr Manley", declared one letter-writer to the *Gleaner*, adding, "He has won the esteem and appreciation of all the Judges and lawyers of the island and also the inhabitants in general . . . In my humble opinion he is entitled to the conference of KC." The writer did not think he was singular in this respect but was "voicing the sentiments of hundreds".[19] Twenty months later, on 15 August 1932, the *Gleaner* was able to report that "The King has been pleased to give permission for the appointment of Mr N.W. Manley . . . to be of the number of HM Counsel for the colony of Jamaica." Congratulations were quick to follow. On 17 August another letter-writer to the *Gleaner* declared: "The name of N.W. Manley is a household name, a name that is the shining light of the Bar and one of the most successful barristers of modern times." At a dinner held in his honour by the Old Boys of Jamaica College in October, the toasts were abundant, but in his reply Manley hinted at a certain dissatisfaction with his life as a barrister. He alluded to the hardships of a profession which made him "eke out an existence on murder and other crimes".[20] Curiously, over the years, Manley developed an intense dislike of murder trials and yet these were the cases in which he was at his most brilliant. Homicides demanded, in his words, "an intolerable degree and intensity of concentration and nervous energy" and so he had to be personally convinced of the innocence of his client. "When one is adversely convinced", he said, "it becomes mere prostitution . . . the artificial stimuli [sic] Spanish fly." And yet, he added, "it must be so! You cannot move, hold, bind, unless your whole self is histrionically engaged . . . Mere words are nothing."[21]

Advocacy and acting are alike. The profession of law, like the other, thrives on the ethos of dash, form and articulation. There is no greater drama than that daily performed in the law courts and, when it came to performance, Manley in full courtroom flight was an actor histrionically engaged. For instance, at the start of one of his most celebrated cases, the final trade mark appeal involving the US-based Vicks Chemical Company and Cecil deCordova et al. of Jamaica before the UK Privy Council in 1951, the Law Lords confessed to being a little startled by Manley's style of address. They had never seen anything as dramatic or as exhuberant, they said, since the days of the celebrated English barrister, Sir Edward Marshall Hall.[22] To emphasize a point, Manley (appearing for Vicks) would thump on the wooden bookstand before him; snatch off his glasses and gesticulate with them. His most characteristic stance was to sway backwards on his heels, gown thrown back with one hand thrust deep into his hip pocket. At other times, he would grasp the stand with both hands, lean forward significantly and expound with great deliberation on his point: "Suppose a man had never heard of the word *Vaporub* in his life, would he have any picture in his mind at all of what it was? I submit that he would have none at all. The words are in antithesis — you can't rub with vapour. The whole cleverness of the name is that the originators chose two words in combination which negate each other . . ."[23]

Since 1915, Vicks had sold a product under the name of *Vaporub*. When a Jamaican company began marketing a similar product branded Karsote Vaporub, Vicks had promptly sued for infringement of their trade mark. Manley lost the first suit to the silver-tongued Sir Lennox O'Reilly of Trinidad, but he won the subsequent appeal in Jamaica and the final appeal before the Privy Council. His submissions to the latter were described by the Lord Chancellor as "the best argument I have ever heard in a trade mark case".[24] The Vicks organization, in their turn, remarked that in all their legal matters worldwide, no lawyer was equal to Norman Manley.[25]

The Vicks appeal was not Manley's first case in England. In 1946, he successfully defended a Jamaican RAF serviceman, Donald Beard, on a murder charge in the Crown Court at the Manchester Assizes. Smiles lit the faces of forty of Beard's uniformed countrymen as they heard Mr Justice Sellars in closing say to Manley: "I would express the pleasure it has been in the Court, and the satisfaction the prisoner must have experienced, to have you appear in this case."

"It has been a pleasure and a privilege to me", Manley replied, "that twenty-five years after being called to the Bar, I have been able to appear in a court in this country, and before you." After his release, Beard told a reporter: "I am profoundly relieved. I never did this thing. I can never express my gratitude to Mr Manley."[26]

The Beard case gained Manley tremendous goodwill among the new and growing migrant West Indian population in Britain, but in his criminal practice in Jamaica, what became known as the Alexander murder case, eclipsed them all. His winning defence of Mrs Alexander, along with her brother, for the alleged shooting of her husband, led Mr Justice Adrian Clarke to tell the accused before discharging them: "If genius is an infinite capacity for taking pains, you have been defended by a genius."[27]

Through long spells of little sleep and incredible application of trial-and-error rehearsals, Manley planned his cases. "He had a sure instinct for planning the strategy of a case," noted the solicitor H.O.A. Dayes. "He always knew what he was doing with it, where he wanted it to go. One could not lead Manley down blind alleys nor cause him to dissipate time and strength on the things which were not vital. He never wasted energy worrying about what the other side would do, but made up his mind what he needed to do with his own case and his opponents, in order to win, and then concentrate on doing it."[28]

"If you were instructing Manley, as I did on several occasions", said attorney-at-law Douglas Fletcher, "you had to have a properly prepared brief. Your presentation of witnesses and your opinion of the law had to be carefully produced otherwise Manley could be very caustic; he did not suffer fools gladly."[29]

A solicitor's association with a barrister, as often as not, had its origins in taking counsel's opinion, but as the solicitor Douglas Judah noted, by 1930 the phrase had almost fallen into disuse, having been

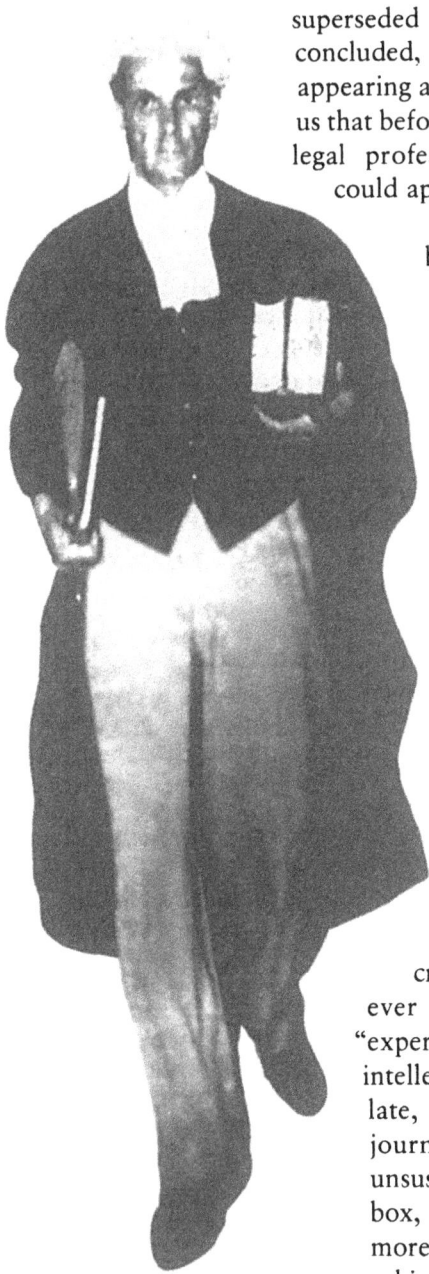

Manley seen leaving the courtroom in 1946

superseded by "taking Manley's opinion". Judah concluded, "Instructing Manley was a pleasure, appearing against him an experience,"[30] reminding us that before the fusion of the two branches of the legal profession, both barristers and solicitors could appear in the lower courts.

When it came to the relationship between barristers and solicitors, it is interesting to note that during the 1940s when the Bar Association resolved that in all criminal matters, in whatever court, counsel need not be instructed by a solicitor but could be approached directly by a client, Manley thought some counsel might take instructions direct, but he personally, "never had, and never would".[31]

Fletcher also recalled that judges had to be very careful how they got into an argument with Manley over either the law or the facts as Manley, by the sheer logic of his presentation, was always able to establish to them, and "not always too diplomatically", said Fletcher, "that they were complete idiots".[32]

Manley was renowned for his cross-examinations which were hardly ever without excitement, and those of "expert" witnessess, especially served as an intellectual treat. He would work long and late, poring over medical and scientific journals, so that by the time the unsuspecting expert entered the witness box, Manley sometimes knew as much or more about the particular aspect of the subject under review than he did. Manley's capacity for long periods of concentrated effort dismayed his colleagues. Time did not matter as long as the job was done. The solicitor V.O. Abendana remembered being engaged in a matter on which he sought Manley's opinion. "Can see you and client Drumblair midnight Sunday," came the reply by telegram. On the stroke of midnight, Abendana and his client arrived at Manley's home for the conference and did not leave until close on 3.00 a.m. when, Abendana recollected, "Manley casually announced that he was going to look over his brief in a case in which he was appearing *today* in the Mandeville Circuit Court".[33]

On another occasion when Abendana was instructing Manley in a case, he arrived late and was not present when the case was called. When Abendana took his seat beside Manley, the jury had already been empanelled. Manley was furious and tore into Abendana. "To make matters worse", said Abendana, "I looked up at the jurors and said, 'They appear to be an intelligent jury'. 'Well', Manley replied, 'if they are intelligent, they will convict'." Abendana tried to assure him that the case was an easy one. "Abendana", Manley snapped, "no case is easy."[34]

This was the quality of the man: no case was easy. He put the same energy, concentration and application into every case he handled, regardless of its importance or who was involved in it. On many occasions, Manley was assigned by the Crown to defend a person on trial for murder. His remuneration in such instances was three or four times less than if it had been a private brief. This made no difference to Manley's commitment; he demanded nothing less than excellence in all his undertakings. It was this total acceptance of his responsibility to his client that caused the *Gleaner* to write at the conclusion of the Walker trial: "Mr Manley must be congratulated as a barrister on the persistent and brilliant fight he has made for the liberty as well as the life of Louise Walker . . . if his remuneration had been ten times as much he could not have worked harder, more conscientiously, more brilliantly."[35]

Women feature frequently in Manley's cases both as clients and witnesses. As clients, he protested the fact that they had to be judged by all-male juries and clamoured for the introduction of female jurors, unknown in Jamaica before 1946 when the Jury Law of 1898 was amended to include women. "No ordinary man can understand the ways and workings of a woman's mind," Manley once told an all-male jury. "He does not understand it. It is sufficient to say that women do things which are peculiar for reasons we, as men, don't understand. And that is why one would like to see women on a jury."[36]

As witnesses in the box, many a woman intrigued Manley. "They make such magnificent liars," he confided to his diary.[37] "It is an observable fact about a certain type of female witness", Manley advised a jury in a closing address, "that while a man will only go the length of telling a 75 per cent lie, they will not shrink from a 100 per cent lie."[38]

Manley was a great defender of the jury system because it involved "the ordinary people in the administration of justice".[39] For Manley, this was "true democracy in action"[40] and he carried it through to his political career when he fought for universal adult suffrage. "I have the greatest faith in the good sense of the common man," he told V.O. Abendana.[41] When it came to addressing juries, "Manley was absolutely marvellous," according to Douglas Fletcher: "He never spoke over their heads and he never spoke down to them. He had the ability to speak clearly and simply and not at great length. A quality which some of our present advocates could well do to emulate."[42]

Over the years, the stories about Manley and his cases multiplied and acquired the status of legend. There are many persons — lawyers and lay-persons alike — who believe that Manley never lost a murder trial; that no man defended by him was hanged. That is not so: neither is the premise that prior to 1938, Manley was a lawyer primarily of the employer class and the events of that turbulent year led him from being a defender of the legally protected interests of the haves to become the defender of the have-nots who lived their lives on the margin of the law. From the outset, Manley conducted cases of every class and category. The courtroom became his classroom; it was here that Manley learnt about his country and his people. In 1923 he confessed, "I'm deplorably ignorant of Jamaica . . . I'm glad for the circuit — it takes me to places I've never been before."[43] He blamed his ignorance on the secondary school system where the pupils were "shut away from life, shut away from the community, ignoring the island's past, its present and future".[44] Manley spoke from experience. "I spent eight years in secondary school", he said, "and left without knowing one single fact about the history of the past, the current history or the possibilities of Jamaica as a country."[45]

The courtroom brought Manley face to face with the people, the communities and the reality of Jamaican life. It was this "human aspect of the practice of law," he said, which interested him most.[46] Take for example the suit involving two neighbours fighting over the erection of a fence:

"You can't put a fence on my land."

"This isn't your land. Your land's in China."

"This isn't your land either. Your land's in Africa."[47]

This pure Jamaican homespun drama runs the gamut of Manley's cases. Here you'll find a witness chewing garlic to ward off the effect of telling a lie and householders parting with their deeds in order to satisfy ghosts in the raising of Spanish jars. But the courtroom is the domain of not only folklore and folly. It is also through a perusal of Manley's cases that we meet an astonishing array of people destined to become household names in Jamaica. From the days of the great King Street retail stores comes what Manley described as a series of "silly Syrian quarrels".[48] But to the Issas, Hannas and Nathans, it was "business" and each would rush to retain Manley before the other had the opportunity to do so. Over the years we meet Marcus Garvey. Was he a bigamist? Was future Olympic gold medallist Arthur Wint guilty of manslaughter? Was the City Printery guilty of sedition when it printed the issue of *Public Opinion* which carried Roger Mais's article "Now We Know" which asserted that the 1944 Constitution was designed to perpetuate Jamaica's colonial status and for which Mais himself was charged with a breach of the Defence Regulation? How does Manley defend the Trade Union Congress officials, Florizel Glasspole and Ken Hill, when they are indicted on charges of obstructing a highway? We meet these, and a host of others who would become leading Jamaican personalities, all in their early, formative years — as jurors, clients or hostile witnesses pitting their wits against Manley in the box.

Manley's cases are also an index of the changing social climate. As the horse and buggy gave way to the motor car, traffic offences began to take on new significance just as murder trials acquired a new dimension with the increased use of firearms. Not only did the nature of the cases change but so did Manley's response to them. In his legal practice, Manley had at first taken the view that counsel had no right to pick and choose for whom he should appear. Later, his political colleagues made it clear that they did not expect him to appear against any well-known member of his party. "I made a rule for myself," said Manley. "I did not, even for clients with general retainers, appear for labour in any matter involving a trade union, and I always appeared for my political associates and colleagues and never against them."[49]

Part of the change was a reflection of his growing involvement in political activity which began in 1938 with his role as mediator in the labour upheavals of May that year. "I knew my own temperament", Manley said, "and well understood that I had entered a new road and would walk it wherever it led."[50] That road led to the launching of the People's National Party (PNP): the first mass-based political party in Jamaica, on 18 September 1938, with Norman Manley at the helm. As leader of the party he played a major role in the steps leading towards self-government in Jamaica. However, in the first election held under universal adult suffrage on 14 December 1944, the PNP won only four seats and Manley himself failed to gain a seat. In the 1949 general election held on 20 December, the PNP increased their number of seats to thirteen with Manley successful in Eastern St Andrew, but it was still not enough to oust Manley's cousin and head of the Jamaica Labour Party (JLP), Alexander Bustamante, from power. It wasn't until 12 January 1955 that the PNP won the general election and Manley became Chief Minister, formally ending his legal career.

Aside from the significant role he played in politics, Manley also laid the foundation for social welfare development in Jamaica. This was through Jamaica Welfare Limited which he was instrumental in forming in 1936. Funds for this islandwide programme of social development and cultural activities came from a cess on bananas exported from Jamaica, which he secured in negotiations with foreign fruit companies. But Manley was not superhuman and before he closed his law office, there were times when his political activities, which included his perpetual struggle with his cousin and political rival, Alexander Bustamante, as well as his commitment to visionary projects such as Jamaica Welfare, diffused his hitherto total concentration on legal matters. For instance, with the launching of Jamaica Welfare uppermost in his mind, Manley found himself floundering during a murder trial: "Nasty experience to stand in court . . . and feel the last ounce go out and silence and pain overtake you — but I bluffed it out."[51]

Bluff it out he might in public, but in private, his wife knew only too well when "a case has been hard hit & it's sticking in your gullet — so jolly hard you can scarcely swallow your dinner".[52]

The effect of Manley's legal career on his wife and children was profound. Norman and Edna had moved house three times before their first year in Jamaica was out. Edna hated housekeeping; she was a sculptress and determined to carry on with her work but was continuously thwarted in her efforts. She couldn't afford to cast in bronze and bags of plaster imported from England took weeks to arrive and spoilt in the process. Above all, Edna felt neglected by Norman who was preoccupied with his legal work which, he said, kept him at it "seven days a week and anything up to twenty hours a day".[53] Early in his marriage, the total will to win took its toll. In October 1923, when he was busy building up his practice, Edna left him and returned to England in frustration taking their child, Douglas, with her. The outcome of Edna's flight was, however, fortuitous. Realizing his wife's lack of personal fulfilment, Manley looked for a house where Edna could have a place of her own in which to work. He found Drumblair where they would live, with one short break, for thirty-eight years. Meanwhile, back in London, Edna Manley's old art teacher advised her to learn to sculpt in wood. She was elated. There was plenty of wood in Jamaica; no more frustrated efforts with imported plaster or worries about the cost of casting in bronze. From now on she would talk with a mallet; let her feelings spring from blocks of mahogany. She sailed back home for Jamaica with her new art tools to carve her own niche in Jamaica's cultural milieu. As for Manley, his family life was now back on a firmer footing and after a harassing day in court, he found Edna "so darned nice" to come home to.[54]

Drumblair became a haven for Norman and Edna Manley and their two sons, Douglas and Michael. Michael Manley would later recall sitting anxiously at the top of the stairs waiting for his father to come home after an especially demanding case. During the Alexander murder trial, however, he was not so passive; the entire family was called on to play a role. It all began when the Crown's expert witness, the Island Chemist, fired several test bullets from the accused's revolver and compared them with the fatal bullets which had killed Elias Alexander. The chemist found ten characteristics which he stated were common to both the test and the fatal bullets. "The possibility of a bullet from another revolver being singularly marked with those ten characteristics is one in a hundred trillion," the ex-Admiralty and War Office munition expert concluded. And he went further. "If a machine turned out one of those revolvers per second, it would take over 317 billion years to get another one like it."[55] Manley was outraged. In a fury of forensic anger, he put the expert's theory to the test. As Michael Manley remembered it: "Dad suddenly arrived home with what seemed to be scores of revolvers and literally boxes and boxes of cartridges. I don't know how many hundreds of rounds were fired into one of two things: a tank of water or a series of Plasticine blocks that my mother built for Dad from her modelling clay. My brother Douglas and I were given the job of retrieving the bullets."[56] The results of Manley's experiments left the "expert" quaking.

When Manley died on 2 September 1969, it was fourteen years since he had practised law. Those years had been spent in active politics before he retired in 1968 after thirty years of selfless service to Jamaican nation building. Although it was his activities as a statesman that captured the headlines and riveted public attention in those years, his skill as a lawyer contened to play a role. In 1957, for example, Manley's masterly renegotiation of the bauxite agreements with the American lawyers who represented the foreign companies operating in Jamaica

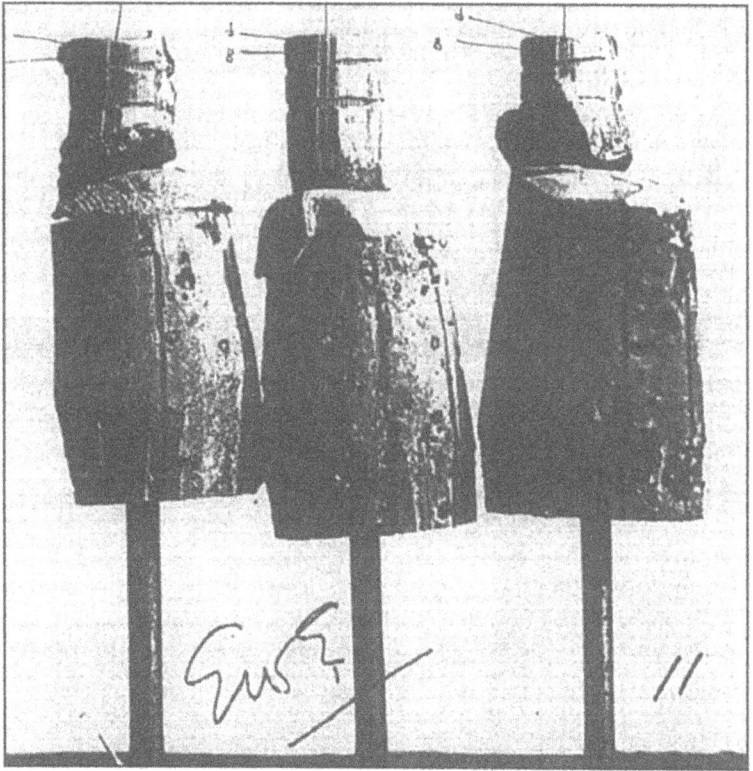

Three of the test bullets Manley fired from different revolvers to compare their markings with the fatal bullets which had killed Elias Alexander

resulted in a six-fold increase in revenue to the country. In March 1959, bouquets were thrown at Manley not only in Jamaica but Trinidad, when he overturned a directive issued by the Commissioner of Police which stated that Jamaican ministers of government and members of the House of Representatives would not be prosecuted for simple misdemeanours such as breaches of the Road Traffic Law. The *Trinidad Chronicle* said that Manley had done well to come out swiftly and determinedly against such an idea of one law for the ordinary man and another for the legislator. The *Chronicle* saw Manley's action as coming at a time when politicians in the West Indies were in danger of magnifying their own importance. The editorial added that Manley had shown that in Jamaica, at least, there was an understanding of the law of the land which applied to all citizens without discrimination.[57]

Manley was given a state funeral as befits one who would be named a national hero.[58] On Saturday, 6 September, his body lay in state before the high altar of the Kingston Parish Church[59] where nearly three centuries earlier the great-great grandparents of the renowned English poet, Robert Browning, were married.[60] The connection is not as obscure as it appears: Manley so admired Browning's work he carried a copy of his *Ring and the Book* into the trenches with him when he fought in the First World War.

"What survives myself?" asked Browning in "Cleon". In Manley's case, one would have thought, stacks of paper — *that* high. But in 1962, surrounded by the forlorn remnants of the great wreck that was the Federation of the West Indies,[61] followed by his party's defeat in the general election held in April that year, Manley went out and burnt "about twenty cubic yards of papers, letters, books, documents, manuscripts . . . I burnt three-quarters of my life — isn't it shocking?"[62]

Why did he do it? Public life had depleted his income to the point where he was forced to sell Drumblair. Since there was no room to store a lifetime of papers, many relating to his legal career, at Regardless, his new, humbler, homestead, the bulk went up in smoke, and with it a valuable chunk of Jamaica's history.

"It was not easy", said Manley, "to remain in politics in Jamaica — not the way I was — without getting into debt."[63]

It is not in the *Law Reports* or *Hansard* alone that the memory of this remarkable man survives, nor in the statues erected in his honour, nor the public places which bear his name. His greatest legacy lies in his doctrine that "there's no answer to hard work. I have always profoundly believed that the road to success is to deliver the goods".[64]

"I had a great time at the Bar," Manley assured his colleagues when they came together to honour him in 1955. "It's good to look back and remember that you helped people in trouble, defended difficult cases and to know that you did a clean job . . ."[65]

A fitting epitaph to the most professional of men as well as a reminder to succeeding generations who choose to follow in the footsteps of Lawyer Manley.

The Spanish Town Courthouse where Manley argued his first case. It was built in 1819 at the southern end of the stately Spanish Town Square, on a site which was originally a cemetery, and later a chapel that was hastily constructed in a religious panic following the destruction of Port Royal by the earthquake of 1692

1

First Time Up

*In Chambers yesterday, before His Honour Mr Justice
Brown, Mr H. Kaye Bryan, Acting Attorney-General, made
an application on behalf of Mr N.W. Manley that he be
admitted to practise as a barrister-at-law in Jamaica. He
pointed out that the papers filed in Court showed that Mr
Manley had passed all the necessary exams and had been
duly called to the Bar in the mother country.*

The Gleaner
31 August 1922

"If I ever told you the story of how I did my first case in court you
would laugh," Manley once told an interviewer. "It was a murder
case, and it happened that I fell ill, and that laid me up for about a
month before the case was heard. And literally I spent one month
studying that case. I suppose I knew every line and letter of the evidence
by heart. I had cross-examined on paper every witness — I filled about
three volumes of notebooks cross-examining the various witnesses. In
this exercise, if you asked a question where the witness could say yes or
no, you then had to fork, and if you got another yes or no, you had to
fork again and proceed. I had written out opening addresses and closing
addresses on different assumptions. I made those addresses before
looking glasses. I opened that case to the jury at least ten times before
the looking glass; and closed it.

"I had never spoken in public until I got up in court for the first
time, because I suffered to an abnormal degree from nervousness. I
could never tell you the agonies. I had written papers at college, but
speak them? I couldn't do it. And that was part of the reason why I had
to make these fantastic preparations."[1]

The day of reckoning was 25 September 1922. Like many young
barristers, Manley depended on the Crown for his first case, that is, as
a court-appointed counsel. In this instance he was assigned by the
Crown to defend sixteen-year-old Joseph Samuels charged with the

murder of Jonathan Kirkwood.[2] They both had been employed as mulemen at Innswood Sugar Estate in St Catherine and had had a dispute over some mules which resulted in Kirkwood being stabbed in the chest by a knife wielded by the accused.

The time had come for Manley to cross-examine a cart-man, James Gordon, who said that he was an eye-witness to the murder. Manley was to recall: "I'll never forget standing up and asking the first question. My tongue swelled, my throat was dry, I stood there with my mouth open. Not a blasted thing; utter silence for about twenty or thirty seconds. And then I felt this great in-pouring of energy and confidence . . ."[3]

"How was it you were able to see everything that happened?" was his first question to the witness.

"I ran up from where I was."

"And you were looking at them all the time?"

"Yes."

"You didn't buck your toe in the cane piece?"

"No."

"You looked where you were running?"

"Yes."

"Then you must have had double sight."

The case was being tried at the St Catherine Circuit Court in Spanish Town before Mr Justice Anthony DeFreitas, Acting Chief Justice. The old brick buildings and shuttered jalousies held a myriad of memories for Manley who had spent a part of his youth growing up there. As a boy of twelve, he had ridden a horse some ten miles each way from his home, Belmont, in the St Catherine hills to Beckford and Smith's (now St Jago) High School in the town. Ever a lover of speed, young Manley was in constant trouble with the police for galloping his horse at full stretch through the town and was once had up for organizing races in the streets. "They didn't do anything," he said, as an old man remembering. "They just talked to me and let me go."[4]

Now, inside the stately Georgian courthouse, Joseph Samuels, only four years older than Manley had been when he had his brief touches with the law, was facing the gravest charge of all: he had pleaded not guilty to a charge of murder. Opening the case for the defence, Manley having licked his initial nervousness, was now calm and deliberate. The prisoner, he said, had acted in self-defence. He had been set upon by several men and beaten; how far he was justified in using a weapon to defend himself was a question of law. He called the prisoner to the stand and let him tell his story.

Manley bought a mare, Firefly which, harnessed to a buggy, took him off to his Duke Street chambers every morning

Samuels narrated how he had been leading his mules up to a little bridge. Kirkwood was ahead, driving his dray, when it got stuck in the trench. As Samuels passed, Kirkwood accused him of 'mashing' his mules and, wrapping his whip around the stick, cried, "I bet I hit you."

Samuels said he turned to run away but Kirkwood called out, "See the little boy here mash my mules."

Several men came up and Kirkwood hit Samuels over the eye with his whip stick. Samuels tried to run but the men penned him up around the dray and started to beat him. He bawled out but no one came to his aid. They were all shouting: "Lick 'im! Lick 'im hard!" He was frightened for his life; he drew out his pocket knife and stuck Kirkwood. He didn't mean to kill him.

Manley called the assistant warden at the St Catherine District Prison to the stand. He testified that when he had examined Samuels on admission, he looked as though he had taken a thorough beating.

In closing the case for the defence, Manley advised the jury that the story, as told by the witnesses for the prosecution, was not one on which they could hang a man; those witnesses were all drawing upon their imagination when they described the stabbing. Each and every one of them had omitted to tell *how* the boy was beaten. Why? If the boy had, without reason, murdered the man, it was only human that the people would have beaten him. They would have no reason to conceal it.

"It might not have been legal", Manley argued, "but it was human. And the reason why they concealed it was because they had all set upon the boy and beaten him. It was purely in self-defence that the boy drew the knife and cut the deceased. Those witnesses for the prosecution were guilty of a felony when they set upon the prisoner and beat him. They should be in the dock . . . ." and he appealed to the jury for the acquittal of the prisoner.

The prosecuting counsel reminded the jury that when several persons saw an occurrence it was almost certain that you would get a different version in some detail from each of them. But on the main issue, it was clear that the prisoner stuck the deceased with the knife, and was responsible for his death.

Complimenting both counsel on the clear and concise manner in which they had presented their cases, the presiding judge told the jury that there were three courses open to them: to find it murder or manslaughter or they might find that it was justifiable homicide.

The jury retired and returned with a verdict of manslaughter. In passing sentence, the judge referred to the youth of the prisoner and to the fact that he was provoked. Samuels was sentenced to six months' imprisonment.

Leaving the courthouse, Manley set off in the buggy drawn by his mare, Firefly, round the Square and out on to the straight, white, dusty road that led to Kingston. Beside him sat his old friend from schooldays, Leslie Clerk. Manley had no intimates: Clerk came the closest to being one. They had met at Jamaica College and found a common ground.

Leslie Clerk in later years

Like Manley, Leslie Clerk read a good deal. They liked horse racing and boxing; both were good swimmers and they shared a love of music. Leslie himself was a professional piano tuner. His uncle, Astley Clerk, owned the Cowen Music Store on King Street where pianos and almost every other musical instrument were sold. Leslie also had remarkable intuitive powers. He could be given an article belonging to someone he didn't know, and after holding it in his hand, describe the owner. Norman, a more rational person, refused to get involved with that sort of stuff. He preferred to talk law and its problems with Leslie, and try to fathom the mysteries of the human personality.[5] It was no surprise then when Manley asked Clerk to share in that moment of truth for all lawyers: the time when they first rise to their feet to address the Court. Half-way through the trial, anxious for some feedback on his performance, Manley had slipped Clerk a note: 'How's it going?' he scribbled. 'Fine.' Clerk responded.[6]

Now, alone with his friend in the buggy, Manley rubbed the dust from his eyes and glanced at Leslie before asking the inevitable, "Well?"

"Well, what?"

"What d' you think?"

"I thought you sat down pretty fast after that first cross-examination."

"I didn't sit. My legs gave way — I fell down!"

They both laughed.

"I wish I could find some bloody way of overcoming this inability to stand up on my own two feet and speak in public," Norman said.

"Then why choose law as a profession?"

"I had great difficulty in deciding what I would like . . ."

"Didn't you want to be an engineer at one time?"

"I had thought of it. I was fond of tools; I loved using my hands, I still do, but it was my family that kept on dinning it into me from I was a boy of twelve that I should become a lawyer."

"Why?"

"I loved argument. Whenever any discussion arose at home, whatever anybody said, I always said the opposite and then proceeded to argue like hell."

"So no misgivings?"

"I can't afford misgivings. This is a problem I have to face. I've got myself committed to a job, and I have to do it, no matter what it costs me.[7] But you know, I was lucky. Coming over on the boat, I came across Sir John Simon, the eminent English KC.[8] He discovered that I had just finished my law training and was returning to Jamaica and he began to talk to me. Like all egotistical lawyers, he had an enormous love of talking about his cases and, of course, I encouraged him. Every day we used to sit down, and we would talk for two or three hours about his cases; his methods, and his

Sir John Simon

techniques. The most valuable thing I learnt was the importance of intensely systematic unending preparation. He told me how he would summon four, five of his associates, and they would sit down at 11 o'clock at night and they would argue until 2.00 in the morning."

"About what?" asked Clerk.

"What is the first question to put to a witness. Just that. Nothing else. In a crucial case, that first question can decide the case. You've got to find one question on which it doesn't matter what the answer is. If he says *yes*, he's in trouble, if he says *no*, he's in trouble; if he says *yes* with a qualification, he's in trouble, if he says *no* with a qualification, he's in trouble. Everything he says, he's in trouble. Imagine, here was a master, talking about his own secrets and explaining the methods he used. Then he gave me a bit of advice."

"What was that?"

"Don't specialize. Simon told me that a competent lawyer, properly instructed, should be able to handle any case. He said it was a piece of advice he himself was given as a fledgling barrister by Sir Frank Lockwood, then Solicitor-General. 'Look at me', Simon quoted Lockwood as saying. 'Tomorrow I'm going to appear in the Admiralty Court, and all I know about navigation is [raising his glass] that port is red'."

In his first month Manley earned 16 guineas, and in the second he earned 25; sums he himself considered "not bad in those days".[9] Then, towards the end of November 1922, he found himself representing the plaintiff in an appeal concerning a breach of contract. The defendants had failed, he would argue, to deliver a load of oranges in time to catch a ship. The appeal came up on 22 November 1922, before Mr Justice Anthony DeFreitas, Acting Chief Justice and Justices H.I.C. Brown and R.T. Orpen. Henry Milne Radcliffe represented the defendants, Motor Car and Supplies Limited. Manley appeared for the plaintiff appellant, Mr George Smith.[10] In this case, the plaintiff sued for £40 damages for breach of contract, and the defendants counter-claimed for £4, being £2 for the hire of the defendants' motor truck for a trip from Gordon Town to Kingston, and £2 for the wrongful use of the same truck on a second trip between the same two places.

In the claim, the learned judge in the court below gave judgment for the plaintiff for £4, and in the counter-claim he gave judgment for the defendants for £4. The plaintiff, Mr George Smith, now appealed against these two judgments.

In the court below, the learned judge found, as a fact, that the contract between the parties was for two trips of the motor truck between Gordon Town and Kingston, and also that the defendants were guilty of negligence in not carrying out their contract on the second trip. He, however, reduced the damages claimed to £4, on the ground that the plaintiff was guilty of contributory negligence.

Analysing the evidence given at the earlier hearing, Manley now argued that "the defendants contracted to carry a load of fruit to the wharf; they altogether failed to carry out the contract. There was no delivery. The carrier of goods cannot call upon the consignee to accept delivery, except at the place of delivery.

"Secondly, the duty of a common carrier is to deliver the goods in a reasonable time. If the carrier delivers at an unreasonably late time, the consignee has the right to refuse the goods and sue for a full value. It does not make any difference whether the carrier is a common carrier or not. The question of negligence on the part of the plaintiff does not arise at all."

Manley noted that the goods which were carried in the truck from Gordon Town on 10 September 1922, consisted of cases of fruit which the plaintiff intended to ship that day to the English markets. Owing to the breakdown of the truck on the second trip, the fruit was not delivered at the wharf, but was taken to the defendants' garage.

Manley submitted that the fruits subsequently became rotten because they were allowed to get wet; that was not negligence on the part of the plaintiff. The defendants said that as soon as the fruits became bad they were thrown away because they had become a nuisance. Manley's submission on this point was that the learned judge in the court below was not right in rejecting the evidence of the plaintiff that there was no market, locally, for this kind of fruit. The true measure of damages, he observed, was the value of the goods. If it was found that the defendants failed altogether to deliver the goods, they ought to be deprived of their costs on the whole.

Radcliffe peered over his spectacles and argued, "What the magistrate meant by contributory negligence was that under the circumstances the plaintiff ought to have done something to minimise the damage. The defendants' contract was to hire a truck for two trips from Gordon Town. The plaintiff saw the truck on the road in trouble. The plaintiff was aware of all the facts surrounding the circumstances; the plaintiff could have got another truck just as well as the defendants." In his view the plaintiff had contributed to the rotting of the oranges. Radcliffe observed that there was no evidence of the truck breaking down through negligence. The oranges could have been saved if the plaintiff had got another truck or done something to have saved entirely the full sum of money he was claiming. The question of rejection did not arise. It was a question of whether the plaintiff had suffered any damages. The plaintiff could have made some attempt to sell the green fruits to other people. The judge in the court below had mixed up contributory negligence with minimising. Under the circumstances, the plaintiff could have minimised his loss. He admitted, however, that there was an agreement to take the fruit to the pier.

The court adjourned for lunch. On the resumption, Manley argued on the question of mitigated damages that "the person who refused to accept the goods was the owner of the goods. With regard to the assertion that the plaintiff should have got a lorry to take away the goods when the lorry had broken down, the plaintiff could not be expected to take any such step until after a contract was broken. The plaintiff is therefore entitled to the full damages of the goods. The plaintiff is also entitled to additional damages."

Manley cited an authority to show that in sending oranges to a wharf, it must be assumed that the plaintiff would derive some profit by the sale of the fruit. He was entitled to some allowance in the discretion of the court. The plaintiff said that he used to sell the oranges at one shilling per box which would make the amount £25. Relying on the terms of the judgment he referred to, it must be assumed that he would make the profit. It was common knowledge that people shipped goods at a profit.

"Assuming your contention is right, Mr Manley", reasoned the acting chief justice, "the court will have to send the case back to the Kingston Court for assessment."

"I will not press the point, Your Honour."

In delivering judgment, Mr Justice Orpen noted that when the truck broke down on the second trip, the plaintiff, although notified by the defendants, did not subsequently accept the fruits, and, as a result, they had to be destroyed. "Now the contributory negligence, which the learned judge in the court below found, is that the plaintiff did not remove the fruit from the garage and sell it in the local market and thus reduce the loss, but I do not consider that such a duty was cast upon the plaintiff," Orpen opined. "After the delay in delivery", he continued, "the plaintiff was legally justified in refusing to accept the fruit, vide *Wren* v. *The Eastern Counties Railway*, 1 L.T.R. (N.S.) 5, where delay in delivery resulting in the loss of a market was held to justify the refusal to accept the goods. In any case, there is no evidence to support the finding that there was any local market for immature fruit plucked for the English market, and the onus of proof of this would be on the defendants. The proper measure of damages in this case should be the amount lost by the plaintiff by the breach of contract, and the evidence on this is the plaintiff's uncontradicted statement that he lost £25. The judgment in the court below should therefore, in my opinion, be varied by entering judgment for the plaintiff on the claim for £25 with costs and solicitor's cost. With regard to the counter-claim, the defendants cannot recover payment for the second trip which they never completed, so that the judgment thereon must be varied to judgment for the defendants, on the counter-claim for £2, with court and bailiff's fees, as they have partly succeeded and partly failed in their counter-claim. Appellants to have the costs of this appeal fixed at £10."

The next day Manley was back in the Court of Appeal, a few yards up the corridor from the Supreme Court. In the barristers' robing room, he was greeted by a newcomer, the man considered the most prominent barrister of the day: J.A.G. Smith. 'Jags' was an outspoken man who enjoyed public speaking and was an immensely successful lawyer and legislator. His success as a barrister was due both to his ability and his persistence in fighting a case. Born in 1877 in Lucea, Hanover, Smith had been called to the Bar in London in 1910 and practised there for nine months before returning home. A black lawyer in an English Court was a rarity at that time, and when he won the appeal case *Rex* v. *Bugler* over which Lord Chief Justice Alverstone presided, both the English and Jamaican legal communities took note. In 1916 J.A.G. Smith had entered politics to become a member of the Legislative Council for Clarendon and harsh critic of government policies that did not meet his approval. The voters of the parish recognized the value of his work and kept him in the Council without a break until his death in 1942. As a barrister, he straddled the Bar, appearing in most of the important causes for a dozen years prior to Manley.

Now, in December 1922, it must have been with some trepidation that the young Manley contemplated facing this formidable opponent in court. Smith was scheduled to argue against Manley in an appeal resulting from a suit brought in the Resident Magistrate's Court at Spanish Town by the plaintiff, Mr Egerton Rickards, a surveyor, for work done.[11] The resident

The Hon. J.A.G. Smith (1877–1942)

magistrate had given judgment by default against the defendant, a Mrs Edwina McDonald. A warrant of levy against the goods of Mrs McDonald was subsequently issued on 17 February, 1908, and was returned *nulla bona* [No goods that can be distrained upon.]

Mrs McDonald took no steps to set aside the judgment from February 1908 to September 1909 when she left island. In April 1910, as the judgment remained unsatisfied, Rickards sold under the Order of Court, some 2 roods and 15 perches of land belonging to the defendant at Porus in the parish of Manchester for £40, and after payment of the judgment debt and costs, the balance was lodged in court to the credit of Mrs McDonald. The purchaser, Henry Patrickson had, since 5 December 1910, remained in undisturbed possession of the land until March 1922, when Mrs McDonald returned to the island, entered on the land and claimed possession.

Mrs McDonald applied to the Resident Magistrate for St Catherine to set aside the default judgment entered against her on 3 February 1908; set aside the sale to Patrickson, and give her leave to defend the action. This application was heard, and subsequently refused by the Resident Magistrate for St Catherine. From this refusal Mrs McDonald now appealed. The outcome was a decision of much local interest. J.A.G. Smith submitted that the resident magistrate had no jurisdiction to order the sale of the defendant's lands: "A Resident Magistrate can exercise jurisdiction only in his parish. The lands in question are at Porus, in the parish of Manchester, and therefore the Resident Magistrate should not have ordered the sale."

Manley took Smith to task: "My learned friend, Mr Smith, has taken the point that a Resident Magistrate of a particular parish has no jurisdiction to order the sale of lands in another parish; but I submit that this could not have been the intention of the Legislature. What would be the position if what my learned friend argues is correct? It would mean this: that a man with land in one parish, could go outside that parish and obtain credit all round, and his creditors in the other parishes would not be able to get the fruits of their judgment. I submit that the Court had jurisdiction to deal with the cause of action, and the power of the Court was not confined to land in any particular parish, so long as there was jurisdiction. A judgment has been obtained against the defendant, and I contend that, as the section stood, the Resident Magistrate had the power to order the sale."

Acting Chief Justice Anthony DeFreitas noted that the law dealing with land jurisdiction of every Resident Magistrate's Court "shall extend to the parish for which the sale is appointed and one mile beyond the boundary line of the parish".

The jurisdiction, therefore, for trying any action with regard to land was limited to the parish and one mile beyond the boundary. Under that part of the law dealing with execution DeFreitas observed that "the Resident Magistrate may make an order for the sale of the estate of interest of the judgment debtor in *any lands* at such time and place and subject to such conditions as the Court shall think fit. Provided always that no such order shall be made where the land to be affected thereby exceeds the value of £200. It is argued that the words *any lands* in this section must be limited to any lands within the parish as the general jurisdiction of the Resident Magistrate to try cases is limited to his parish. I do not think this argument is sound," DeFreitas opined. "The limitation under section 86 is made *for the purposes of this part of the Law*, that is, that part of the Law which gives the Resident Magistrate jurisdiction to try a case with regard to land, and I see no reason why this limitation should be extended to the words *any lands* in section 223, which is for the purpose of giving effect to a judgment, and in which the only limitation is that the lands must not exceed £200 in value . . . . If the limitation were put upon the words *any lands* in section 223, as there is no procedure under the Law for transferring a judgment from one Resident Magistrate's Court to another, a judgment creditor would in a case like the present be deprived of one of the means of enjoying the fruits of his judgment — a result which I am sure was never intended by the Legislature.

"I am therefore of opinion that the sale of the debtor's interest in the land in this case was within the jurisdiction. The appeal must therefore be dismissed with costs."

One can only speculate that Manley showed little outward emotion following his triumph over Jags in the Court of Appeal. Manley was a shy man who kept his feelings to himself, but privately he must have experienced a deep-rooted sense of fulfilment: he had justified his mother's faith in him. Up to the time of her death, Manley had been an uncontrollable teenage terror who defied discipline and had a thoroughly disreputable reputation. His mother's death dealt him a cruel blow. He turned over a new leaf and fought hard at the job of self-reformation and to excel in the profession for which she had thought him best fitted: a barrister-at-law. And what would Manley's father have thought? For he too loved argument, but as one of the most celebrated litigants of his time. How this shaped his son's character is one for the geneticists; it is safe to say that due to his father's passion for the law courts, Norman Manley's life was irrevocably changed from what should have been a privileged upbringing to one of hard struggle.

2

A Litigious Charmer

*On the evening of the 22nd inst. Mr T.A.S. Manley died at
Roxburgh. By his death the parish has lost a valued friend
and supporter, as for many years he carried on an extensive
fruit and produce business by which he gave employment to
a good many people in the parish. The congregation of
mourners who assembled in the Wesleyan Chapel at Porus,
on the day of his funeral, and followed from the chapel to the
grave, told of the place he occupied in the heart of the
people. Mr Manley was a keen businessman and his mental
abilities far above the average. In his courage and intensity
of purpose, and in his grasp of a subject, he left most far
behind. To his sorrowing wife and children is extended the
sympathy of the entire community.*

The Gleaner
25 March 1899

Norman Manley was only six years old when his father died and the
event would change his life dramatically. Ironically, the father of
the man who would become the most famous lawyer in the land
squandered his hard-earned wealth on lawsuits.

When pretty, petite Margaret Ann Shearer from Hanover had
married the charming thirty-eight year old Thomas Albert Samuel
Manley from Porus, Manchester, she had pledged her troth to a
prosperous businessman known throughout Jamaica and a pillar of his
community. Thomas Manley was a man of great personal charm and
hospitality who had a lot of American friends, mainly importers, who
often visited his home, Roxburgh, to strike a deal for the Manchester
orange which had become popular in the United States for its size and
flavour and was exported to a considerable extent by 1895.

After the wedding on 15 January 1890 at the King's Church in Westmoreland,[1] Thomas took Margaret to his comfortable mountain home, four miles up a rocky, winding ascent from the quaint roadside village of Royal Flat near Williamsfield. Roxburgh exuded all that Thomas had worked and strived for. There were four well-furnished bedrooms, the master room having an Arabian bedstead and marble top dressing table. The dining room sported silver dinner and breakfast sets, electro-plated dish covers, an ice-cooler and a "large safe". Lace curtains draped

Manley's mother, Margaret Ann Shearer, born at Blenheim, Hanover

the windows of the carpeted drawing room with its five rocking chairs, two dozen cane-seated chairs, revolving book case, Carl Otto piano and Mason and Hamlin organ.[2] For transport there were four buggies and several mares in addition to other livestock. There were also Thomas Manley's personal pets: a mastiff and a collie who were trained by him to hold visitors at bay until he gave the order to relax. Pimento barbecues and large water tanks for both domestic and pasture use surrounded the house which was raised above a cellar to offer magnificent views over the table-land.

It seemed a perfect life, except that Thomas Manley had one major flaw: a fatal love for litigation. Over the years, he wasted his money on lawsuits; every possible issue he took to the courts. So fond was he of the law that the day before his wedding he had drawn up a marriage settlement with Margaret (the daughter of an Irish pen-keeper, Alexander Shearer of Blenheim and his Jamaican wife, Ann Margaret, née Taylor) who had come to Porus to be the postmistress. The settlement revealed Thomas Manley's extensive holdings: Roxboro (later Roxburgh) Castle Plantation in Manchester, "containing by survey 383 acres"; land at Arcadia Pen in Porus, another parcel of land on the main road to Mandeville, 137 acres at Chisholm's Mammee Gully in Clarendon and a further 317 acres known as Breadland Pen in the same parish. Additionally, Thomas Manley had insured his life for the sum of £300 with the London Assurance Company and had acquired five shares in the American Hotels Company.[3]

Manley's father, Thomas Albert Samuel Manley

Thomas had come a long way from his birth as an illegitimate country boy from Porus, born with little or no prospects in 1852. "He was a mulatto", said Norman Manley, reflecting on his father's pedigree: "a straight cross between a black woman and a white man. He was a bright boy who worked his way up to become one of the leading produce dealers in Jamaica. It's the family legend that from a youngster he showed great business acumen. He was supposed to have gone to market with his mother's donkey and come home with a mule he had swopped for the donkey!"[4]

Thomas grew up as a country boy with his mother. His father was an English travelling salesman from Yorkshire who fathered several children in Jamaica. In addition to Thomas there was Samuel Smith Manley[5] who became a well-known baker and shopkeeper in Black River and John Wilfred Samuel Manley who owned a store in Porus, having established himself on a lot of land he purchased from the old Trowel plantation.[6] Finally, there was a girl, Emma, who later married an Alberga.[7]

The three Manley brothers — Thomas, Samuel and John — were all self-made and remained close throughout their lives, supporting each other in their various business ventures. It was Thomas, however, jovial but stubborn, and with a passion for taking chances, who was the most successful. He became a far-sighted and aggressive businessman who early recognized the potential market for Jamaican fruits and spices overseas. Thomas purchased and planted land both in Manchester and Clarendon to become one of the first farmers in Jamaica to begin an export trade in agricultural produce with the United States. The surplus he sold locally in stores he built for the purpose.

The year he married Margaret Ann Shearer, Thomas, together with his brothers Samuel and John Manley and Margaret's father, Alexander Shearer, purchased Belmont in St Catherine.[8] The property had been auctioned in Kingston on 13 June 1890, and Thomas Manley, acting on behalf of his family, had been the highest bidder with a sum of £1,710. Belmont consisted of a substantial stone-built dwelling house and the usual outbuildings, but what had put a gleam into Thomas

Belmont is advertised for sale

Manley's eye was the abundance of logwood (a profitable source for dye which had tremendous export value in the 1890s) and the fact that an estimated 2,000 tons of roots were ready for digging. As soon as Belmont had become a family concern, the ever industrious Thomas had gone into the logwood business and ended up in the Kingston Circuit Court. He was not represented by the man who had been his solicitor and legal adviser for over a decade, John T. Palache, but by Godfrey G. Gunter, the Mandeville-based solicitor. The reason for the change in legal representation was profound. Thomas Manley, wounded beyond reason at losing three lawsuits in a row, had turned around and sued his own solicitor, John T. Palache, for negligence.[9]

Before the breach, it was a common sight to see Palache, a short and rather stout gentleman clad in a loosely fitting black alpaca jacket, rolling sailor-like from his office by the old Brooks Hotel across the village green to the Mandeville Courthouse, with the equally stout, but taller, Thomas Manley in tow. They'd take no notice of anyone else, so engrossed would they be in discussing either Manley's latest lawsuit or how to make people eat more vegetables. Both were pioneers of the 'Grow More Food, Eat More Vegetables' campaign. Local labourers learned from them how to plant and cultivate and were given plants and seedlings in unstinted quantity.

On 27 June 1891, Thomas Manley wrote to Palache charging him with various gross breaches of professional duty, "the result of which has wrecked my whole future prospects and today I am deprived of my good name and truthfulness on which my business was hitherto carried on".[10]

One year later, on 19 June 1892, Thomas Manley appeared before the Supreme Court of Jamaica, claiming £5,000 as damages in respect of injury alleged to have been sustained by him through the professional negligence of John Palache. In his statement of claim, Thomas Manley charged Palache with failure to exercise due care, diligence, and professional skill in the conduct of three litigations, in all of which

Manley was unsuccessful. The case was tried before Mr Justice Lumb and a special jury. The trial occupied nine consecutive days, during which Palache insisted that there was no way any solicitor worth his salt could act on Thomas Manley's behalf. According to Palache, Thomas would select his own witnesses, examine them himself and personally escort them into Kingston on a daily basis to attend court. Additionally, said Palache, Thomas would furnish him with written notes of what he expected each witness to say in the box. Palache further revealed that if a case didn't go as Thomas Manley expected, he would get up and try to take over the proceedings himself. How could any reasonable lawyer continue to represent such a client? At the end of the hearing, judgment was accordingly entered for Palache. Thomas promptly appealed and moved the court either to enter judgment in his favour or to allow a new trial. The appeal was dismissed and Thomas, nothing daunted, appealed to the Privy Council in England and lost again, the decision being given in favour of Palache with costs.[11]

Despite the demands of his legal and business affairs, Thomas Manley's home life prospered. Margaret bore him four children: Vera, Muriel, Norman and Roy who were all born at Roxburgh with less than five years separating the first from the last. Norman was born on 4 July 1893 and Thomas ensured that the *Gleaner* recorded the event for posterity: "BIRTH Manley — At Roxburgh, the wife of T.A.S. Manley, of a son."[12] On 17 September 1893, he was baptized Norman Washington at the Porus Methodist Church by the Reverend Harvey Swithenbank.[13] The good Reverend could never have guessed that twenty-eight years later, the babe in his arms would marry his own daughter, Edna Swithenbank, after he himself had married Margaret Manley's sister, Ellie. Nevertheless, all that lay in the future. For the moment, what Margaret had to say about her husband's propensities is not recorded. When the case regarding the Belmont property came to trial, she was three months pregnant with Norman and dutifully accompanied her husband and his solicitor, Godfrey Gunter, to court.

The Kingston Circuit Court at that time was situated in Harbour Street. Business in judges' chambers then, and for many years afterwards, was not transacted *in camera*. Chambers were open to the public, and it was here that young solicitors and articled clerks learnt the first elements of the practical side of their profession by hearing how able seniors conducted interlocutory matters. On 20 January 1893, Thomas Manley appeared in court charging one Charles Burke with obtaining money by false pretences.[14] In September 1890, Manley had entered into an agreement with Burke to receive Belmont logwood at

Spanish Town and forward it to Kingston for threepence per ton commission.

Mr Barrister Cargill addressed the court on Burke's behalf. "The first question which the jury will have to decide is the amount due by Burke to Manley. The plaintiff said that he had entered into contracts with the defendant to forward logwood from Spanish Town to Kingston. Now, the plaintiff does not seem to know what a contract is. His idea seems to have changed as time went on . . ."

It was all Gunter could do to put a restraining arm on Thomas; of course he knew what a contract was, and he jumped to his feet and told them so. Mr Justice Northcote slammed down his gavel: "Sit down, Mr Manley!" As with most of Thomas Manley's lawsuits, the verdict against him was a foregone conclusion. Some of the receipts for the wood were missing; others were illegible. Burke told the court that "Manley was suffering from bad eyes" at the time. Perhaps an early indication of the diabetes that finally carried him off six years later?

Throughout the month of March 1899, Thomas had been ill, suffering from a severe attack of diabetes. At 7.00 p.m. on Wednesday, the 22nd, he succumbed.[15] Many probably wryly thought that the litigious Thomas would have appealed the judgment. "I vividly remember a storm of weeping and sobbing in the house on realizing that he was dead," Norman Manley was later to recall. "I don't remember the funeral, I just remember that."[16]

Thomas Manley's demise, at age 47, was announced in the Gleaner,[17] advising "American papers, please copy" — a reminder that Thomas Manley's final adventure had been the financing of a shipment of oranges and pimento bound for New York. The ship foundered in a storm at which point it emerged that Thomas had not insured his valuable cargo. Thomas side-stepped this final prospect of ruin by departing this earth, leaving his family almost penniless.

Following the death of her husband, Margaret Manley penned a personal note to the Gleaner thanking her "numerous friends and acquaintances for their kind letters of sympathy received by her from them in her bereavement".[18] It was dated 8 April 1899, Roxburgh. Then she packed her bags, left her four children with her sister, Mary, and took a steamer passage to America where she got a job as a postal telegraphy clerk in Washington. Unable to support her family on her American earnings, Margaret Manley returned home. "I remember her coming back," Norman Manley reflected. "That's when we moved to Kingston with the idea of trying to get me an education at Wolmer's. Just before I was nine years old, I entered Wolmer's and I was there for nine months. Meanwhile, my mother, who was a very strong-minded and energetic woman, had come to some arrangement with her family and moved us all to Belmont where she took charge of the property."[19]

Of his mother, Norman wrote later that she "had one fixed determination in life — to see that her children got a good education".[20] Belmont, he said, "was a hard place to manage. It was quite undeveloped and like so many of the old, derelict places in Jamaica it carried on as best it could with a little of everything. Logwood, sold after being cut into lengths of heart wood with the bark and sap chipped off; a few cattle; a few tenants; a little cocoa. Singlehanded she managed all these things and even found time to persuade the authorities to allow her to open a post office at Belmont itself which she took charge of. She made all our clothes, made jellies when guavas were in, kept a small chicken farm and ran things with firm efficiency".

Capable and decisive Margaret Manley may have been, but she couldn't compensate for the absence of a father in Norman's life. "I was by nature a rebel," he later confessed.[21] And when he succeeded, at thirteen, in winning a half-scholarship to Jamaica College, he became in his own words, "the ringleader of all the mischief makers in the school. At one time I was reported simultaneously by all seven masters. How I survived, I don't know. It was only because old Simms [the headmaster] deeply sympathized with my mother, and knew what a struggle she had with her family, that I wasn't expelled".[22] This went on until Norman was seventeen years old, when, at the early age of forty-two, Margaret Manley died of pernicious malarial fever. Her faith in her son's future, which Norman later mourned "had so little to support it," prompted him to turn over a new leaf and he startled Simms by announcing that he meant to try for the Rhodes Scholarship. "And being a very ruthless young man", Manley subsequently admitted, "I deserted all my old friends and made myself an utter terror in the school in favour of law and authority![23] About three months after that, several pupils reported me. Simms sent for me and said: 'You know, Manley, it is a very laudable thing to keep order, but I do ask you to remember that mercy must temper justice.' I never forgot that," Manley laughed in later life. "Mercy must temper justice."[24]

Manley's personal desire to succeed was greatly influenced by his mother's ambitions for his future. He settled down to win the Rhodes and put to positive use the traits he inherited from his father: courage, intensity of purpose and mental abilities far above the average.

Chinese immigrants

3

A Chinese Controversy

The ship Epsom, 650 tons, Capt. Buckland, left London on
31 July 1853 for Australia, from there to Hong Kong, to take
on the Chinese immigrants intended for Jamaica.

Falmouth Post
8 August 1854

As 1922 drew to a close, the solicitor, Mr Lewis Ashenheim, briefed barrister Manley on the defence of three Chinese charged with setting fire to their Kingston premises at No. 13 West Queen Street, with intent to defraud. Ashenheim was by this time in the forefront of practising solicitors. Born in Kingston on 7 May 1873, he was admitted to practice as a solicitor of the Supreme Court of Jamaica in February 1896. He went into partnership with Mr A. J. Corinaldi and rapidly won recognition for his sound knowledge of law and impressive court deportment. In May 1912, Ashenheim ended his partnership with Corinaldi and joined the firm of Farquharson and Milholland, the firm's name being changed to Milholland, Ashenheim and Stone.

The defence of the three Chinese was the first of many cases Manley would argue on Ashenheim's behalf. Over the years the two men would become, according to Manley, "old friends" who enjoyed the thrust and parry of debate and ritually played bridge at Drumblair with Ashenheim's uncle, Louis Alberga, and others throughout Holy Thursday night until nine o'clock Good Friday morning when Edna Manley would serve a breakfast of bacon and eggs.[1]

The arson case was significant in that a spate of fires had destroyed the premises of several Chinese shopkeepers in Kingston during the early 1920s, giving rise to the suspicion that they had been deliberately set for the purpose of gain, that is, the collection of insurance. On examining the evidence given at this and other trials, it appears that some Chinese shopkeepers were the victims of discrimination, malice and jealousy, partly as a consequence of business competition, and that some fires may well have been wilfully set by competitors to burn the Chinese out of business. To better understand the ramifications of the case, something of the Chinese and their status in Jamaica at that time must be told.

The first Chinese had arrived in the island in August 1854 as indentured labourers to work on the sugar, coffee and pimento estates. It had taken the ship *Epsom* 108 days to reach Falmouth, Jamaica's bustling north-side port, after it had left the then British Colony of Hong Kong Island on 21 April with 312 immigrants, all male, aged between sixteen and thirty-eight.[2] Another group of Chinese immigrants arrived from Panama on 1 November 1854 when the brig *Vampire* docked at Falmouth with 107 survivors of some 1,042 contract labourers who had been hired to work on the Panama railroad. The majority had died as a result of the harsh conditions there.[3] By January 1855, a good number of these immigrants had deserted the estates and were seen walking about the towns begging for alms. Interviewed by a local newspaper, one Chinese said that he had left the estate in Clarendon

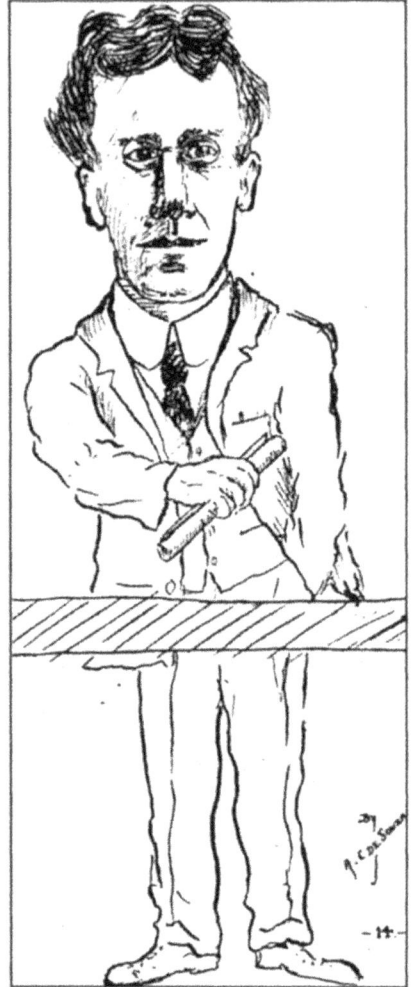

The solicitor, Mr Lewis Ashenheim (1873–1941)

where he had been placed because the overseer refused to grant him such supplies as he was led to believe he would have received, independent of his wages.[4] Before long, the Chinese had set up small grocery shops or gone into market gardening. Over the years they were joined by fellow immigrants who, like their brethren, soon left the estates on which they were settled and set themselves up in business.

The local Chinese shop not only supplied rural Jamaicans with everything for their domestic and agricultural use, but it served, with its inevitable copy of the *Gleaner*, as a centre for discussion on such diverse topics as politics, the weather, the latest crime and the best way to grow yams. But "Lawd ah massy! Look! de ooman she a wear trousiz," was a comment often hurled at the Chinese women who did not immediately surrender their traditional loose brown oil-silk trousers. For their part, they would plod on regardless. Up and down; down and up, hour after lagging hour, heedless alike of banter and rudeness, and sometimes coarse insult, until they and their husbands became permanent fixtures in the community. Little by little the shops thrived and expanded as the Chinese became popular with their customers because they extended credit, sold goods in quantities which the labouring classes could afford and good, quick service was no trouble. Pennies really did contain four farthings, and so a farthing or ha'penny's worth of goods could be bought. Selling a ha'penny's worth of saltfish, a gill of salt butter, and giving away a glass of water, or a bit of fish to go with the bread or crackers, were things unheard of before the Chinese kept shop in Jamaica. H.G. deLisser, however, noted in 1910 another point of view: that one of the secrets of the Chinese grocer's success was that "he robs your oil and gives you a biscuit and you go away thinking you have got something for nothing".[5] This ambivalent attitude continued and more than once flared into anti-Chinese riots. In July 1918, for example, riots which started in St Catherine and St Mary spread as far afield as St Ann and Clarendon.[6] Nevertheless, many Chinese worked their small retail groceries into sizeable stores and then into wholesale houses. Their children went into commerce and played pivotal roles in Jamaica's professional, civic and cultural life. On 28 July 1922, George Tai Tenn Quee became the first Chinese to practise law in Jamaica when he was enrolled as a solictior of the Supreme Court.[7] It was in April of the same year that the Parochial Board of St Andrew announced that the time had come for the Central Government to take steps to prevent the landing in Jamaica of Chinese immigrants. They couldn't afford to close their eyes, they said, to the fact that the Chinese held the monopoly in the grocery trade and the bakery, laundry, restaurant, pastry and ice-cream businesses, "taking bread out of the mouths" of the local populace.[8] It is against this background that Manley argued the first of his "Chinese" arson cases.

In Kingston, the largest concentration of Chinese was in the western district. According to Ashenheim's brief, on the night of 31 October 1922, a fire had started in a shop in West Queen Street owned by Ernest Chin Chung. The Kingston Fire Brigade received the alarm around 9.45. Within two minutes, chief officer Malcolm Dunn and his men were at the scene. The inside of the building was on fire; smoke was issuing through the roof. Dunn ordered a fireman to break the

Mr Justice Anthony DeFreitas

street door of the shop. He struck one blow with an axe and was preparing to swing a second when a voice said, "Don't chop; see keys here."

Dunn took the keys from a Chinese whom he later learned was the proprietor, Ernest Chin Chung.

On entering the shop, Dunn said that he noticed a strong smell of kerosene oil. The police investigated and later that night, Chung and his two assistants Ah Fat and Ah Bow, were arrested and charged with arson.

The case came up for trial on 10 January 1923 when the Home Circuit Court resumed its sitting before Mr Justice Anthony DeFreitas, Acting Chief Justice, with Mr John St John Yates, Acting Assistant to the Attorney-General prosecuting. The three accused pleaded not guilty.[9]

In opening the case for the prosecution, Yates admitted that the evidence was of a circumstantial nature but, he added, "the Crown will prove by the conduct of the accused, that they were the originators of the fire. For example, when Chung was asked to give some assistance to extinguish the flames, he threw down the bucket. Why did he not want to save his property? The suggestion of the Crown is that the fire was deliberately set, and for the purpose of gain".

Officer Dunn was the first witness to take the stand. He said that on entering the premises he saw a fire in the north-western portion of the shop; there was a strong smell of kerosene oil. How long did it take the firemen to put out the flames? About five minutes. And then?

"I examined the north-western corner of the premises and found a burnt barrel. There were small pieces of wood alongside the barrel and some kerosene tins. When I returned to the station my clothes and boots were wet with kerosene oil; for days after, they reeked of kerosene."

It was Manley's turn to question the fire chief. Officer Dunn agreed with Manley's suggestion that if there were tins of kerosene oil about, it was probable that they would be spilt; and if the oil spilt and mixed with the water and he went walking about the premises, the mixture might be splashed on his clothes. Asked where the fire had started, the officer replied, "In the north-western corner of the shop."

"And what were the walls in this section made from?" enquired Manley.

"Brick," replied the fire chief.

"Not a very sensible place to set a fire — was it, Officer, considering that there were other walls made of wood?"

The witness hesitated; Manley sat down. No further questions.

Police Detective Sergeant James Hamilton Irving was on the stand. He described in detail how he had found pieces of charred board in the north-western corner of Chang's shop and "in the centre of the pieces of board was a barrel; inside the barrel were small pieces of board, up to about nine inches long, some charcoal, rolled newspapers, socks, cloth, caps and rolls of toilet paper. On top of these things, was a tin of kerosene oil. On top of the tin was a small straw basket. The straw smelt of kerosene. Close to the barrel were five tins and a galvanized iron bucket. Four of the tins were opened, and the unopened one was labelled *kerosene oil*. Two of the tins smelt of kero-maize oil, and the other two smelt of maize oil. In the bucket there was a liquid smelling of kerosene; there was water mixed with it. In the liquid there were several lamp wicks, silk thread, and a pair of lady's evening shoes. I also found three rolls of toilet paper about one and a half yards from the West Queen Street door. They smelt of kerosene. I took samples of the articles found in the shop to the Island Chemist."

Cross-examined by Manley, the witness said he went to the shop to ascertain the cause of the fire. He observed a lot of goods packed up and scattered about. He made a selection of the goods in the shop, selecting the articles which smelt of kerosene. He confirmed that the fire appeared to have started by a brick wall.

Manley leaned forward and shot out his chin.

"I suggest to you that your observations were for the purpose of manufacturing a crime?"

"No."

After some amount of prodding, the detective admitted that he would not have placed some of the articles where they were found if he should set a fire. The whole affair, he concluded, was suspicious.

The court adjourned for lunch. On the resumption, Kenneth R. Brandon, Clerk of Courts for Kingston, explained that when persons wanted kerosene licences, they applied to him. None of the prisoners had applied for a licence, and he produced the records themselves which showed that no licence had been granted to 13 West Queen Street. Cross-examined by Manley, Brandon agreed that an application could get lost or mislaid.

The next witness for the prosecution, Acting Deputy Island Chemist, Everard Noel Richards, related how he had been asked to examine various items: two rolls of toilet paper which smelt of kerosene; two rolls of sansilk; some lamp wicks; bits of wood and some bundles of socks which appeared to have been wet with kerosene.

"If your fingers touch them how long will the smell last?" The judge asked the witness.

"Oh, some time," replied the chemist.

The judge looked downcast: "I am sorry because I just touched them and the smell is on my fingers. I'll have to bear it."

Manley allowed the collective outburst of laughter to fade before he began his cross-examination:

"Were the rolls of toilet paper soaked through and through?"

"No, sir. I'd say about half an inch."

"Would you say that if the rolls had fallen into kerosene oil they would have the same smell?"

"Yes, and I go further. It would be the same if they had fallen in water and kerosene."

Daniel Clare, a pedlar, said he rented the piazza from the accused, Ernest Chin Chung. On 31 October last, he was on the piazza and saw Chung at about 11 o'clock the morning with a dray load of goods. Chung went out and came back once or twice that day. When he left the piazza at 6.30 p.m. Chung was not there. According to Clare, Chung wasn't feeling good that day; he had heard him ask someone to buy cerasee.

As the prosecuting counsel sat, Manley rose and asked the witness to explain cerasee.

"Is a bush, sir, for making bath or drinking", he replied, adding, "boil cerasee tea good for bellyache."

Rhoda Walters, a barmaid, was on the stand. She said that she was employed at the rum bar next to Chung's shop. On the night in question, she saw fire coming out of there. She got three buckets of water and poured it on his roof before the fire brigade arrived. In going to fill the fourth bucket, she saw Chung standing near the pipe, "And I say to him, 'You can't help me put out the fire?' And I give him the bucket, and him put it down and say something I don't understand."

Manley watched the witness play out her testimony. Then it was his turn to cross-examine.

"Miss Walters, did you have any difficulty in throwing water on the roof?"

"Yes."

"What sort of roof is it?"

"Zinc."

"So the water must have run off?"

"Yes."

"Did you think that while you were doing that laudable task, it was of no purpose?"

"No."

"Miss Walters, can you explain how the light of the fire came through a concrete wall, wooden windows and zinc?"

"The zinc was curling up."

"The bar in which you work is Bethune's bar?"

"Yes."

"Which did the better business — your bar or Chung's?"

"You needn't answer that," instructed DeFreitas.

Manley heeded the warning and sat down.

Gershon Johnson, a tavern keeper, said he remembered the night of the fire. He was going upstairs outside his place when he saw the smoke going up. He stood for two minutes looking at it, and then gave the alarm. He went out into the grass yard behind Chung's shop. Chung was there. He said to him, "You standing up there, instead of going to give assistance?"

Just then, he said, he heard the fire brigade coming, and Chung moved to his own yard. He saw Rhoda Walters throwing water on the shop. He heard when she asked Chung to come and assist her. She gave him the bucket, and he threw it on the ground. Chung was fully dressed. The roof of Chung's shop was about ten feet from the ground. When the fire was out, he went into the shop with detectives Robb and Rose. At the north-western corner he saw a large quantity of single matches scattered about. He heard Chung say, "It's bad luck. I'm sick and those two fellows are careless". Johnson recalled at that point he said to Chung, "Bad luck, eh? How about the matches that were scattered about and the kerosene oil?" Chung replied that the fire brigade must have bounced down those matches.

Manley began his interrogation of the witness:

"Why did you go into the room?"

"Because it interested me. I'd seen smoke from that shop before."

"Why did you not tell the magistrate that at the preliminary hearing?"

"I wasn't asked."

"Don't you think it was a piece of officiousness on your part to have gone into the room?"

"That's what you might think."

"You have a bar nearby?"

"Yes."

"And you didn't like the competition?"

"Every man is entitled to live."

"You were interested in assisting the police?"

"Yes, knowing that I wasn't insured like others."

"As a loyal citizen you went in?"

"Yes."

"You say that the detective asked you to come in and show them where the fire started?"

"Yes."

"Where did you see the fire?"

"Leaping up to the roof."

"What was the roof made of?"

"Zinc."

"And the walls?"

"Brick."

"And do you ask the jury to believe that you saw fire leaping up to the roof?"

"Yes, I saw it coming up through the crevice."

"The flames were coming through the crevice?"

"No, sir."

"Where did you see those flames?" intervened the judge.

"Between the foundation and the sill."

"Don't shuffle with me sir, or I'll commit you to prison!" threatened DeFreitas, as he hauled up his white cuffs and pushed back his wig in an effort to cool off. "Is where you saw the flames?" he repeated, slipping now into the vernacular.

"In the shop."

"I know in the shop; where did you see them through?"

"Through the roof."

DeFreitas sighed. Manley turned back to the witness and asked, "How high up your staircase were you?"

"I was on a level with the zinc."

"You told the police that you saw where the fire started?"

"Yes."

"Did they come to you, and ask you, or did you go to them and tell them?"

"They came to me and asked me."

"When did you hear the fire alarm?"

"When I was talking to Chung."

"You heard the alarm of fire while you were talking to Chung?"

"No, sir."

"But that is what you have just said."

"I sent the alarm when I saw the fire from the staircase."

"Did you see Ah Fat and Ah Bow there before the fire was put out?"

"No."

"But you told the magistrate that you did?"

"It was a mistake."

"Is that the only mistake you have made in this case?"

"I don't know."

"Is it also a mistake when you said you saw Chung there before the fire was put out?"

"No."

"Did the basket and barrel look suspicious to you?"

"Yes."

"And that was why you were officious enough to insinuate that Chung set the fire?"

"I said it was suspicious."

"Doesn't it occur to you now that if that basket was on top of the tin of oil, it must have been burnt in some way?"

"Yes."

"Don't you think it must have been put there afterwards?"

"Yes."

"Did you put it there?"

"No, sir."

Johnson was re-examined by Mr Yates for the prosecution who asked: "What was your object in going to Chung's room that night?"

"To see justice done."

"Even though the heavens fall!" Manley muttered *sotto voce*.

The court adjourned. The following morning the case for the prosecution continued when Joseph Bethune, another tavern keeper, took the stand. His premises adjoined those of the accused, Ernest Chin Chung. He went into Chung's shop, he said, after the fire, and saw caps, socks, and so on, in the north-western portion of the shop. He didn't remember seeing such items in the north-western corner before.

Quizzed by Manley, the witness said that Chung never sold kerosene oil in his shop.

John Reginald Howie took the stand. He told the court that he was an accountant employed by Mr B.W. Boyd, the local agent of the World Auxilliary Insurance Corporation. He produced an insurance policy which he said was the one issued by Mr Boyd's company to the accused, Mr Chung. The stock in trade of the accused was insured for £500 and the fixtures at £100.

Cross-examined by Manley, the witness said that Mr Ashenheim had made a claim on the insurance company on behalf of Chung for £132 in respect of stock in trade and £25 for fixtures. The company's representative had had the stock valued after the fire. It was valued at £455 and the fixtures at £200.

"That was £55 over and above what he was insured for", submitted Manley, "and that after the fire?"

"Yes," the witness replied.

Detective Nehemiah Robb was sworn in. He recounted how he himself and Detective Rose went to the scene. The articles, now in court, were in the north-western portion of the shop. The burnt barrel was amongst the articles. There was kerosene oil near the barrel and a straw basket on top of the barrel. Cross-examined by Manley the witness said the tavern keepers Bethune and Johnson came in the shop after he had been there. Had he asked Johnson to come into the shop and show him where the fire occurred? No. Was it possible for anyone to have gone into the shop and put the basket in the position it was? Yes.

This closed the case for the prosecution. Manley submitted that on a joint indictment such as that against the three accused, there was no evidence to go to the jury. The only evidence against the accused was that one was owner of the shop and the other two were there in the course of their ordinary duty and that when the two left for home a fire occurred. There was no evidence to show that the three accused jointly set the fire. DeFreitas was adamant; he would not withdraw the case from the jury. Manley bowed in acquiescence and opened the case for the defence. His eyes swept around the courtroom before settling on the jury:

"Jamaica is a country where there is this peculiar fallacy", he said, thrusting one hand deep into his pocket, "that wherever there's a fire, there's a Chinaman." And he called Ernest Chin Chung to the stand.

Chung said that he had been in trade in Jamaica for about nine years. He had bought the West Queen Street business in May the previous year for £300 and made many improvements. At the time of the fire he valued his stock at about £500. He was not in financial difficulties; he did not know how the fire occurred. Two or three days previous to the fire he had been ill with fever but, in spite of that, he used to keep an eye on the business. On the day of the fire he got some bush and boiled a bath. He went to the shop around 8.50 p.m. to collect the day's sales then returned to his room nearby. His two assistants came home about twenty minutes later. They were all in bed when he heard someone call out: "Fire! Fire!" He peeped through the window and saw his place on fire. He put on a pair of slippers and went out in his sleeping clothes. He walked through the Princess Street grass yard and into West Queen Street. He took his keys and attempted to open the shop door but a fireman stopped him. Chung related how he had run back to the grass yard calling out: "Water! Water!" He saw Rhoda Walters in the bar. It was untrue that she gave him a bucket. Yes, he sold kerosene oil. He used to buy and sell about twenty tins a month. He paid money to his merchant Mr Soltau to get a general trade licence, and another to sell kerosene. He did his cooking in the shop, at 10 a.m., 3 p.m. and 7.30 p.m. His cooking stove was next to a cistern, standing on a box in which he stored the articles for cooking. Next to that was a barrel in which he kept charcoal.

The court adjourned for lunch. On the resumption Yates cross-examined Ernest Chin Chung who insisted that when he was taken to the Sutton Street Police Station he was wearing his sleeping clothes. Whilst he was there, a Chinese friend, who lived opposite, brought him a pair of trousers and a jacket. Rhoda Walters never gave him a bucket of water, so he had none to throw away. He did not light the cooking stove on the day of the fire. He did not observe any fire in it. He could not say how the articles got into the barrel. He had not left any unopened tins of oil in the north-western portion of the shop.

Manley called Mr William Soltau, a wholesale merchant, to the stand. Chung had been his customer for about five or six years, he testified; he had found him straightforward and he paid up regularly. Soltau confirmed that Chung bought kerosene oil from him, and had requested a general licence. He had instructed his clerk to look after the matter.

Manley turned to face the jury. "On the evidence of the prosecution, you will have to ask yourselves this question: Is it credible that the accused would have put down the articles, if they intended to burn down the place, in the way in which they were found? They are either lunatics or someone put the articles there in order to make up a case against the accused. The case for the prosecution is rotten. So many lies have been told by their witnesses that I will not embark on the task on finding out who is the greatest liar. Can you rely on the evidence of the woman Walters? She said that she had offered the accused a bucket of water to throw on the fire but he threw it away. The evidence shows that the witnesses acted either out of malice or they lost their heads. The conduct of the police shows that they had acted like hysterical schoolboys. The witness Bethune gave the most untrustworthy evidence, and so it goes on. The Crown says it's a lie that the accused

Chung was ill, but they themselves called a witness, a pedlar, who said yes, he was ill, and he had asked for cerasee. It is not for the prisoners to show how the fire occurred. It is quite possible for the fire to have occurred in this way: one of the accused might have been smoking and at night when the place was swept up, the lighted end of a cigarette might have caused a fire. All this is quite possible. With regard to a motive for setting the fire, I submit that the Crown has not proven any motive. On the evidence, if the place was burnt down, the accused would have lost £380. Do you think that a shrewd Chinaman would have set a fire to sustain such a loss? The prosecution, I submit, have failed. I leave the case confidently in your hands. Thank you."

Yates replied that there was no question about it, a fire had taken place in the shop, and the question was whether the prisoners, or any of them, had set the fire. How did the fire occur? Chung had stated that he did not see any burning charcoal in the stove that evening. One would have expected an innocent person to have given a truthful account about his movements. He had lied. He told the detectives that he was ill for three days, yet they had witnesses who had seen him carrying on his business as usual. The accused said that when he came out to the fire, he was in his night clothes. The witnesses for the prosecution had stated that the accused was fully dressed. In all these cases of arson it was difficult to obtain proof. The facts were before the jury and it was for them to say whether they would convict the prisoners or not.

Without hearing the judge's summing up, the jury returned a verdict of not guilty in respect of the three prisoners.

The presiding judge, Anthony DeFreitas, nodded in agreement, "I concur with the verdict," he said.

The three Chinese were discharged.

4

An East Indian Affair

Celebration and registration of Hindu and Muslim
marriages were given legal sanction by the House of
Representatives yesterday as the Opposition joined with the
Government in giving unanimous approval to a Bill that
provided for the appointment of marriage officers from
among priests of these two faiths . . . for many years the East
Indian community in Jamaica has been making
representation to have the terms of the Indian Immigrants
Marriage and Divorce Law changed and to establish a code
of rules to apply to Indians imported into Jamaica as
indentured workers.

The Gleaner
5 December 1957

Indians, called East Indians in the West Indies, had come to Jamaica initially as indentured labourers to supplement the declining local labour force following the emancipation of the slaves. Immigration began in 1845 and continued until 1921. The Indians laboured under contracts, at the end of which they could return home or settle in Jamaica. By 1889 the East Indian population numbered 10,000. This number progressively increased over the years as more and more Indian immigrants opted to stay in Jamaica, contributing to the country's racial mixture and popularizing new tastes in food such as "curried goat" which became a Jamaican speciality.

At the end of their indentureship contract, many Indians reverted to their ancestral occupations, some became farmers or fishermen, while others returned to the trades of barber, goldsmith and iron-smith. Several became money lenders, and a few, Sadhus (holy men) in the Hindu tradition, living on alms and spending their lives in meditation and singing devotional songs.

Though an overwhelming majority of the labourers were Hindus, followed by Muslims, priests were never recruited to satisfy their religious needs. Some priests did come, but only as indentured labourers

A group of early Indian labourers

who practised priesthood as a part-time profession. Furthermore, Hindu and Muslim marriages were not legally recognized by the colonial government in Jamaica at the time. Because of this many Indians converted to Christianity but this was primarily for convenience; not from conviction.[1] From 1940, Dr J.L. Varma, founder of the East Indian Progressive Society, appealed to three successive secretaries of state for the colonies and three governors of Jamaica to have Hindu and Muslim marriages recognized. "No one did anything", Varma recalled, "until 1957 when Norman Manley was Chief Minister. I approached him about this handicap and he saw to it that a law was passed under which Hindu and Moslem priests could be gazetted as marriage officers."[2]

Varma's petition would have stirred Manley's memory. In the 1920s, early and arranged marriages continued to be the custom among the Indian immigrants. Parents still considered it their moral responsibility to marry off sons and daughters, and were always on the lookout for prospective matches. The changing pattern of their lives, however, led to inevitable modifications, sometimes with dire results, as John Rajkumar discovered on 16 January 1923, when he found himself in the dock of the Spanish Town courthouse, charged with the abduction of Estella Naddijohn.[3]

Henry Isaac Close Brown was the first Jamaican to become a Supreme Court judge. He was respected for his steadfastness and integrity

Mr Justice H.I.C. Brown, a most able lawyer and jurist and Acting Senior Puisne Judge, presided over the hearing. Mr John St John Yates, Acting Assistant to the Attorney-General, said he appeared with his learned friend the Hon. J.A.G. Smith for the prosecution. Manley had been retained for the defence. Smith called his first witness, Estella Naddijohn, to the stand.

In a soft voice, the sixteen-year-old recalled that in September 1922 she was living with her uncle, Solomon Lateefe, at Congreve Park. Her aunt was sick and she was caring her. John Rajkumar came to the yard and told her uncle that he wanted to marry her. Lateefe said he could give no answer, he was not her father. Rajkumar said all right; he would go and see her father. The next time she saw the defendant, he gave her a ring, but she refused to put it on. Estella Naddijohn held up her slim hand and pinched her skin as she related how Rajkumar forced the ring on her finger. The next day, she said, "I take off the ring and give it back. Him use a vulgar expression and go away". She subsequently met Rajkumar one Saturday at the Spanish Town market and they went to her uncle's house. Her father was also there. She prepared dinner and after they had eaten, her father took off his belt and gave her two strokes. She ran off into the bush to hide. Rajkumar found her and said that her father would beat her if she returned.

"John ask me to go home with him," she narrated. "I say, no, I go to my cousin at Bog Walk." Rajkumar told her to meet him at the Spanish Town railway station. She went to the station and he bought a ticket for her and they travelled to Bog Walk. Rajkumar hired a car but instead of taking her to her cousin, he took her to his home and carried her in the coffee piece. She spent the whole day there. "Him give me breakfast, but I don't eat it."

In the evening, she went up to the house and had to sleep in the same room as Rajkumar. The next day she was taken back to the coffee piece. At night she was brought back and slept in the same room with the accused. Next morning she was taken back to the coffee piece. She told Rajkumar that her family would come for her; for answer, she said, he hid her further in the coffee piece. Eventually, her uncle came and took her home.

Manley began his cross-examination of Estella Naddijohn, gently enquiring, "Where is the ring?"

"My father give it to the police."

"Were you at Congreve Park on the occasion of the second visit of the prisoner to your father?"

"Yes."

"And that was the occasion when the ring was introduced?"

"Yes."

"And the ring was put on your finger in the presence of everyone?"

"It was forced on."

"How was it forced on you?"

"Well . . . I tell them I don't want any ring and my father and mother don't consent."

"Didn't you hear Lateefe invoke the Almighty God to witness the agreement?"

"No."

"And the date of the wedding announced?"

"No."

"And there was general rejoicing that night?"

"No."

"Was there not singing?"

"Two of them were singing; I went to sleep."

"Did you love John at first?"

"No."

"You say you didn't love him?"

"No."

"Not even a little bit?" Manley coaxed.

Estella dropped her eyes, "Well . . . I didn't hate him."

J.A.G. Smith saw the smile spread slowly over Manley's face, accentuating his long upper lip. Estella's father, Dennis Naddijohn was called to the stand.

Questioned by Smith, Naddijohn confirmed that Estella was born on 30 November 1906. Her mother was called Sancherri. No, they were not married at the time, but he had married her since. Who registered the birth of the child? His father. Yes, he knew the defendant, John Rajkumar. He came to his yard and asked for Estella's hand in marriage.

He said, no, she was too young. Rajkumar approached him a second time when he was visiting his brother-in-law at Congreve Park. Rajkumar turned up with his father, and asked permission to marry Estella, but again he refused. They were there until the night when they had dinner. He told Estella that she must return home and he gave her two strokes. She ran into the bush and he was unable to find her.

Cross-examined by Manley, the witness said that he was a good father to his daughter. He had not beaten her before.

"Is it the custom among your people for sons to come and ask for a daughter in marriage?" asked Manley.

"I don't know. I born in Jamaica."

"You remember getting a letter containing a charge for one pound and seven shillings."

"Yes."

"And in that letter it said that you would have to pay the money because you broke up the marriage agreement?"

"Yes."

At this stage the court adjourned for luncheon; on the resumption Solomon Lateefe took the stand. He remembered the day his niece, Estella, went to market and came back with the prisoner. Her father gave her three strokes with a belt and she ran away. They couldn't find her that night, or the following day, which was a Sunday. On the Tuesday he went to the prisoner's house at Linstead and brought Estella home.

Cross-examined by Manley, Lateefe said that when the prisoner and his father came to ask for the hand of Estella in marriage, there was no feast; there was no singing. He told Estella to throw away the ring since there was no consent.

The case for the Crown was closed; Manley opened for the defence. "The Crown has charged that Estella Naddijohn was unlawfully taken away from her guardian or parents without consent. The defence will prove that the prisoner never took away the girl, but she went away, because of the treatment of her father, to Linstead. Your Honour, I call John Rajkumar to the stand."

Rajkumar recalled that after Estella's father had consented to the marriage during his visit to Congreve Park, Lateefe told him to get an engagement ring and they would fix a date for the marriage. Mrs Lateefe measured the girl's finger in order that he could get the ring. He went back to Congreve Park that night and a number of them gathered to carry out the contract. After he and Estella had stated that they were willing to be married, Mrs Lateefe put it to the gathering whether they had any objection. There was none and Mrs Lateefe asked the blessing of the Almighty on the contract. There was singing and drinking and everyone enjoyed the evening. The wedding was fixed for 11 December. Subsequently he heard that the girl's father had changed his mind and wished to break off the marriage. It was said that a man named Adolphus had told certain tales on himself and his father.

He next visited the house one evening after meeting Estella at the Spanish Town market. Her father, to whom he had rendered a bill for breaking off the marriage, became irate because Estella was determined *not* to break off the engagement or to give back the ring. He gave her a beating and she ran off. Next morning, while travelling on a train to Bog Walk, he met Estella at Spanish Town. They travelled together to Bog Walk and there they took a motor truck to Linstead, Estella paying her fare. Estella said she wanted to see his house and then she would decide. On their arrival at his home, his sister put up Estella in her house. He never slept with Estella. Two days later Estella's uncle came for her. She didn't want to go; she told her uncle that she had run away because her father had beaten her.

Cross-examined by Smith, Rajkumar said that his love for Estella had ceased when the father refused. It was not a pleasant surprise for him to meet her on the train at Spanish Town. He did not, even for old time's sake, pay her fare from Bog Walk to Linstead. All his folks were surprised to see her. They agreed to put up Estella until her family came for her.

William Tankia took the stand. He testified that Rajkumar boarded the train with him at Grange Lane and Estella joined the train at Spanish Town. The couple journeyed to Bog Walk. Cross-examined by Smith, Tankia said that he gave Estella his seat because he knew she was intimate with the defendant and he thought he would like it.

Walter Wilson, the next defence witness to be called by Manley, said that he was the driver of a motor car and lived at Linstead. He had picked up the defendant and Estella Naddijohn at Bog Walk and taken them to Linstead. She had asked him how much he charged and he said two shillings.

Manley told the court that the father of the accused was also a witness but he was so deaf, he did not propose to call him.

Justice Brown frowned: "I don't think, Mr Manley, you should mention why you don't call a witness. You either call him or you don't."

"It shouldn't have been mentioned at all," Smith chimed in.

"Then I will call the witness," retorted Manley in the heat of the moment.

Robert Rajkumar, father of the defendant, said that he went to Lateefe and asked him about a girl to marry his son. It was an Indian custom for the fathers or parents to arrange the marriage of their children. Lateefe told him that he had a niece and he would agree, but he could do nothing until the two young ones met each other. Lateefe told him to send up his son the following Saturday and he did so.

Smith began his cross-examination, "Lateefe must have found it difficult to make you hear what he had to say?"

"Sir, I don't hear."

"You know, I understand that you are not deaf?"

"I don't understand your question. It is not in my language."

"You heard and understood Mr Manley very well," Justice Brown cautioned.

"Estella came to your house?" asked Smith.

"Yes, on the Sunday."

"Didn't Estella's uncle come to you and ask if the girl was there?"

"Yes, and I told him she was."

"Why didn't you give her up then?"

"She went to hide in the coffee piece."

"But couldn't you and John catch her and give her up?"

"She wasn't a dumb thing, sir."

Manley tugged the collar of his robe as he got up to address the jury.

"This is a most damnable and wicked attempt to make up a case," he opened. "The whole prosecution is a farrago of nonsense. The chief point — the only issue in this case — is whether the prisoner went to the home of Estella and induced her to leave the care and protection of her guardian to go with him to his own home. There are two sets of facts before you: that by the prosecution and that by the defence. You will have to consider the motive for the prosecution. They are people who have money for they can afford a private prosecution. The defence submits that the prisoner took the train at Grange Lane while Estella took the train at Spanish Town. If this is true then it is clear that Estella did not change her affection towards the accused. Then there is the evidence of the feast that marked the marriage agreement. Even Estella admitted there was singing, though several witnesses for the prosecution have tried to twist the truth in order to make out that there was no marriage agreement.

"Against that, there is evidence that the agreement was broken off. It is clear that such an act aggravated the father, and when the girl protested, the father gave her a beating which caused her to run away and spend a whole night in the bush.

"You are no doubt sorry for the girl and the position she has been placed in by her parents, first by breaking off her engagement, and next by forcing her to go into the witness box. There is another important point on which the prosecution has failed to act. Although I submit that this is not a court of morals, the prosecution should have got a doctor to examine the girl. The same people who have money enough for a private prosecution could have obtained a doctor's certificate."

Manley moved for the acquittal of the prisoner on the evidence which he denounced as "demonstrably false".

J.A.G. Smith replied: "You have been treated for quite a little while to what might, in an abstract way, have been very interesting, but it was purely an attempt to cloud what otherwise must be a very clear issue. You do not have to deal with well-sounding platitudes, but a clear-cut issue. Are you satisfied that the girl was under 16 at the time? If you are, then the next question is whether she was induced to leave her father's home by the prisoner. It does not matter whether she was engaged or not. Sufficient it is that without the consent of her father, it was an offence. It was admitted that the father never consented, and even if the girl had agreed to go, it does not alter the position. The offence is complete, and no honest body of jurors will allow themselves to be deceived by any platitudes. If you believe that the prisoner persuaded the girl to leave her parents, that is sufficient."

In his summing up, Justice Brown pointed out that "the law under which the prisoner is charged is an ancient one enacted to protect young girls from being led away from the care and protection of their parents. The evidence is absolutely of a contradictory nature. One side or other is lying; it is for you to say what side you believe".

At 2 o'clock the jury retired to consider their verdict. They returned two hours later with a verdict of not guilty. John Rajkumar was discharged.

5

A Soap Opera

At first the Jews were concentrated in Port Royal, but after the destruction of much of that town by the earthquake of 1692 many of the survivors migrated across the harbour to the new city site of Kingston which supplanted Port Royal as the commercial capital. From the early eighteenth century onwards, the great majority of the Jews in Jamaica were retail traders in Kingston.

R.D. Barnett and P. Wright
The Jews of Jamaica
Tombstone Inscriptions 1663–1880

Abraham Dolphy was a merchant and former vice president of the United Congregation of Israelites in Jamaica. As for soap: "I know nothing about soap; I don't deal in soap," he told barrister Radcliffe under cross-examination in the witness box of the Supreme Court. Dolphy was blinking rapidly now, the perspiration dripping from his forehead. He'd been stupid, he admitted that. When Inspector King had read the summons, charging him with conspiracy, he was in such a state, he could have dug his eyes out, he said. If only he could call back time.

The time was 24 January 1921; the place: Abraham Dolphy's

Abraham Dolphy

store on Harbour Street in Kingston. Enter Thomas Griffin, a local representative for Lever Brothers and engaged to Dolphy's niece.

"Mr Dolphy, sir, I have 2,000 boxes of soap belonging to Lever Brothers which I can sell you for £2,500," Griffin announced, showing him a cable from Lever Brothers authorizing the sale.

"It's out of my line", Dolphy replied, "and too large a quantity."

Griffin smiled: "Listen, I can resell the soap in a few days and make a profit of £500.

41

We can split the proceeds. And since I'm about to marry your niece, well, the profit will come in very handy. I'd buy the soap myself, but I don't have the money."

Dolphy hummed and hawed and finally yielded: "All right. I'll advance you the £2,500 on condition you repay it in three days. You can keep the profit."

The two men exchanged cheques, Griffin postdating his to 26 January. On that day, Dolphy received a note from Griffin, asking him not to cash the cheque before 2.45 p.m. Dolphy waited and went to the bank shortly before it closed. The cheque was dishonoured. Dolphy went after Griffin but he wasn't at his office, nor at home. He found him, two days later, at his niece's house, and blasted him for having issued a cheque which had no funds to meet it.

"Why worry?" said Griffin. "You have the 2,000 boxes of soap. They're at Frank Lyons's wharf. Here, I'll give you the order right now." And he signed it: Lever Brothers Ltd. T. Griffin, 28 January 1921.

Down at the wharf, Frank Lyons had another story:

"I can't give you what I haven't got, Dolphy; there is no soap."

Dolphy consulted his solicitors, who demanded delivery of the soap from Lever Brothers, alleging that their client had bought the soap from Thomas Griffin, one of their agents. Lever Brothers refused to deliver the soap, and entirely repudiated the alleged contract between the two men.

On 5 April, Dolphy and Griffin were jointly charged with conspiring to cheat and defraud Lever Brothers of 2,000 boxes of soap.

"Imagine, a man of my age and standing being so charged," Dolphy told the court. "What happened next?" asked Manley in cross-examination.

"I was advised by my solicitor, Mr Samuel, to settle the matter for £1,000, that being the costs and expenses incurred by Lever Brothers in connection with my claim against them. I also signed a deed by which Lever Brothers and myself released each other from any claims we had against each other."

That, Manley had written in an earlier Opinion, "was an agreement of the worst sort".[1]

Dolphy then sought to recover his £2,500 from Griffin. Hence the hearing now being conducted in the Supreme Court before His Honour, Mr Justice R.T. Orpen. Manley, instructed by Millholland, Ashenheim and Stone, appeared for the plaintiff, Abraham Dolphy; H.M. Radcliffe, instructed by the Solicitor-General, Mr W. Baggett Gray, represented the defendant, Thomas Griffin.[2]

Dolphy continued answering questions posed by Manley. As far as he knew, Griffin had authority to sell the soap, and to take money in payment. He had no reason to believe that Griffin had not paid Lever Brothers for the soap.

"Why did you agree to the settlement?" Manley asked.

"I opposed the settlement, but I was pressed by my family, especially my wife who was in a delicate state of health at the time. And, acting on the advice of my solicitors, the matter was settled. I received no part of the £2,500 I advanced to Griffin. I never entered into any agreement with Griffin to defraud Lever Brothers. If I had known that there was no soap at the wharf, I would not have taken the delivery order."

Henry Milne Radcliffe, KC

In the cross-examination by Radcliffe, Dolphy was asked:

"At the time it was suggested to you that you should buy the soap, didn't you consider it cheap?"

"I told you, I know nothing about soap."

"But the offer was an alluring one?"

"I told Griffin I wanted no profit. If he gave me back my £2,500, I would have been perfectly satisfied."

"You bought the soap the day you gave your cheque?"

"Yes. But I wanted no profit."

"So you were a purchaser of soap, and not a lender of money?"

"Quite so, sir."

"Then I take it that you considered that the 2,000 boxes of soap that were lying at Lyons's Wharf was your own property?"

"I thought so, sir."

"So you looked all the time for the soap, not the money?"

"I looked for the soap, but if I did not get the soap I wanted back my money."

Continuing, Dolphy said he would not have loaned Griffin £2,500 without security.

"Don't you think if the transaction was a straight one, you would have got some document from Griffin on the 24th of January for the soap?" questioned Radcliffe.

"I admit that I did a stupid thing. I could not have done a more ignorant thing."

"If you'd got back your money on the 26th, there would have been no soap deal?"

"That is so."

"In other words, it was the money or the soap? The cheque that Griffin gave you, if that were cashed, you would have released Lever Brothers?"

"Yes."

"And the moment the cheque was not met at the bank, you laid claim to the soap?"

"Certainly."

"Why didn't you make out the cheque to Lever Brothers?" asked Mr Justice Orpen.

"That has learnt me a lesson, sir", Dolphy replied mournfully, "indeed it has."

Re-examined by Manley, Dolphy said he would not have paid the £1,000 settlement with Lever Brothers at the point of a bayonet. It was paid through pressure of his wife.

Manley called Robert W. Taylor, a Kingston storekeeper, to the stand. In answer to Manley's question, Taylor said that he knew Thomas Griffin. "On the 26th January 1921, he came to my store and told me that he had received instructions from Lever Brothers to sell 2,000 boxes of soap which he would let me have for £1,500. I told him I had no money at the time. Griffin asked me if I knew of anyone who had the money as he would be able to sell the soap and make £500 profit in a few days. I suggested that he go to Mr Abraham Dolphy or some other person with spare money."

Cross-examined by Radcliffe, Taylor said that it was suggested that he should purchase the soap and that Griffin would sell same and share the profit.

Alexander Davis was next on the stand. He was the overseer at Mona Estate. Yes, he knew Griffin; he'd made him a proposition regarding soap. "He told me he'd made £500 profit on 2,000 boxes of soap which he'd bought with borrowed money, but the party to whom he had sold the soap, hadn't paid him. Griffin asked me for a loan of £1,500. He would pass over the acceptance from the party who had bought the soap, and we would share the profit. I told him I had no money."

Manley said that this closed the plaintiff's case.

Radcliffe called no evidence on behalf of the defendant, and asked for judgment on the grounds that the plaintiff's evidence did not support his statement of claim: "On the face of a document, which the plaintiff has signed, he has given a release to Messrs Lever Brothers with respect to the claim for 2,000 boxes of soap. There is no question about the money being advanced to Griffin as a loan. The correspondence shows that the plaintiff is claiming the soap from Lever Brothers on a contract and the question about a loan is an afterthought and not borne out by facts." In short, Radcliffe submitted, Dolphy could not both lend Griffin £2,500 and purchase soap from Lever Brothers for the £2,500 with one cheque. "I cannot see what claim Mr Dolphy has against the defendant, I therefore move for judgment," he concluded.

The court was adjourned for one week when Mr Justice Orpen delivered judgment:[3] "The defendant, Mr Griffin, in his statement of defence, alleges that the agreement between the plaintiff, Mr Dolphy, and himself was an illegal one, in that by it, it was intended to cheat and defraud Messrs Lever Brothers of soap to the value of £2,500. Therefore, Mr Dolphy cannot recover any money paid to him in pursuance of the agreement.

"No evidence of any weight has been produced before me to support the allegation that Mr Dolphy was mixed up in any fraudulent or illegal transaction to cheat Messrs Lever Brothers. It is a serious matter to make a statement of this kind against a businessman or indeed anybody, and it should not be put on the files of the court unless the defendant believes that he is able and is ready to prove its truth.

"The only evidence which I have before me as to the transactions between the plaintiff and defendant is that of the plaintiff, Mr Dolphy.

"No evidence has been produced before me as to what became of the soap between 24th and 28th January, or whether it was really ever in existence at all on the 24th. Mr Frank Lyons could have been called to give evidence on this point but the court is left absolutely in the dark as to this matter. The fact however remains that the plaintiff never got delivery of the soap.

"As to the propriety or otherwise of the dropping of prosecutions on the payment of sums of monies, I hesitate to make any remarks, as I have only the plaintiff's evidence before me, but speaking generally, I am of the opinion that it is a most improper procedure and one liable to gross abuse. If a charge is true, the criminal should be punished, and if untrue, the accused should have his character cleared, and this can only be done by having a full hearing of the evidence.

"The plaintiff states that he was most unwilling to sign the deed of release and pay the £1,000, and that he only did so under the strong persuasion of his solicitor and his wife and family. I accept the plaintiff's evidence as to the motives which actuated him in signing the release.

"In cross-examination, Mr Dolphy insisted that he was a purchaser of the soap from Mr Griffin, as an agent of Lever Brothers, and not a lender of £2,500 to the defendant. Mr Dolphy said he had a right to hold Lever Brothers to the bargain, unless the defendant's cheque had been cashed, in which case he would have relieved Lever Brothers of the transaction, but as the defendant's cheque was not met, he demanded delivery of the soap from Lever Brothers.

"Mr Radcliffe has argued Mr Dolphy accepted the delivery order on 28th January in lieu of the defendant's cheque and therefore he cannot now sue on the dishonoured cheque, and his only remedy is against Lever Brothers for the soap.

"In the statement of defence, Mr Griffin states that plaintiff knew that Lever Brothers had got no consideration for the order for delivery of the said soap. In other words, he admits that he had never paid over the £2,500 to Lever Brothers.

"Mr Dolphy absolutely denies this. He states that he had no reason to believe that Mr Griffin would not pay Lever Brothers for the soap, and I can hardly imagine that Mr Dolphy would accept the delivery order, unless he believed that the defendant had paid in the £2,500 to Lever Brothers' account.

"It is clear then, that the defendant, Mr Griffin, knew when he handed over the delivery order to the plaintiff in lieu of defendant's cheque for £2,500, he was handing over a document which was useless for the purpose of getting possession of the soap, so that he was giving no consideration for his cheque.

"Regarding the transaction between the plaintiff and the defendant as a loan of £2,500 which would be quite consistent with the evidence, the plaintiff would be quite entitled to recover the £2,500 on the dishonoured cheque of the defendant. Mr Dolphy's subsequent conduct in demanding the delivery of the soap from Lever Brothers would be quite consistent with his belief that the £2,500 had been paid over by defendant to Lever Brothers, and I have no evidence before me which would cause me to disbelieve that he thought this was the case.

"Mr Dolphy however contends that the original transaction was a purchase from Lever Brothers, and regarding it as such, I consider he is still entitled to recover from the defendant the £2,500 which he handed over to Mr Griffin for the purchase of the soap, and which sum the defendant on his own pleadings admits was never paid in by him to Lever Brothers, and therefore can be treated as money paid to the defendant for the use of the plaintiff.

"I therefore give judgment to the plaintiff, Mr Dolphy, for £2,500 with costs."

6

This Land is My Land

Land is the only source of the material life of the people. It provides food and shelter. It furnishes work and wealth. It is the basis of all production, of all development, of all security, of all growth. It is in very truth the root of our being.

Norman Manley
Public Opinion
May 1943

On 28 March 1923, Norman Manley took his seat in the Supreme Court. Behind him sat the Mandeville-based solicitor, Godfrey G. Gunter, who had been close to the Manley family, having replaced John Thompson Palache as Thomas Manley's legal adviser when Manley had sued Palache for negligence as his solicitor in 1892. When Gunter had briefed Norman Manley on the special jury case which was about to be heard, the bright young barrister had been caustic:

"It's a waste of time; the case should not be brought at all."

Gunter explained that the plaintiff was a Chinese shopkeeper in Williamsfield, Manchester.

"A fire?" asked Manley, looking up in that odd, quirky way he had.

"No. Well, not directly," said Gunter. "He's claiming damages from my client, Mrs Alice Jones, a rival shopkeeper, for slander."

"Slander?"

"She accused him of having burnt down a previous shop he rented from a Mr Heron."

"Ha!" Manley scoffed.

The special jury case of *Isaac Lin Kin Chow* v. *Alice Jones* to recover damages for slander got underway in the Supreme Court on 28 March 1923 before His Honour, Mr Justice R.T. Orpen.[1]

Barristers John St John Yates and H.M. Radcliffe, instructed by the Hon. H.A.L. Simpson, appeared for the plaintiff; Manley instructed by Godfrey G. Gunter represented the defendant.

H.A.L. 'Corkfoot' Simpson was a shrewd solicitor — 'Corkfoot' because he had an artificial leg, having lost the genuine article to the 1907 earthquake. Many persons went cold when questioned by Simpson. He did not bully nor raise his voice, but his searching questions and chilling sarcasm had the desired effect.

Yates opened for the plaintiff, Lin Kin Chow. He contended that in the small community of Williamsfield, the defendant's accusation that he burnt down a shop would certainly damage the reputation of his client whom he then called to the witness stand.

The bright-eyed, ruddy-cheeked Lin Kin Chow was all impatience as he told the court that he carried on a grocery business at Williamsfield in premises rented from a Mr Stephen Miller. Mrs Jones carried on a similar business next door. Before that, he had rented another shop from Mr Heron. That was burnt down in December 1921. There was a magisterial enquiry, but no steps were taken against him.

On 24 April 1922, he saw the defendant, Mrs Jones, and Mr Miller standing in the passage near his yard. Miller told him that Mrs Jones would not allow him to put up a fence between the two properties. Lin Kin Chow was adamant; he had to have a fence, he said, to keep his children from running all over the place. Mrs Jones got in a temper:

"I won't allow you to put up any dirty box fence," she told him.

"This is my land," he replied.

"This isn't your land. Your land's in China."

"This isn't your land either. Your land's in Africa."

"If Mr Miller himself put up the fence, I will pull it down."

"Cho, Mrs Jones, why you go on like that?"

"I don't know why you Chinese come to live here."

"Me is Chinese all right, but you is a damned old mule."

"You burn up Mr Heron's shop, now you want to burn up this one."

"What you say? I burn up shop? You can prove it?"

At this stage, said Lin Kin Chow, Mrs Jones went inside her shop saying that she was going to give him hell.

"And me say, very politely, 'Mrs Jones, I is quite ready to receive all the hell you can give me'."

Lin Kin Chow was then cross-examined by Manley:

"Didn't your wife complain often to Mrs Jones about your being drunk?"

"No."

"Didn't Mrs Jones have to save you from drowning in a pond one day when you were drunk?"

"No."

"You weren't as bad as that?"

"How can a drunken man keep business?"

"Didn't Mrs Jones rescue you from the railway line one day?"

"No."

Lorrel McLeod, a United Fruit Company worker at Williamsfield, then took the stand. He testified that he had heard Mrs Jones tell Lin Kin Chow that he had burnt the other shop down, and now he had come to burn this one.

McLeod was followed by Harold Bolton, a bus driver. He too testified hearing Mrs Jones tell Lin Kin Chow not to put up any fence because he had already burned down one shop and she didn't want her place going up in flames.

Manley stood to cross-examine Bolton:

"What was the first thing you heard on arriving at the shop?"

"I heard Mrs Jones say: 'Don't put up any dirty fence there'."

"And what else did you hear?"

"Mrs Jones say: 'I won't have you burn down this place as you did the last one'."

"Did you hear Lin Kin Chow say, 'I can stand all the hell you can give me'?"

"No."

"Did you hear Lin Kin Chow call Mrs Jones, 'a damned old mule'?"

"No."

"Do you know a man named Delapenha?"

"Yes."

"I put it to you that when you arrived, everything was over, and that you talked the matter over with Delapenha?"

"I have no cause to lie."

"To what extent have you profited by coming here and saying all this?"

"I don't know."

"You don't know? I suppose you do it for charity!"

Manley sat down amidst the titters and chuckles.

Ferdinand Delapenha, a coachbuilder from Mandeville, was sworn in. He said he had heard Mrs Jones tell Lin Kin Chow that she wouldn't have him put up the fence, as he would burn down the place the same way he burned down his previous shop.

The case for the plaintiff was closed, Manley opened for the defence and called Alice Mary Jones to the stand. She deponed that on 19 May, she had received a letter [produced] from the solicitor, Mr

Simpson, asking her to apologize to Lin Kin Chow. Three weeks later, a writ was served on her. She had not replied to the letter, not knowing what to apologize for. She consulted her solicitor, Mr Gunter, who replied to Mr Lin Kin Chow's solicitor denying that Mrs Jones had used any slanderous language.

Manley called Frederick Taylor, a corporal of police stationed at Williamsfield, to give evidence. He said he was standing in front of the station, nearly opposite Mrs Jones's shop, when the incident was supposed to have taken place. He did not hear any loud talking. He heard only when the plaintiff said: "You say I burn down the shop?" At that time Lin Kin Chow was on the road. He did not hear anyone reply. He did not see Delapenha, Bolton or McLeod until about fifteen minutes later, going from the railway station to Lin Kin Chow's shop. At that time, Lin Kin Chow was in his shop talking loudly. He did not hear Mrs Jones say anything. Her shop was nearer to him than Lin Kin Chow's. He stood at the spot, in front of the police station, for about half an hour.

Cross-examined by Radcliffe:

"Why were you standing for half an hour?"

"I was station guard."

"Did Mr Lin Kin Chow appear annoyed when Mrs Jones accused him of burning down his previous shop?"

"Yes."

"Do you know the plaintiff well?"

"Yes. He once charged me for assault."

As Yates sat, Manley got up to re-examine the witness.

"And what became of the prosecution, Corporal?"

"The case was dismissed."

"What was it about?"

"Mr Lin Kin Chow came to the police station one night drunk. He was disorderly. I ordered him out. He would not go; I had to put him out."

"And was that the only occasion on which you saw him drunk?"

"No, sir. I've seen him drunk several times. On one occasion I had to go and remove him from the railway lines."

"What was he doing there?"

"He said that he was trying to drown himself, sir."

Laughter swept across the courtroom.

Frederick Davis, a carpenter, next testified, corroborating the last witness. Cross-examined by Yates, Davis said that Lin Kin Chow was in his liquor on the day of the alleged slander:

"Plaintiff's face was red as blood."

"What's the colour of your face when you are drunk?" asked Yates.
"I don't know, I'm never drunk."

"As red as mine, or was it the colour of the fire which burned down the shop in Williamsfield?"

"It was as red as blood, I say."

The witness remained grave in spite of the obvious attempts of judge, jury and spectators to muffle their mirth.

"What made you say that the plaintiff was drunk?" asked Mr Justice Orpen. "Did you see him drinking on that day?"

"I saw himself and others in the bar most of the time."

Addressing the jury, Manley submitted: "This whole case is a misunderstanding. I submit that the case should not have been brought at all. Defendant said to the plaintiff: 'You have no land here, your land is in China.' Then we have the plaintiff's retort made in the same strain. So far as damages are concerned, I don't know in what way the plaintiff has suffered. I suggest that the plaintiff is not deserving of anything after calling the defendant 'a damned old mule', but assuming that you find for the plaintiff, which I very much doubt, you should award the most infinitesimal damages that it is possible for you to award. I feel sure that after all you have heard, I can leave my case confidently in your hands."

Radcliffe replied: "My learned friend submits that there was a misunderstanding. I submit that if there was a misunderstanding, it is a pity that when the plaintiff's solicitor wrote to the defendant, she did not go next door and have the matter ventilated. But no, the defendant appreciated the fact that there was cause for action, and I submit that the plaintiff's case has been fully established. The defendant charged the plaintiff with having committed a diabolical criminal act, and I urge that whether or not special loss has been suffered by the plaintiff, he is entitled to damages."

The jury retired to consider their verdict. After an absence of ten minutes, the jury filed into the court and returned a verdict in favour of the defendant, Mrs Jones, with costs.

Godfrey Gunter smiled with satisfaction at young Manley's courtroom performance. Two months later Gunter had even more reason to be pleased with his old friend's son when he attended the Jamaica Law Debating Society dinner at the South Camp Road Hotel. The event brought out the best legal talent of the island; nearly all members of the profession were present. On this occasion, Manley had been asked to toast 'The Legal Profession'.[2]

"When I was asked to make the toast", he declared, "I was told that it had always been the custom for juniors to do so. Why? Perhaps,

I thought, it was because of the audacity of junior members of the Bar."
And with all the polish of a well-rehearsed actor, Manley quoted an
altercation between a youthful F.E. Smith, who later, as Lord
Birkenhead, became Lord Chancellor of England, and Judge Willis, a
sanctimonious English County Court judge.

"F.E. had been briefed for a tramway company which had been
sued for damages for injuries to a boy who had been run over. The
plaintiff's case was that blindness had set in as a result of the accident.
The judge was deeply moved. 'Poor boy, poor boy,' he said. 'Blind. Put
him on a chair so that the jury can see him.'

"F.E. replied coldly: 'Perhaps your Honour would like to have the
boy passed round the jury box?'

" 'That is a most improper remark,' Judge Willis retorted angrily.

" 'It was provoked', said F.E., 'by a most improper suggestion.'

"There was a heavy pause, and the judge continued, 'Mr Smith,
have you ever heard of a saying by Bacon — the great Bacon — that
youth and discretion are ill-wed companions?'

" 'Indeed I have, your Honour; and has your Honour ever heard
of a saying by Bacon — the great Bacon — that a much talking judge is
like an ill-tuned cymbal?'

"The judge replied furiously, 'You are extremely offensive, young
man'; to which F.E. concluded: 'As a matter of fact we both are; the only
difference between us is that I'm trying to be, and you can't help it'."[3]

"With all modesty", Manley continued, after a pause for applause,
"I think there is a very good reason why juniors should propose the
toast of the legal profession, because, fresh from the Inns of Court,
juniors are the best persons to have proper ideals of law and justice.
There is a great love and regard for the profession. The instant one
becomes a member, one enters a brotherhood which holds a greater
power over its members than any other brotherhood in the world. We
have not only the privilege of being members of the brotherhood in
Jamaica, but also of the English brotherhood: the greatest in the world."
Manley called upon the gathering to honour the toast, not as men
drinking to themselves, but to something bigger than themselves.

Sydney Jacquet, like all the others present, pushed back his chair,
climbed to his feet and raised his glass. As he did so, sundry whispers
might have run through the room as Manley had recently won a case
against him: *Jacquet* v. *Parish Board of Portland*.[4]

Sydney Jacquet was a solicitor of the Supreme Court, and had a
comfortable house at Richmond Hill, half-a-mile above the town of Port
Antonio, the capital of Portland. In August 1920, an epidemic of Kaffir

pox or alastrim (a disease which closely resembled smallpox, but had a negligible mortality rate) broke out in Portland. At first, the Parish Board of Portland isolated patients at Olivier Park in tents; hardly a satisfactory solution. The patients were subsequently moved to the market night shelter in Port Antonio which soon became overcrowded. Faced with the urgency of housing hundreds of patients with a contagious disease, the Board, with the government's consent, found a site where they established a Kaffir pox hospital. It was 300 yards from Sydney Jacquet's gate. He was not amused.

Jacquet sued the Parish Board of Portland first for damages, alleging that he lived in constant fear of contracting the disease, and secondly, for an injunction to restrain the defendants from using the said lands and building for a hospital. Radcliffe represented Jacquet at the hearing; Manley appeared for the defendants, the Parish Board of Portland. In order to succeed, Jacquet had to satisfy the court either that the hospital itself was a nuisance, or that the manner in which the hospital was being run had created a nuisance.

First, Manley submitted, the plaintiff alleged that the hospital was improperly established. According to Sydney Jacquet, there were no proper sanitary conveniences and the hospital itself was so near to the road as to be a menace to his health. Manley told the court that a fortnight before the place was opened, the building was repaired and proper sanitary arrangements provided. The hospital was on an elevation from twenty-five to thirty feet above the road and was about thirty-six feet in from the road. The hospital lands were surrounded by a wire fence and the building itself enclosed by another fence outside of which the patients were not allowed to walk except when being discharged. Apart from Jacquet himself, his servants and his adopted daughter had constantly used the road since the hospital was opened two-and-a-half years earlier, and none of them had contracted the disease. Additionally, there was no evidence to show that any visitor to the plaintiff's house, or any other user of the road, had been infected with Kaffir pox. In his view, Manley said, the plaintiff could not claim damages as he had suffered none. Continuing, Manley admitted that the building was not exactly a pretty one to look at and he noted that on one occasion, Mr Jacquet had taken his telescope and scanned the hospital only to find blankets hanging on a line to dry, and this he found both unsanitary and objectionable. But the blankets, Manley explained, had been washed in hot water and soaked in Jeyes' disinfectant before they were hung out to dry. This, Manley contended, was safe, if a little unsightly. Surely Mr Jacquet did not expect the Board to provide a drying room so that when he took up his telescope, he wouldn't see blankets hanging about? True enough, it was said that if the Board had the money, it would have selected another site, but they did not, and they had to keep within their means. The section of the Law requiring the local Board of Health to act in certain cases of infectious diseases did not include Kaffir pox. Manley noted that when the rules under the Law were made, Kaffir pox was unknown to the medical profession in Jamaica and so it could not be said that the Law contemplated it.

Manley argued that the only way a properly conducted hospital could in itself be a nuisance would be through the spread of the disease in its vicinity, no matter what precautions were taken. The only way this could happen, he argued, would be by aerial transmission of the disease. The evidence on this point rested with Dr John Moseley for the plaintiff and Dr Ludlow Murcott Moody for the defendants. Moseley believed that Kaffir pox was airborne; Moody maintained that the disease was contagious, but not airborne. Moody, who was later to become Manley's brother-in-law, marrying his sister, Vera, was the government bacteriologist and one of those brilliant Jamaicans who had studied medicine in England (King's College Hospital, London) and walked away with all the prizes: the Huxley Prize for Physiology in addition to the Leather and Warneford Prizes in 1915, the Todd Prize for Clinical Medicine, and the Tanner Prize for Obstetrics in 1918. Moody was a quiet, reserved man, but with a

Dr Ludlow Murcott Moody

mischievous sense of humour, and a tendency to tell stories with a sly ending that left the laughter to break out long after he had left the room. "Why can't I remember jokes?" Norman once asked his wife, Edna. "Moody's head must be a storehouse of them."[5]

Responding to questions put by Manley in court, Moody, in a manner which was quiet and unhurried, presented a report published by the Pasteur Institute in Paris, to support his opinion that Kaffir pox was not an airborne disease. Next, he supplied statistics which showed that the chances were over 1,000 to 1 against a recently vaccinated person getting Kaffir pox. "And if the disease were contracted", Moody added, "it would, in all probability, be very mild."

"In this case", Manley submitted, "the plaintiff, Sydney Jacquet, refused to be vaccinated."

Manley then proceeded to deal with the law as it applied to nuisances and cited the case of *Winterbottom* v. *Lord Derby* as to the rights of a private individual in the case of a public nuisance. The next question was whether a smallpox hospital was per se a nuisance? He submitted it was not, on the strength of authorities as far back as fifty years, if they used smallpox as an example. Of course, if it was not properly managed, a hospital might become a nuisance. Even a baby's nursery might be a nuisance for that matter. Nuisance and annoyance were two different things. The plaintiff was an ordinary member of the public and was entitled to no more protection that any other ordinary, reasonable citizen. On the Law and on the evidence, Manley submitted that the defendants had fully established their case.

Radcliffe replied that with regard to the cases cited in case of nuisances, all turned on the special circumstances of the case. What one judge would find a nuisance in one case, another judge would not. With regard to the medical evidence, they had the opinion of Dr Moseley, who spoke of the danger of germs being carried from the hospital to the plaintiff's house by air. Mr Jacquet also gave evidence as to the prevailing winds. Dr Moseley considered that the germs were airborne and he gave in support of his opinion, a case in his hospital where a patient on one floor of the hospital had allegedly contracted the disease from another patient isolated on the lower floor. There was also the evidence of Dr Burke who said that one of the staff of the hospital had contracted the disease.

At this point, the judge implied that this would be quite likely owing to contact as Dr Burke himself had said that he believed the disease was contagious but not airborne. "But they disinfect themselves", argued Radcliffe, "and it goes to show the danger all the more from the plaintiff's point of view." Proceeding, Radcliffe said that even if Mr Jacquet had got vaccinated it would not have altered the position as far as an injunction went. "It was stated by Dr Moody that vaccination minimized the chances of contracting the disease," remarked Mr Justice Orpen. Radcliffe said that might be so, but while a hospital might be necessary in a town, a proper site should be selected for it. Many things had to be considered. Dr Moody could not say there was no possible chance of infection. The members of the Board themselves appreciated the fact that the place was not suitable for a permanent hospital. One of the Board members had said so in his evidence, though he said it was a matter of urgency at the time and because the place was going cheap. Yet, although it was a matter of urgency in 1920, they found them in 1923 still carrying on the hospital there. Radcliffe submitted that there was never a selection at all. The road to the place was a narrow one and with all these diseased people going up and down, was it to be expected that they were going to jump to one side and give Mr Jacquet the way? Radcliffe said the only remedy was for the Court to grant an injunction.

Two weeks later, Mr Justice Orpen delivered judgment: "An isolation hospital reduces the risk for every inhabitant of the district. It is, in fact, a necessity", he said, "and though the individual must be protected, the public advantage should not be forbidden unless the danger and injury to the individual are clearly proved. In this case, the plaintiff has not satisfied me that the present hospital constitutes an appreciable danger to public health or is a nuisance, in the legal sense, to his property . . . neither has the plaintiff satisfied me of the truth of the theory of aerial connection of the disease. The evidence on this point is that of Dr Moseley for the plaintiff and Dr Moody and Dr Burke for the defendants. Dr Moseley believes that the disease of Kaffir pox can be airborne, whereas both Dr Moody and Dr Burke believe that the disease cannot be airborne but is only contagious. Here we have a conflict of experts and I gladly adopt the words of Bowen, L.J. in his judgment in the case of *Fleet* v. *Metropolitan Asylums Board* 27 L.R. 363 in which he says: 'It would be most dangerous to form an independent opinion on a scientific question from the smatterings of science that might be picked up during the hearing of a case', and he held in that case that the plaintiff had failed to prove the theory of aerial dissemination of smallpox, and that they had therefore not been able to show that there was appreciable danger from the hospital."

As for the injunction, Mr Justice Orpen quoted the words of Fitzgibbon, L.J. in the case of *A.G.* v. *Rathmines and Pembroke Joint Hospital Board*, 1904 1. L.R.I. 161 in which he said: "To sustain an injunction, the law requires proof by the plaintiff of a well-founded apprehension of injury — proof of actual and real danger — a strong probability amounting to a moral certainty that if the hospital be established, it will be an actionable nuisance."

Orpen then quoted from the case of *A.G.* v. *Nottingham Corporation* L.R. 1904 1 Ch. D.673 where J. Farwell quoted the above words of Fitzgibbon and added: "Defendants in the present case are entitled to the benefit of the observation that the hospital has been open and received patients for the last six months during the last half of which it has been full, and no mischief has at present arisen therefrom . . ."

Orpen continued, "in the present case involving Sydney Jacquet the hospital has been open for over two years, and there is no evidence of any mischief arising therefrom . . . I therefore find that the plaintiff has not satisfied me that the hospital itself is a nuisance. The action is dismissed with costs".

The judge, however, concluded: "I may add that I greatly sympathize with the inconvenience and discomfort which the plaintiff has suffered, owing to this hospital being placed in the vicinity of his dwelling house and I hope the defendants will see their way to cease using the present building as an isolation hospital as soon as the present epidemic of Kaffir pox has passed away. That this was their intention is clear from the correspondence which took place between them and their landlords, the managers of the Titchfield Trust, and which Mr Manley placed in evidence."

We can only speculate on what thoughts, if any, of the recent case ran through solicitor Jacquet's mind at that dinner as he drank the toast to his profession raised by young Norman Manley.

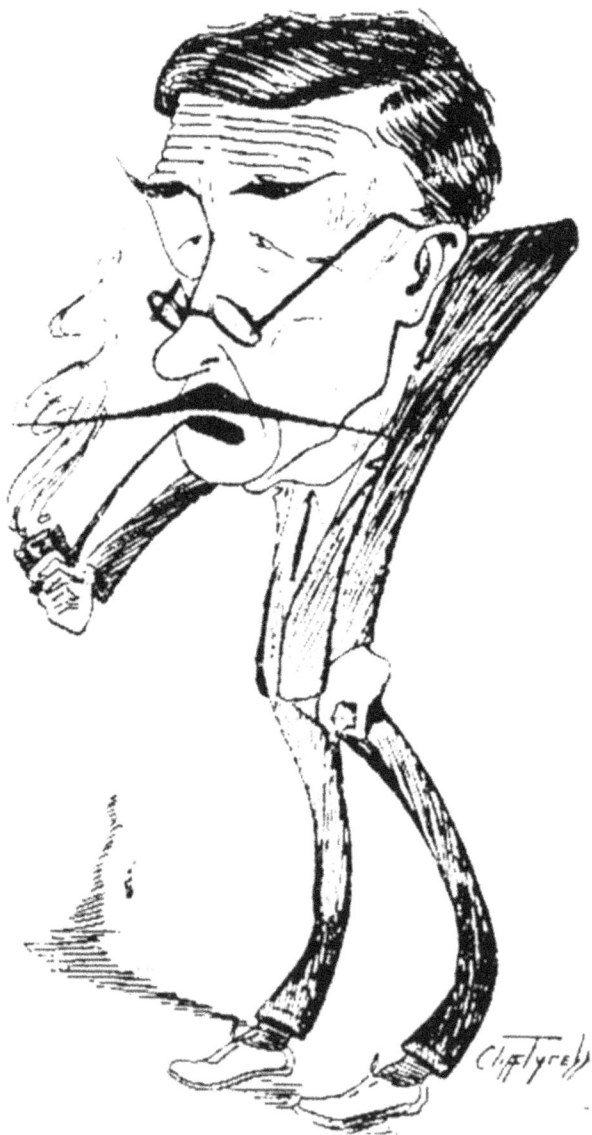

Augustus Bain Alves as seen in a Gleaner *cartoon by Cliff Tyrell*

7

Money by Menaces

Law to the legal practitioner . . . is a tool, dangerous and double-edged, a weapon to be judiciously handled, to be reverentially cared; to be treated with that shade of feeling commonly reserved for a living creature, to be used sparingly and only in dire straits, and whenever possible to be kept in the background, a silent threat for the adversary, an imminent fear to oneself, a hidden nuisance to the grave arbiter.

Norman Manley
On 'The Use of Precedents' in Jamaica Law Notes
October 1924

Augustus Bain Alves was one of the best-known trade unionists of his day. So it seems ironic that when he appeared in a case, he was a witness for the employer versus one who claimed to be a disgruntled employee. Though it could be argued that it was just this question of employment that the case turned on, another seemingly simple affair which brought out Manley's sharp wit and revealed the well-known Bain Alves playing detective.

Bain Alves was a skilled cigar maker and one of the few Jamaican trade union organizers who emerged from the ranks of skilled workers themselves. He was founder and president of the Longshoremen's Union No. 1 of the Jamaica Federation of Labour, and in June 1918, published a resolution in the *Gleaner*, which he forwarded to the governor, asking for the official recognition of labour unions. Bain Alves was also a city councillor who enjoyed the cut and thrust of debate, participating in the debates which were a feature of the weekly meetings of the Universal Negro Improvement Association (UNIA) set up by Marcus Garvey in 1914. In 1922, Bain Alves turned his talents to managing the Queen's Hotel in Kingston. On 3 March, he was called out to the verandah where he found one Charles Gaussen puffing nervously on a cigarette.

"Look here", said Gaussen, "I understand you have influence over Nanco? I want you to get £60 from him for me, so that I can go to New York, otherwise I will give some funny evidence against him that might be serious."

Bain Alves was to recall this conversation on the witness stand of the Home Circuit Court on 18 May 1923. Gaussen had since been arrested and charged with demanding money by menaces from John Nanco, a Kingston merchant.

Mr Colin McGregor, an eager young barrister from Mandeville, who had been admitted to the Jamaican Bar in December 1922, instructed by Mr Aston Simpson, appeared for the prosecution. Manley, instructed by Mr E.V. Clarke, represented the accused, Charles Gaussen.[1] The presiding judge, Anthony DeFreitas, sat back to referee the two young adversaries.

According to McGregor, Charles Gaussen had gone to Bain Alves at the Queen's Hotel and told him that he could give damaging evidence against Nanco in respect to a fire which occurred at his store in January 1923. He subsequently received a cheque for £60 on condition that he did not give evidence in the case. "It was", concluded McGregor, "a clear case of blackmail."

Mr Colin McGregor. He became Chief Justice of Jamaica in 1957

"What was your reply to Gaussen's request?" asked McGregor as Bain Alves continued with his testimony.

"I said, 'All right, I will see Mr Nanco immediately'. And Gaussen replied, 'Tell Nanco if he doesn't give me £60, I will give evidence that he set his Harbour Street store on fire'."

"And then?"

"I went downtown and told Nanco what Gaussen had said. He gave me a cheque for £60. Knowing that Gaussen would come back to the hotel, I bored two spy holes between the wooden portion of my office and a bedroom. When Gaussen returned, I took him into my office and gave him a chair parallel to the spy holes. I showed him Nanco's cheque for £60 and told him that Nanco said he must put the threats in writing. I gave him a sheet of writing paper."

"Did you tell him what to write?"

"No."

"After Gaussen finished writing, I told him to write out a receipt for the cheque and say what he was getting this £60 for. I then asked my porter, Battling Irons, to get me a penny stamp which I stuck on the receipt, and Gaussen wrote his name across it. Later, Gaussen came to my office in a passion and said, 'This is a fraud. The bank has stopped the cheque. I am going to the police'. I told him, 'You don't dare face the police, because you are the centre of a conspiracy to send a decent man to prison for the sake of £200 offered by the insurance company'. Gaussen cleared out. Next day, about 10 a.m. I met him in front of the *Gleaner* office talking to the news editor and a staff reporter. Gaussen called me to one side and said, 'For God's sake don't tell these gentlemen what I have written on the documents, because I understand that a warrant is out for either me or Nanco. Ask Nanco to give me some money and let me go away immediately'. I replied: 'Ask him yourself'."

Manley, elbows in, wig set squarely on his forehead, began his cross-examination of Bain Alves:

"Have you ever been in the police force?"

"No. I have never been a policeman in my life, nor in the detective force."

"Don't you think you have missed your vocation?"

"I don't know."

"Don't you think you are clever?"

"Yes."

"Clever enough to put a man in prison?"

"No, to save a man from prison and to break up a conspiracy. I was not anxious to put Gaussen in prison."

"When first did you hear of the conspiracy?"

"On the 3rd of March when Gaussen told me that he had been to the police."

"You knew that Mr Nanco's store was burnt?"

"Yes."

"You are a city councillor and president of a labour union?"

"Yes."

"So you are a man of some public influence?"

"It's a matter of opinion."

Continuing, Bain Alves related how he had read in the *Gleaner* that Gaussen had brought a civil suit against Nanco for unpaid wages. The first time Gaussen came to see him at the Queen's Hotel on 3 March,

Gaussen had asked him to get a settlement of the civil suit. Gaussen said he would settle for £60. When he told Gaussen that the matter was *sub judice*, Gaussen shifted his ground and made the threat.

"Did you threaten to kick Mr Gaussen out of your office?" asked Manley.

"No. I thought it was well that Nanco should know what was happening. I didn't want to see a man's reputation ruined — to go to prison — and he and his wife and children to suffer. Of course, sir, you know some wives wouldn't mind a man going to prison." Manley let the laughter subside before asking:

"So you decided to meddle in the matter?"

"I thought I should meddle in the matter, because I didn't want to see a man go to prison. I was once assaulted by a big man after making a political speech . . ."

He was cut short by the judge who said that was irrelevant to the case.

The prosecution called John Nanco, a furniture dealer, to the stand. He said that on 18 January last, his store in Kingston was burnt. Yes, he knew the accused, Gaussen. Was he ever employed at his furniture store? No, never. Had Gaussen filed an action against him for wages due. Yes. The action was filed in *forma pauperis* in the Supreme Court. The action was for £117 and he was defending the action.

Nanco recalled how he had gone to the Queen's Hotel on 9 March and given Augustus Bain Alves a cheque. He went inside a bedroom and saw the accused in an adjoining room — Mr Alves' office — through a spy hole. He heard Mr Alves ask Gaussen to put in writing all the threats he had been using before he would deliver him the cheque. Mr Alves did not dictate anything. He also asked Gaussen to write a receipt for the cheque. Nanco said he then walked out of the bedroom, into the office, and said to Gaussen:

"You are not going to give any evidence against me?"

Gaussen replied: "No, that's all right now."

Cross-examined by Manley, Nanco said that he had arrived in Jamaica in 1921 from Bristol in England. He met Gaussen the same month, and a year later, he became Gaussen's sub-tenant. Had he sent away some of his wicker furniture to Havana with his brother-in-law, he was asked, to which he replied in the affirmative. Did Gaussen travel with the furniture? No.

"Wasn't Gaussen on board the same ship?" questioned Manley.

"Yes", Nanco admitted, "but not with my furniture."

"What has become of the wicker chairs in Havana?"

"They are in the hands of a customs broker."

"Is it a fact that the customs authorities objected to the landing of the furniture because they were greatly undervalued?"

"When my brother-in-law arrived in Jamaica he told me that the customs in Havana wanted to add to the valuation."

"Didn't you employ Gaussen at your store to pack up the furniture?"

"That's an infernal lie."

"Mr Nanco, if you use such language again, I will commit you to prison," the judge rebuked.

Continuing his evidence under cross-examination by Manley, Nanco said that he never employed Gaussen in Jamaica or in Havana. He was surprised when Gaussen set up a claim against him for £117 for wages.

"I put it to you, that having failed to dispauperise him, you now seek to trap the accused?"

"No."

"And you locked the door and threatened him with violence if he did not sign the document?"

"No."

"Is it not a fact that Gaussen came there in an endeavour to settle the civil suit in order to go to New York?"

"No."

"If you were to get the accused in prison would you not kill the civil action and any other matter in connection with the fire?"

The witness looked around and shuffled about the witness box. It was obvious he had no answer.

The case for the prosecution was closed and Manley opened for the defence. Addressing the jury, Manley submitted that Nanco decided to make a shipment of furniture to Cuba and for some weeks before, Gaussen was in Nanco's store engaged in the packing. Gaussen went with the furniture to Cuba and there was some difficulty with the customs. Gaussen's funds were exhausted and when he returned to Jamaica he approached Nanco with regard to what he owed him. Nanco promised settlement. It was never made. Gaussen brought an action in the Supreme Court to recover £117 for moneys due. He filed the action in *forma pauperis* and Nanco endeavoured to get the court to dispauperise him. In support of the application, there were affidavits from people who had mythical addresses.

"How do I know?" asked Manley. "The fact is, that when the addresses on the affidavit were investigated, it was found that the addresses were vacant lots. In one case the lot was covered with *roast pork* [a type of cactus]. The application failed. Gaussen went to Augustus Bain Alves, as a man who had some influence over Nanco, to get him to settle the civil suit. What Alves and Nanco said took place", Manley asserted, "is wholly untrue. The whole episode is a made-up story, and I don't think you will accept it. The true facts of the case should be investigated; it is a disgrace that such an incident should take place in the community."

The foreman of the jury here intimated that the jury did not want to hear the defence, but one juryman rose and dissented. Manley proceeded with the defence and called Frank deMercardo to the stand.

"I'm an auctioneer," deMercardo explained. "I know Charles Gaussen — he was my partner up to the early part of last year. He left me to go with Mr Nanco in respect to a furniture business in Cuba. Before he left, I saw him in Nanco's store packing furniture. I went with Gaussen to George and Brandy's wharf two weeks before he sailed. I heard him making enquiries about the freight of the furniture to Havana."

Manley called Charles Gaussen to the stand and let him testify on his own behalf: "In February 1922, Nanco offered to employ me as a manager to take some furniture to Havana. Before sailing I asked Nanco for something in writing about the terms of employment. Nanco said not to worry; it was perfectly all right. He was supposed to come with me, but his wife is a jealous woman, and said he couldn't go, so he sent his brother-in-law, John Perrier, instead. When Perrier and I contacted a customs broker in Havana, he refused to pass the goods. According to him they were undervalued. I told Perrier to send a cable to Nanco telling him what had happened. After a month went by, I asked Perrier for my pay. He said the furniture was still in the Customs House so how could I expect any pay? I told Perrier, 'That's not my business. If Nanco blundered in undervaluing his goods, it's not my fault'. I remained in Havana until the middle of August. When I returned to Jamaica, I was broke. You know, sir, Havana is an expensive city to live in. I went to Nanco's store and complained about how badly I had been treated. Nanco never paid me bad mind."

At this stage the foreman of the jury interposed. They had arrived at a unanimous verdict, he said. They did not want to hear any more evidence. A verdict of not guilty was returned and Gaussen was discharged. Smiling broadly, Gaussen left the box and went to shake Manley's hand.

8

Of 'Panya Jar' and Drop Pan

*During the past week the town of Lucea was kept in a
considerable state of excitement, in consequence of a report
that a Spanish jar ['Panya jar'] containing a large quantity
of gold coins had been discovered in a yard about a mile
from the town. Preparations on an extensive scale were being
made for the purpose of taking up the jar and its contents. . .*

The Gleaner
26 January 1869

Norman Manley's sister-in-law, Mona Swithenbank, thought that
law was sometimes "just a game" for Manley. "He was brilliantly
clever," she mused. "He had this absolutely clear brain and he used his
powers to help people. At the same time, I think he thought some of us
very silly and very gullible, and how right he was: we are silly and
gullible."[1] Three cases handled by Manley in the summer of 1923,
illustrate the type of gullibility to which we are prone.

It was a fine sunny morning in May 1922 when Ellen Smith, a
housewife of Frankfield, Clarendon, saw two men come into her yard.
One was holding a bundle of papers bound by several elastic bands. He
introduced himself as Jocelyn Davis, also known as Habow. "At least,
that's what they called me in Cuba," he said. "It means a man with a bad
colour. But my real name is Jocelyn Victor Ledford Davis. And I'm here
to tell you that there is hidden treasure in this yard."

"How you know?" the startled householder asked.

"I was over by your neighbour, Mr Elliott, and I spied it," said
Davis. "In every parish there's hidden treasure, and the government
sends me to take it up."

Davis then offered Mrs Smith £400 for the little spot where he said
the treasure was buried. She refused to sell.

"If you refuse to sell", he informed her, "the government allows
me to take it up on their behalf."

"It's funny you should offer £400 for such a small spot."

"Because there's hidden treasure there," said Davis as he pointed out a square spot like a door mat. "Get me a fork and shovel, Mrs Smith."

"I don't have a shovel."

"A hoe will do."

Ellen Smith dutifully brought a hoe and fork and Davis took out a silver tripod from a leather bag and stuck it in the ground.

"Him spy through it like a surveyor," Ellen Smith told her husband later that evening. "Then him get excited and tell me: 'This is one! There is another!' And him point out four spots, saying they contain Spanish jars full of gold." Ellen Smith described how Davis had dug the last spot, and when he had got down about eighteen inches there was a grating sound.

"Ah, Mrs Smith, do you hear the fork striking the jar?" he asked.

She said, yes.

"It's a large jar. I don't think we can take it up today. It must have thirty thousand dollars in gold."

"How you know?"

"I know."

Davis said if she didn't give it up, it would mean trouble, for he would have to report it to the Government Treasury in Kingston. "I will take up one for the government, but I won't tell them about the other three," he told her. "You pay me £40 and I will take up two for you. The third I will take up for myself — half for me; half for you."

"I don't have £40."

"Then give me £4 to buy the quicksilver to detain the jars."

Ellen Smith handed over the money.

"I'll be back in two weeks with the quicksilver," Davis promised, warning, "Mind you don't trouble the spot."

Despite the warning, Ellen Smith and her husband went to the spot and dug, but found no jar. Two weeks later, Davis returned with some stuff looking like logwood water saying it was the quicksilver.

Ellen Smith made up her face: "I never see quicksilver that colour."

"It's the kind used to take up jars," Davis explained, as he sprinkled it over the spot.

Davis was subsequently arrested and charged with obtaining money by false pretences, and hired Norman Manley to defend him. J.A.G. Smith and Colin McGregor appeared for the Crown.[2]

"Did you ask Davis about your £4 when he came with the logwood water stuff and poured it over the spot?" Manley asked Mrs Smith on the witness stand of the May Pen courthouse on 6 June 1923.

"No. Him promise to come back the next week, to raise the jar."

"And you believed he would take it up?"

"I was moving under two opinions."

"You were doubting, yet hoping?"

"Yes."

"Why did you wait three months before going to the police?"

"I wasn't well. And even then, if I didn't have some boldness, I wouldn't have reported it to the police. All I wanted was the sergeant to be present when Davis come to take up the jar. If no jar come up, the sergeant would see I get back my money."

The jury without retiring found Davis guilty.

"And very properly too," Mr Justice Orpen commented. "The crime was a mean, dirty one, namely deceiving ignorant people about jars of treasure hidden on their land. It is fortunate that their foolishness did not involve them in further loss." And he sentenced Davis to eighteen months imprisonment with hard labour.

"A foregone conclusion," commented Leslie Clerk to Manley after the trial. "Why did you accept the brief?"

Manley looked him in the eye: "Counsel has no right to pick and choose whom he should appear for."

"Rather a simple point of view, don't you think?"

"Perhaps. But I feel strongly about it."[3]

"What's next?"

"In court?"

"Yes."

"Spanish jars!"

"Again?"

"Yes, but this time an appeal involving the judgment of nonsuit which raises a very interesting question as to the true construction of section 183 of the Resident Magistrate's Law."[4]

"That is a section", Manley argued, in the Court of Appeal on 2 July 1923, "which provides that a resident magistrate might nonsuit in every case in which satisfactory proof has not been given entitling the plaintiff or the defendant to the judgment of the court. My submission is that if the plaintiff made out a *prima facie* case, and the defendant failed to discharge the burden of proof devolved on him, in the circumstances the appellant was entitled to judgment. This is a case in which the plaintiff went into court on a written contract for the sale of half an acre of land, a house and furniture for the sum of £130. The defence to the action was that the defendant did not deny making the document but he was induced to make it under fraudulent circumstances: that he was invited to part with his deeds in order to satisfy ghosts in the raising of Spanish jars."

"That's not the defence in the case," argued J.A.G. Smith, representing the respondent.

"Well, that's how I understand the defence", retorted Manley, "the defendant's case was that he never received any money, and that his title was obtained from him by fraud. The pretence alleged was that it was necessary to give the document so as to make it more easy to get at the Spanish jars deposited on the land. The resident magistrate, in his reasons for judgment, supports what I say. He said that the defendant asserted that the document was required (so he was told) to lock up the spirit. In short, the defendant had made an allegation which amounted to a crime. The resident magistrate concluded that the defendant had failed to satisfy him in respect to the circumstances under which he parted with the document. He had failed to discharge the duty devolving on him, so that if the plaintiff proved the contract and the defendant failed to prove fraud, the plaintiff must be proved to be innocent."

Extracts from evidence given at the trial were here read by Manley. According to the plaintiff's story, she resided at Elderslie in St Elizabeth and, wishing to acquire the property located at Cambridge in St James, she visited the district and there the bargain was concluded and the sum of £130 was paid over. The defence was that no money passed and that a fraud was played on the defendant in respect to the raising of Spanish jars.

Manley said the magistrate should have come to a conclusion one way or the other and should not have nonsuited the plaintiff as he had done.

Smith raised the point that having regard to the nature of the claim and the amount involved, the resident magistrate had no jurisdiction. He contended that the magistrate had exercised his discretion in nonsuiting the plaintiff and it was a charitable view he had taken in not giving judgment for the defendant which he could have done.

"Mr Manley," began the Acting Chief Justice, Anthony DeFreitas, in delivering judgment. "The Bench desire to thank you for your able and interesting argument in interpreting section 183 before their unanimous judgment against you is delivered. We agree that section 183 of Law 28 of 1904 has not displaced the rules as to burden of proof or presumption which are well recognized, and to which we have referred, and our decision is not to be taken in any way sanctioning any such belief. We think that the resident magistrate's judgment is to be supported on the ground that there was a conflict of evidence as to the payment of the purchase money of £130. It was necessary for the plaintiff to prove the payment of that sum of money to the defendant. She gave *prima facie* evidence of the payment, but we think that his *prima facie* evidence has been so shaken by the evidence and surrounding circumstances in the case that we are not prepared to say that the resident magistrate was not justified in vesting himself on section 183, and ordering a nonsuit. The appeal is dismissed with £10 costs to the respondent."

Panya jar not my line, Manley no doubt thought, as he closed the file, opened another and prepared to argue an appeal on behalf of George McCarthy, David Wellington and Charles McFarlane, charged with assisting in the conduct of "drop pan" lottery.[5]

Drop Pan is an illegal numbers game played in Jamaica. It originated among the Chinese and is so named because tickets numbered from 1 to 36 are put into a pan, and the pan "dropped" as a means of drawing the winning number.

In this case Manley submitted that the appellants were wrongly charged. "There is no evidence that they assisted in the conducting of a public lottery, and if the case were proved, it would be that they were engaged in gaming rather than conducting a public lottery. The men were found together, but I submit that the finding of a lottery ticket is a presumption that it was bought, and I maintain that the evidence tends to show, if anything, that the appellants were *playing* not *assisting* in the running of a lottery."

Manley went on to refer to the evidence given at the trial and pointed out that there was no mention whatever of the appellant Wellington. The only evidence was that he was found in a group where money was being counted and tickets were being sorted. It appeared that McCarthy and McFarlane were convicted and fined £25 or 30 days on the same evidence on which the magistrate convicted Wellington.

In arguing the case for the Crown, Colin McGregor maintained that "the appellants were found sorting tickets and counting money. On the evidence of the police alone, it was open to the magistrate to convict". McGregor went on to refer to the specific evidence against the appellants McCarthy and McFarlane but admitted that the evidence against Wellington was so weak that he could not support the conviction against him.

"If you don't support the evidence against Wellington", submitted the Acting Chief Justice, Anthony DeFreitas, "is it not more difficult to establish the case against McCarthy and McFarlane?"

McGregor said he couldn't take the case any further.

"If the case failed against Wellington, it must fail against the two other appellants," Manley insisted.

"Seeing that it has been submitted by counsel that the sustaining of the conviction of Wellington would be unsafe", the chief justice noted, "it would appear to the Court nonetheless safe if the conviction against the two other appellants was upheld. If the additional evidence against Wellington is very slight, it is equally so with regard to the other appellants. It is quite possible that the defendants assisted in the conduct of the lottery, but there is not sufficient evidence on which a conviction can properly be sustained. I agree with Mr Manley that the conviction against Wellington cannot be sustained and go further to say that it would also be unsafe with regard to the other two appellants. The appeal must be allowed."

9

Motor Madness

The first motor car that reached our shores was owned by Mr L.D. Baker, at Port Antonio, in 1900. Mr E. Nuttall, the well-known Kingston solicitor followed Mr Baker, and in the winter of 1903 imported a steam car locomobile. Of the owners of gasolene cars, Dr Henderson was the first in the spring of 1904 with a Duryea, soon followed by Mr Griffith of Black River with a 14 horse power Orleans car.

The Gleaner
29 January 1906

Who brought the first motor car into Jamaica? "I considered myself the first resident in Jamaica to import a car," Mr H.W. Griffith of Hodges Pen, St Elizabeth, always maintained. "Four cylinder cars were only put on the market at the end of 1902, and I placed an order for a four cylinder New Orleans, French-hooded, at the beginning of 1903, and received delivery of same at Black River in July that year."[1]

Mr H.W. Griffith's 'New Orleans', said to be the first motor car brought to Jamaica

Shortly after, according to Mr Griffith, Dr G.C. Henderson imported a three-wheeled vehicle and then, in November 1903, an Englishman named Wright visited Jamaica with a two cylinder Peugeot of French manufacture. Both Griffith's and Wright's cars were exhibited at the Paradise Pen show in Westmoreland on New Year's Day, 1904, when the owners were requested to drive around the show ring, "Which we did", Griffith recalled, "much to the delight and amusement of those present."

Mr Griffith's car was certainly the first to be registered in Jamaica: No. M-1. "It was in 1905 that Mr Nuttall had a steam car," said Griffith. "He assembled it himself."

Sir Sydney Olivier (Governor of Jamaica 1907-1913) thought otherwise. If his memory served him correctly, it was in 1904 that "Mr Ernest Nuttall used to glide sedately about the Liguanea Plains with Mrs Nuttall in a small steam-driven gig. That same year, Mr John Lockett of Troja had a primitive chain-driven Buick which was the first petrol-driven car I ever rode in the island. I remember it as a rather musical ride".[2]

In those days local restrictions were put on the landing of petrol which had to be sent to Rockfort and stored there. For this reason, Griffith took his New Orleans back to England in 1906 and brought back a Turner Miesse steam car, manufactured at Wolverhampton. This he shipped back in 1909 and brought out a Napier which he used for some 150,000 miles before he put it aside in 1922 for a four cylinder Buick.

By 1923, the motor car was well on its way to becoming an integral part of Jamaican society. Those who could afford to, employed chauffeurs, who often sneaked off on little jaunts of their own, sometimes with disastrous consequences. Take, for example, the time a chauffeur-driven car collided with a horse-drawn bus. Under such circumstances, who is responsible? The owner of the car or the chauffeur?

Manley was faced with the question in October 1923 when the action was heard of *Vassall* v. *Owen*, in which the plaintiff claimed the sum of £50 for injuries to her bus, harness and horse, caused by the negligent driving of the defendant's motor car.[3]

Manley appeared for the defendant, Lieutenant Owen. Mr R.W. Bryant, representing the plaintiff, set the scene: "The bus was standing at the left-hand corner of Temple Lane and the Parish Church at South Parade. The motor car, driven by the defendant's chauffeur, David Saunders, turned the corner from Orange Street in a reckless manner.

The driver of the bus, Ferdinand Rose, yelled out, 'Be careful', but the chauffeur ran right into the bus, hitting the horse in the head and severely injuring the coachman, who had to be sent to hospital. The vehicle itself was badly damaged. The incident took place at 5.30 in the afternoon."

Presenting evidence for the defence, Manley noted that on the day in question, Lieutenant Owen, the harbour master, along with his wife, left the Royal Mail building at about 12.30 p.m. in his new Dodge motor car driven by David Saunders. The couple left the car at the foot of West Street and sent back the chauffeur with instructions to take the vehicle to the garage at the Royal Mail building and to pick them up at 6.30 p.m. at the Ordnance Wharf. Saunders failed to turn up, and on information received, Lieutenant Owen went to the Sutton Street Police Station where he saw the car. Examination of the speedometer showed that after Lieutenant Owen left the car, it had done between 19 and 20 miles.

Samuel Wray, a corporal of police, testified that on investigating the collision he found the chauffeur was drunk. He prosecuted the chauffeur on two charges upon which he had been convicted and fined.

Manley addressed the court: "I submit, Your Honour, that under the circumstances the defendant, the master, is not responsible for the acts of the chauffeur, his servant. The chauffeur disobeyed his master's instructions. He deviated from the course he should have taken, and embarked upon an unauthorized journey. The master cannot be held liable."

Mr Bryant submitted that "The chauffeur was acting in exercise of his duty and was in charge of the car with his master's authority. The deviation was not such, in time or place, to relieve the master of the liability. I suggest that at the time of the occurrence, the chauffeur was on his way to meet his master. There is no evidence of 'joy riding' or of what took place between 2.30 and 5.30 p.m."

Justice Orpen had the last word: "I am satisfied that the chauffeur was not performing his duty as a servant when the accident happened. It is a matter of only five minutes from the garage to the Ordnance Wharf, and if the chauffeur had been going for his master he would not have been in the vicinity of South Parade one hour before the time. I am extremely sorry for the plaintiff, but I have to find in favour of the defendant."

Judgment was accordingly entered for the defendant with costs.

Motor cars at this time shared the highways and byways not only with horse, mule and donkey power but also with the tram car, all of which were road hazards for pedestrians, as barrister Radcliffe, representing the West India Electric Company, explained in the Court of Appeal in 1923:[4]

"A tram car was proceeding from Cross Roads in the direction of Camp. The driver saw the plaintiff coming along the road about two chains way. He crossed over the track and a motor car came along. The plaintiff got frightened and, jumping back, hit the side of the tram car."

"The plaintiff claimed the sum of £49 2s 6d for damages for negligence", he continued, "and the judge of the Kingston Court awarded the full amount. I submit that the plaintiff failed to prove negligence and that the judge was wrong in awarding damages without any evidence of loss. For instance the plaintiff said he lost £2 per day in not being able to look after his dairy and measure lands. The plaintiff has not proved any loss. If he had paid someone to do his work it would be a different thing."

Manley, representing the plaintiff respondent, Mr F. Greenwich Sharp, argued that "the motorman stated that when he saw the old gentleman ahead, he checked his car, and sounded his gong. What the learned judge said was that he ought to have gone further, and by anticipating danger, taken steps to prevent it. So long as there was reason to anticipate danger, it was the duty of the driver to have checked his speed". Manley contended that there was plenty of time for the driver to have stopped his car. The position was that the plaintiff saw the motor car coming towards him, became frightened, stepped back to avoid it, and the tram car came upon him.

Additionally, said Manley, the road was not a normal one: "The car line runs on the left hand side, right up against the edge of the bank. It is a dangerous road, and as such drivers have to be very careful. Extraordinary precautions have to be taken in case of danger. It was not done in this case."

Acting Chief Justice DeFreitas noted that the plaintiff said that he was dazzled by the light of the car and he stepped to the right.

"It is immaterial whether the plaintiff struck the front or the side of the car", argued Manley, "the driver saw from a distance what was before him, it was his duty to take the necessary precaution. The judge was perfectly right when he took the view that the driver should have slowed down. It is a view which any reasonable person would take. I don't see how the court can disturb that finding."

Manley suggested another element which the court had to consider: the fact that the incident took place at night.

"Why did the plaintiff not cross the road?" asked DeFreitas.

"He might have realized that it would have been dangerous," Manley reasoned. "It was the duty of the driver to have anticipated danger and to have taken precaution to prevent it." He had seen the motor car coming from the opposite direction.

"The evidence showed that the motor car was some distance away," DeFreitas commented.

"But the speed of the motor car was ten times faster than the tram car", argued Manley, "and I submit that there was every reason for the driver to have anticipated danger. I submit that the judgment is sound in law and should not be disturbed."

Radcliffe said his learned friend's suggestion as to danger might have been a good one if there was any evidence to support it. Where was the evidence of danger?

"Mr Manley very rightly mentions the condition of the road as being a danger," Justice Brown observed.

Radcliffe argued that there was nothing to show the driver any danger, considering the distance the motor car was from the man. He could not see how it could be suggested in the circumstances that the driver could have anticipated danger.

The court reserved its decision until 9 March when, in a short, oral judgment, Acting Chief Justice DeFreitas concluded: "It is clear from the evidence that the defendant's tram car was driven with due care and had safely begun to pass the plaintiff, while the plaintiff was on a clear road in a position of safety and the tram car was continuing to pass the plaintiff when he put himself in contact with the side of the tram car that was moving on fixed rails. He put himself in such contact because he was dazzled by the distant lights of an approaching motor car which there was no reason to apprehend would reach him before the tramcar had completely passed him. It is obvious that there is no evidence in the case of negligence on the part of the defendants, and therefore the judgment in favour of the plaintiff cannot stand. Judgment is entered for the defendant with costs and solicitor's costs in the court below, to be taxed. The respondent must pay the appellant's cost of this appeal, fixed at £10."

Justices Brown and Orpen concurred.

As cars were now the fastest type of vehicle on Jamaican roads, their speed became an issue with other road users. Acting Corporal Cyril Francis, attached to the Sutton Street Police Station, had one passion in life: bagging drivers who exceeded the speed limit of 12 miles per hour. He became known as the "Speed Cop"; the pedestrians' idol and the drivers' nightmare. On 15 December 1923, he stopped the driver of a car travelling along Harbour Street:

"May I see your licence, sir?" he asked.

"No, you damn well can't."

"Can I have your name, sir?"

"You know damn well who I am."

"Would you be the solicitor, John Henry Cargill, sir?"

"You know that I am."

"Then you won't be able to plead ignorance of the law, will you, sir? I'm charging you with exceeding the speed limit along Harbour Street."

Cargill retained Manley to defend him.[5]

Before His Honour, H.C. Robinson, of the Kingston Resident Magistrate's Court, the Speed Cop described how he first saw Cargill on King Street, and followed him along to Harbour Street. Cargill was doing about 19 miles an hour, he said, and he had witnesses to prove it.

Manley called Cargill to the stand. He insisted that he was not exceeding the 12 miles per hour speed limit: the Speed Cop and his witnesses were "abominable liars". The resident magistrate glowered; Manley swiftly changed gear:

"Mr Cargill, what were your movements on the day in question?"

"I went to see Dr Moody. My back was hurting; I was not in a mood to drive fast."

Cargill said that after leaving the hospital, he had driven along North Street and down Orange Street and around South Parade. When he got to King Street there was a constable on point duty. He signalled to the constable and he passed him down. He saw another constable at Barry Street, and another at Tower Street. From King and Tower Streets, he never exceeded the speed limit to his office on Harbour Street. There was a bus in the middle of the road, just in front of Kinkead's store. The Hon. W.A.S. Vickers [Custos of St Andrew] was getting on the bus. Cargill insisted he was driving very slowly along Harbour Street when Francis stopped him and said that he was going to run him in for speeding:

"He said I was doing 19 miles an hour on King Street. It's a downright lie."

Asked why he hadn't produced his licence as requested, Cargill said it was in his bag at his office.

Cargill was cross-examined by Inspector O.F. Wright for the prosecution: "Are you suggesting, Mr Cargill, that Corporal Francis is untruthful?"

"Yes."

"What did your speedometer read?"

Cargill shrugged his shoulders; he had to admit that his speedometer was broken.

"You know that you can exceed the speed limit and yet you are not driving dangerously?"

"Yes."

"You know that Mr Michael deCordova of the *Gleaner* had been prosecuted also?"

"Yes, I heard his opinion too."

"You know that Colonel Pinnock has also been prosecuted?"

"I was in court when he was fined."

"You had to stop in King Street?"

"Yes."

"You didn't stop in Harbour Street?"

"No."

Manley called Andrew Horatio Aguilar for the defence. He said that on the day in question he was standing in front of his store on Harbour Street with Mr Edgar DaCosta. There was a fair amount of traffic in Harbour Street. He saw when Cargill passed by in his car; he was driving at a steady pace, not more than 12 miles per hour. Francis was about 15 yards behind him.

Manley next called Edgar DaCosta for the defence. Yes, he saw Cargill driving along Harbour Street at the time of the incident. There were several buses in the street, Cargill was driving slowly. He heard the Speed Cop's horn, then he saw him coming from the direction of King Street chasing Mr Cargill.

Cross-examined by Inspector Wright, DaCosta acknowledged that he had a brother named Vivian. No, he did not remember if his brother was fined for improper conduct at the Half-Way Tree courthouse. How did he feel about the police? Well, he was not particularly well disposed towards them. He had told the Speed Cop that Mr Cargill was not exceeding the speed limit.

Manley submitted that there was no evidence to suggest Cargill was speeding along King Street. "But immaterial to that", concluded the resident magistrate, "I consider that there is quite enough evidence for me to convict and we have the admission from Mr Cargill that his speedometer was broken. The Speed Cop has been doing good work in Kingston. There is a certain element which is out to 'down' Corporal Francis. All I can say is that it will be a very sorry day for Kingston if the Speed Cop's position is taken away from him. Thanks to Corporal Francis, people can walk the streets of Kingston more freely. The witnesses for the defence state that the Speed Cop was behind Mr Cargill in Harbour Street. It is quite clear that the witness DaCosta is against the police. I have to find the defendant guilty of exceeding the speed limit. He must pay a fine of £8 or seven days imprisonment."

Cargill was next charged with not producing his licence when called upon to do so by Corporal Francis. He pleaded guilty; was admonished and discharged. The charge against Cargill for exceeding the speed limit in King Street was withdrawn.

Three weeks later Cargill and the Speed Cop were back in the Kingston Resident Magistrate's Court, but this time the roles were reversed. The Speed Cop, Acting Corporal Frances himself was in the dock, charged with exceeding the speed limit on his motor cycle in East Street.[6] John Henry Cargill was prosecuting!

There was no doubt about it. A string of witnesses relished the opportunity of testifying against the Speed Cop who had no rebuttal: he wasn't on duty at the time. Justice Brown found him guilty.

Cargill, having had his moment of glory, said he was not asking the judge to punish the defendant, but to admonish and discharge him.

Justice Brown concurred.

Speed, in all its forms, had a fascination for Manley. Indeed, it led to one of his vices. He loved the feel of a powerful engine and he loved to drive at an outrageous speed. In 1923, Manley himself had learned to drive and was after a car. He was spending a lot on car hire: £8 a week when travelling the circuit. He was, he thought, becoming quite an expert driver, but after a fashion that fancied ditches, as many a pedestrian observed as Manley chalked up the dust along the roads.

10

Compelling Evidence

*When, in England, the news broke of the happenings in
Jamaica in October and November 1865, and particularly of
the official massacre of a large number of the peasantry in
an orgy of 'suppression', and of the illegal Court-martialling
and execution of George William Gordon, some public-spirited
men formed the Jamaica Committee, supported by a
subscribed fund of £10,000; and sought legal opinion as to
the 'steps open to them to assist their fellow subjects in
Jamaica to obtain the protection of the law; and if this has
been broken, to bring the guilty parties to justice'.*

Ansell Hart
Monthly Comments, *July 1968*

On 1 November 1923, Norman Manley journeyed to the parish of
St Thomas to attend Court. He knew the Morant Bay courthouse
to be a symbol of the extraordinary steps Jamaicans would take if denied
what they believed to be justice, but he was at the time woefully
ignorant of the details which led to what is known in history as the
Morant Bay Rebellion of 1865.[1] As he was to later note in a debate: "I
spent eight years in secondary
school and left without
knowing one single fact about
the history of the past."[2] "I'm
deplorably ignorant of Jamaica,"
he remarked on another
occasion. "I'm glad for the
circuit — it takes me to places
I've never seen before."[3]

Manley, over the years,
would come to extend and
deepen his knowledge of the
Jamaican past and it was during
his time in politics that the two

*Morant Bay courthouse. The statue of Paul Bogle
was sculpted by Edna Manley in 1965 to
commemorate the rebellion of 1865*

leading protagonists of that nineteenth century event, Paul Bogle and George William Gordon, were to be named the first national heroes of an independent Jamaica. As Norman Manley mounted the courthouse steps that November morning, he could not have dreamt that forty-six years later he himself would also be immortalized by his countrymen, joining the pantheon of national heroes of the new nation, to be buried beside the monuments to the heroes of Morant Bay.[4]

Despite his limited knowledge at the time, it would not have been lost on the lawyer and future lawmaker that a perceived lack of justice was at the heart of the Morant Bay rebellion since its central symbol, the courthouse, had been fired by an angry mob. Thomas Harvey, of the Society of Friends in London, who visited Jamaica after the rebellion concluded that the major reason for the uprising was "the entire loss of confidence in the administration of justice as between employers and employed and between the higher and lower classes; and the generally arbitrary, irritating and excessively indiscreet conduct and bearing of the magistracy and other persons of authority". It was a significant fact, he noted, brought incidentally to light by the Royal Commission established to examine the events, that the people had established courts of their own for the settlement of disputes, appointed justices and constables, issued summonses and levied pecuniary fines.[5] It was in the new day that had dawned in the wake of the rebellion that young Jamaicans like Manley had been empowered to serve the cause of justice. That is what he had come to do that morning, having been assigned by the Crown to defend two parishoners of St Thomas charged with murder.[6]

The Hon. E. St John Branch, KC arrived in Jamaica on 24 September 1923, to take up his appointment as chief justice

The brothers, Charles and Daniel Scott, had pleaded not guilty to the murder of Rebecca Payton at Bowden Road on 13 June 1923. John St John Yates was prosecuting for the Crown. He opened with an announcement that, after much consideration, he had come to the conclusion that there was not sufficient evidence against a third man, Loderick Peters, who had been charged along with the brothers Scott. He would therefore enter a *nolle prosequi*.

"Bring up the accused," ordered the Chief Justice, Mr E. St John Branch.

"Mr Peters", the judge addressed the

prisoner, "the attorney-general has entered a *nolle prosequi* in the charge against you. You are discharged."

As Peters was vociferously greeted by the large gathering of his friends outside the courthouse, Charles and Daniel Scott were placed in the dock.

The right of challenge was freely exercised by both sides before a jury was selected. The foreman, Rudolph Burke,[7] a planter, must have eyed Manley keenly. He was six years Manley's senior, and one-time cricket, football and track captain at Jamaica College, Manley's Alma Mater. Burke was also a record holder for the quarter-mile and would have read, with a certain amount of satisfaction, of Manley's record time of 10 seconds flat for the 100 yards at the Inter-Secondary Schools Championship Sports in 1911. Apart from being a Jamaican record, it had made Manley one of the fastest schoolboys in the world. But any reflections by Burke would have been cut short when the attorney-general began to outline what he termed a most foul and diabolical murder. He called fourteen-year-old Luther McKenzie to the stand.

McKenzie stated that Rebecca Payton was his cousin. She was the gate woman at Bowden railway crossing and a higgler who sold bread, buns and ginger beer. McKenzie slept at her house. On the 12th of June last, he went to bed at 8 o'clock. There was only one room with two beds. He awoke at about 1.30 a.m. and heard footsteps on the verandah and a man's voice say,

"Give me a sixpence of bread."

Miss Payton replied: "I gone to my bed. I can't get up."

The voice said: "If you don't get up, I kill you."

There was a kick on the door. It flew open. A man with a flashlight stepped up and fired a revolver.

"I see the man who fire the shot right now — in the dock — the one with the white jacket," McKenzie shrieked. And he pointed to Daniel Scott. "Him fire the revolver twice. Miss Payton fall to the floor when the first shot take her. When the second shot fire, the lamp go out. As Miss Payton fall, I jump over her and through the window." McKenzie described how he had tried to run away along the railway line but was grabbed by a man who took him back to the house. It was the same man who had fired the revolver. And once again, he fixed his eyes on Daniel Scott.

When they reached the house, McKenzie said that he saw a man standing in the road. Inside the house he observed blood on the floor and bed but there was no sign of Miss Payton. There was no light in the house, but that same man, Daniel Scott, lit the lamp.

"Him say I must help search the place. Him take a pan from the table with money in it, and a blue cloth thread-bag which also have money."

The witness was shown a thread bag and testified that it was the same one. "Me know it by the two small holes," he concluded.

According to McKenzie, Scott also took a blue paper bag from the starch pan and put it in his pocket. Then he helped himself to a pair of silver bangles. Scott left him then with a warning that if he talked, he would kill him. McKenzie remained in the house until daylight when he went to Phillipsfield and asked a friend, John Williams, to accompany him to Miss Payton's house. "We search the house, the kitchen and yard," he testified. "We find Miss Payton body in a patch of cane." Williams went with McKenzie to the police station at Port Morant and made a report. Subsequently, "Me go to the police station at Port Morant. The police them show me seven men. Me pick out Daniel Scott. Him fire the revolver that night."

Questioned about the other prisoner, Charles Scott, McKenzie said that he picked him out as the man he saw standing in the road. How did he identify Charles Scott?

"Him shorter than the other man."

At this point, Manley requested that the prisoners be made to stand together for comparison. They were the same height.

Continuing McKenzie said: "Me also pick out another man — James Wilson."

"Why did you pick out James Wilson?" asked the judge.

"Because him the same height as the man I see on the road."

James Wilson was called and made to stand next to the brothers Scott.

"I will make a note that Daniel Scott is half a head taller than Wilson," the judge noted, "and that the two Scotts are the same height."

The Crown prosecutor continued to question the witness about the identification parade and how he came to pick out the prisoners. McKenzie said that the first time he saw them, they were facing him. He didn't recognize any of them, but when their backs were turned, he picked out Daniel Scott as the man who fired the revolver.

Examined by the court, McKenzie explained that he pointed out Charles Scott at the identification parade after he had picked out James Wilson because he thought he resembled the man he saw outside the house.

Dr Frederick Richard Evans, the District Medical Officer for Plantain Garden River District, said that when he examined the body of Miss Payton he found several injuries which included a round wound below the collar bone that went below into the chest breaking two ribs and turning upwards into the shoulder blade where he found a .38 calibre bullet. Death was due to haemorrhage and shock. The deceased might have lived for, say, five minutes.

Dorcas Anderson was sworn in. She said that she lived with the prisoner Daniel Scott at Aelous Valley. Both Daniel and his brother Charles left home on Tuesday, 12 June with a donkey. They returned about 6.30 or 7.00 the following night. That same night the police came and arrested Daniel. The witness was shown the blue thread bag. She said it belonged to Charles Scott; he had had it for some time.

Reuben Edwards, a lineman employed by the United Fruit Company testified that early on the morning of 13 June, he was "at the cotton tree, near Willie Wong's shop in Port Morant. Peters say I must call him if I see any truck pass, for him have two friends who stay the night to send away. Peters bought drinks, combs, pocket knives and a pipe which him give to the two men. Andrew Wheeler's truck come along and Peters put Daniel at the head of the truck and Charles at the tail, and them go off". At this point the witness identified the two prisoners in the dock as the men Peters had sent on the truck.

After taking the oath, Detective Bygrave detailed the events which led to the defendant's arrest: "I went to Charles Scott's house. He came out, and as he saw me, shut the door. I pushed the door and stepped in. I had no intention to arrest him at this time. I asked Scott if he went to Port Morant the morning before and he said no. I then arrested him on a charge of murder. He said, 'Massa, do as you like. I don't know the place Bowden'. I searched Charles, and asked him for the clothes he wore the day before. In the pocket of the trousers I found a thread bag with nineteen shillings and sixpence in it. I took Charles to the police station at Morant Bay and went to Daniel Scott's house. He was putting on a pair of trousers and smoking a new pipe. I said, 'You have a new pipe smoking? Let me see it'. He threw it away in the coffee-piece and I arrested him on a charge of murder. I cautioned him. He replied, 'Massa, me don't know what you call so'. Before the incident of the pipe, I asked Daniel if he were at Port Morant and came off at White Horses. He said he slept at White Horses."

Cross-examined by Manley, the detective said that he was at the police station when the boy McKenzie did his identification."The boy walked right up, facing the men in a line, and pointed out Daniel Scott as one of the men. I must say, I don't know why I should have to attend an identification parade. That is no place for a detective."

"I would like to get evidence from some officer of rank who was present at the identification parade," the chief justice requested.

Sergeant Major Hinds said he was present and was called to the stand. He described how Luther McKenzie had looked up and down the line before going up and pointing to Charles Scott. He had pointed out another man before picking out Daniel Scott.

Adella Campbell, a niece of the deceased, was next on the stand. She identified the blue thread bag as belonging to her aunt. How could she be certain? She had handled it often, she said, and knew it by the fish-line string and the fabric which was a remnant of one of her aunt's dresses.

Robert F. Coombs was called by the Crown and told the court that he was a planter and lived at Morant Bay. He testified: "I knew Rebecca Payton. She sold bread for me at Bowden Crossing. I went to the police station at Morant Bay and was shown a blue thread bag. It belonged to Miss Payton."

"Are you quite sure?" asked Yates, the counsel for the prosecution.

"Yes. I handled that bag many times. Miss Payton put my bread money in it."

Constable V.J. Ingram was sworn in and told the court: "On Saturday, the 18th of July, I was station guard. There were in custody, Hugh Wallace, Stanford Archer and Charles Scott in one cell, and Daniel Scott in the next cell but one. Archer reported that he heard Charles Scott call to Daniel and ask if he was fretting. Daniel said no, because he heard that Peters was spending a lot of money to get them off, and he had heard that the little boy was sick and he hoped he would die, as he was the only witness against them."

The court adjourned until the following morning. The prosecution continued its case with Hugh Wallace. He said that he had been placed in the same cell with Charles Scott and Archer. He heard Charles Scott ask someone in the next cell: "Are you fretting?" The answer was no, because Peters had told him that he had spent lots of money to get them off. He also knew that the boy was sick and might die, and since there were no other witnesses, they might get off. At this point, the witness said, the other prisoner in the cell, Archer, turned around and exclaimed: "Oh, so you kill de woman! I'm going to tell the station guard." Scott replied, "Don't bother with that, for the whole of us are men." Archer, however, called the station guard who in turn called the sergeant major, and the statement was repeated to him in the presence of Charles Scott.

The case for the Crown was closed and Manley opened for the defence: "The main evidence on which this case rests is that of the young boy, Luther McKenzie, who has testified that he saw a tall and a short man, and not two men of the same height, as the prisoners are.

Then there is the question of identification. The same boy swore that he had some difficulty in pointing out the prisoners, and, as a matter of fact, as you have already heard, he pointed out another short man, previous to pointing out one of the prisoners. Take careful note that he could not make them out on seeing their faces, but only after their backs were turned."

Manley said that he would call attention to the evidence of Detective Bygrave who testified that the boy walked straight up and pointed out Daniel Scott as one of the two men engaged in the killing of the unfortunate woman.

"This", said Manley, "is damnable perjury and an outrage on the country. I speak strongly gentlemen, because I feel strongly over such an amazing attempt to deceive the Crown and you. Then we have the thread bag which, by the way, one witness for the Crown identified as belonging to the prisoner Charles Scott. This thread bag, you must remember, was said to have been found in the pocket of Charles Scott by the same Detective Bygrave, the truthfulness of whose evidence is very questionable, and not such as should be accepted against people whose lives are at stake . . . I submit gentlemen, that there is no evidence in this case to support the charge, having regard especially to the conduct of the police." Manley called the prisoner, Daniel Scott, to the stand. Scott described how he had left his house with his brother and a donkey and made their way through Danver's Pen to Negro River where they met one Bogle. They continued through Seaforth, White Hall, Golden Valley, Taunton, and then to Sunning Hill, where he sold the donkey to a Percival Domay. They remained there till about 5 o'clock when they went to Port Morant to see Loderick Peters about the sale of a piece of land at Aelous Valley. They slept at Peters's house that night and left at about 6.30 in the morning. They went to Willie Wong's shop where they bought two knives, a pipe and a comb before taking a truck to White Horses. They walked the rest of the way home, reaching about 6.30 p.m. Detective Bygrave came the same night and arrested him. He was in bed when he came. He told Bygrave that he was at Port Morant the day before. He was taken to the police station where seven of them were put together for identification. A little boy came up and looked but did not point out any of them. The boy was taken away and brought again; this time their backs were turned to the boy and he pointed him out. He also pointed out another man. Detective Sergeant Irving pointed to his brother Charles, and asked the boy if he did not see that tall man there. The boy said no.

Charles Scott, the other accused, next gave evidence corroborating his brother and flatly denying ever having any conversation with the witness Wallace, who was a prisoner in the same lock-up with them. He said he had the conversation with the other prisoner, Archer, whom he told: 'We black men won't help one another'."

Manley then called a banana buyer, Percival Domay, to the stand and he confirmed that he had bought a donkey from the two brothers. He was followed by Phillip Bogle who testified as to having met the two prisoners at Negro River Bridge at about 7.30 a.m. going in the direction of Sunning Hill.

Loderick Peters was sworn in. He said he was a labourer living at Port Morant. He knew both accused — had known them for about four weeks before the incident. He had met Daniel first at Aelous Valley and they had spoken about the sale of some land. Both the accused came to his house at Port Morant about 6.30 in the evening on 12 June. They told him they were journeying from Sunning Hill where they had sold a donkey. Peters told them he would be coming to see them about the land business and he put them up for the night. He awoke about 3 o'clock and heard Charles coughing and heard Daniel speaking to him. At 6 o'clock he woke them up, as arranged, for their transportation by truck. If they had gone out during the night they could not have returned as he had a very bad dog. He gave a statement to the police and was subsequently arrested and taken to the lock-up at Morant Bay.

Cross-examined by Crown prosecutor Yates, Peters said that on the night the prisoners slept at his house, Daniel said he was hot, and asked for the door to be left half open. He knew Stanford Archer — he was in the lock-up along with himself and Wallace. He never told any of the Scotts that he was spending a lot of money to get them off; neither did he tell Charles Scott that the little boy was sick. There was no means of communication between them as prisoners, and so they could not talk together.

Yates sat down.

Manley got up to address the jury. He confined his argument to three points: identification; the alleged possession of the thread bag and the alleged conversation that took place between the accused, Charles Scott, and the other prisoners, who were in the same cell with him.

"On the question of identification", he said, "the Crown cannot get away from the well-established fact that one of the men who was present at the killing was shorter than the other, whereas the difference in the height of the two accused is within a quarter of an inch."

Manley made good use of the fact that a witness for the Crown, Dorcas Anderson, had sworn that the thread bag, which they had heard so much about, was the property of the accused Charles Scott, and above all, it was said to be found on the accused by no other person than Detective Bygrave, on whose evidence they dare not rely, having regard to what had taken place at the identification parade.

Manley then proceeded to deal with the alleged conversation. He administered severe strictures on the police for what he termed fraudulent methods of investigation, that is, to get one criminal to extract a statement from another, and then put it forward as evidence against such a one at his trial, especially in a case where the life of the accused person was at stake. As for the evidence of the man Wallace, Manley deemed it "a gross lie, a mere invention and should be treated as such". He concluded: "The rule of criminal law is as old as the hills and as fair as the hills, and on the face of such evidence that has been put before you by the Crown, I confidently appeal to you to find the prisoners not guilty."

The Crown prosecutor, John St John Yates then rose and addressed the jury for twenty minutes. He lost no time in marshalling the salient points in the case, paying particular attention to the three phases dwelt on by Manley.

"Among other things," propounded Yates, "whatever lamentable lapses may have occurred at the identification parade, or slight differences in the evidence given on this point, the insurmountable fact remains that the boy, Luther McKenzie, who had a full view of the man who fired the shot and killed the

Acting Attorney-General Yates, on the defensive at the law/n/ court

woman, swore that that man was Daniel Scott. This witness also gave a very fairly satisfactory account as to the presence of the other accused on the spot at the time the killing took place, and I now tell you, subject to the direction of the learned judge, that it does not matter which of the two fired the shot that did the killing, as long as you are satisfied that the two prisoners were both there for one common purpose, then both of them can be found guilty of the charge."

As to the thread bag, Yates noted that it was identified by three different persons who were very familiar with it as the thread bag of the deceased, Rebecca Payton. Additionally, the boy, Luther McKenzie, actually saw the bag being taken from the table and transferred to the bosom of the accused. He would like to point out that there was no dispute as to the bag being found in the possession of the accused and taken from his pocket by Detective Bygrave. The prisoner and his concubine, the latter a witness for the Crown, had sworn that the bag was his but he did not think the jury would be moved by this.

Mr Yates concluded: "Now, gentlemen, much has been said by my learned friend, relative to what he terms an invention and a gross lie on the part of the man, Wallace, who had a conversation with the prisoner, Charles Scott, whilst they were locked up together in the same cell. But, gentlemen, you as Jamaicans are competent to judge. Do you think there is a Jamaican who would go into the witness box before his God, and without rhyme, reason or reward, swear away the lives of two of his fellow men? I certainly do not think, gentlemen, that Jamaica has fallen so low, and I feel justified in saying that such an act would be impossible. In conclusion, I must remind you that, notwithstanding all that has been very properly urged on behalf of the prisoners, you are called upon to perform your duties according to your oath and I feel confident that you will have no difficulty on the evidence to bring home the charge to the accused."

The chief justice summed up: "I must say that the case has been handled exhaustively and fairly by both counsel whose method of analysis is most commendable. There are, however, two little points on which I disagree with both gentlemen. First, as to the remark of the attorney-general, relative to the impossibility of a man inventing such a story as that told by the witness, Wallace. Personally, I would not like to go so high, as I do feel that it is possible, although improbable. Secondly, I think Mr Manley has put the case against the police too high, although I admit that there was a lack of care and intelligence on the part of the police at the identification parade. The most senior official possible should be present, with book in hand ready to make notes of all that transpires. I think that the inspector of police should himself be present to carry out these parades, and not the detectives engaged in working up cases. I also think there should be more men lined up."

The chief justice continued his summing up drawing special attention to the salient points and reminding the jury that it was not for the defence to prove the innocence of the prisoners, but for the Crown to prove their guilt.

The jury retired to consider their verdict. After an absence of twenty minutes, they filed into court and returned a verdict of guilty of murder against both prisoners.

Charles Scott shouted, "I'm not guilty and will hold my opinion." Daniel Scott was silent.

The chief justice donned the black cap and passed the death sentence.

Six weeks later, the two brothers paid the extreme penalty within the walls of the St Catherine District Prison.[8] They insisted to the last that they were innocent but the Privy Council, on investigation, found nothing to justify clemency being extended.

On Christmas night the brothers were heard to sing carols, but come 27 December, they went to the gallows without a murmur. They made no special request for their last breakfast, refusing to eat before they joined the procession to the gallows which had been specially constructed so that they could be executed together.

Edwin Charley started to manufacture local cordials and aerated water in Spanish Town in 1892. He transferred his business to 62–64 King Street in 1906, but the building was destroyed in the disastrous earthquake the following year. When the premises were restored, Edwin Charley started to blend his famous brand of Charley's rums

Edwin Charley's bottling factory and Kingston headquarters on King Street

11

A Rum Letter

No other island of the Caribbean, no other country in the
tropics, produces rum of quite the same flavour as the
Jamaica liquor. Yet manufacture and blending, storing and
ageing, also contribute; also play their part . . . in the course
of two and a half centuries, the rum-makers and dealers of
Jamaica have learnt all there is to be learnt about producing
the famous Old Jamaica Rum. When one speaks of Jamaica,
one thinks of rum.

Planters' Punch, 1937–38

Where there's rum, there must be sugar, and both commodities sustained the extensive business of rum merchant Edwin Charley, whose shipments of rum in the early 1920s were the largest from the island. An idea of his export trade can be gleaned from two shipments made in one week of 300 puncheons to Glasgow, Scotland and 429 to London, valued at £30,000.[1] Unlike many rum merchants in Jamaica, Edwin Charley was not merely a buyer and seller of rum; he was a distiller. He owned Innswood Estate in St Catherine and controlled the quality of his rum from the cultivation of the sugar cane to export of the final product. Beside his extensive business in bulk rum, Edwin Charley operated a large bottling factory on King Street.

In August 1923, Edwin Charley received a letter purporting to have been written by Mrs V.C. Alexander, asking him for a loan of £20. The money was to be placed in an envelope, addressed to 'Unknown' and sent to the General Post Office where Mrs Alexander would collect it.

V.C. Alexander was an auctioneer, real estate and commission agent, and had been since 1908. Amongst his notable transactions were the sale to Messrs. Lindo Bros. of J. Wray and Nephew for £200,000 and the Pusey Hall Estate for £65,000.[2] Edwin Charley went to V.C. Alexander and showed him the letter. The matter was immediately reported to the postal authorities.

Later, a Mr Scardefold Hanson turned up at the post office and asked if there was any letter addressed to 'Unknown'. He was told that there was none. The next day he returned to make a similar enquiry, and was interrogated by a detective. Hanson asserted that he was sent for the letter by a man but his explanation was not accepted by the detective and Hanson was subsequently arrested and tried. The acting resident magistrate believed the evidence for the prosecution, and Hanson was convicted.

When the case came up for appeal, Manley represented Hanson and argued two grounds against the conviction:[3] "Hanson is charged with attempting to receive money by false pretences, but I submit that the alleged attempt to obtain the money has not been sufficiently brought home to the appellant. The burden of proof in this respect rests with the prosecution. The second, even stronger ground, is that there is no evidence to show that the appellant had made the pretence, and if he made the pretence, it was false. The pretence was that the appellant forged the letter. I contend that the prosecution must prove that Mrs Alexander did not write the letter or authorize it to be written. Before the appellant can be convicted, it is essential that Mrs Alexander goes into the witness box, and says that she did not write the letter, or authorize it to be written; and that she did not authorize any one to go the post office for a reply." Evidence was given by V.C. Alexander, stating that the signature to the letter was not that of his wife.

The chief justice said he gathered that the allegation was that the appellant went to the post office to obtain the fruits of the letter.

"That is the allegation," Manley confirmed.

"But it has been shown that at the time the letter was written Mrs Alexander was abroad," the chief justice commented.

"The fact that Mrs Alexander was abroad", argued Manley, "does not preclude the fact that she had written the letter. Whilst abroad, the lady might need money and write someone requesting that the letter be written to Mr Charley."

"That is an ingenious argument, Mr Manley", commented the chief justice, "but it would have to be left to a jury to say whether they believed such a story."

Continuing, Manley argued: "There is no evidence to show that the appellant was the person who caused the letter to be sent, and his conduct is more consistent with innocence than guilt. He is an intelligent person, and if he had written the letter, is it to be supposed that he would be so clumsy as to go to the post office to ask for the reply himself? The Crown has not discharged the burden of proof devolving on it, and there is no evidence to show that the Mrs V.C. Alexander mentioned in the letter is the Mrs V.C. Alexander mentioned in the evidence. I insist that there is no evidence as to the falsity of the pretence."

The Chief Justice, Mr E. St John Branch, raised a bristly brow. He was a sportsman and enjoyed the chase, whether it was enticing the tricky calipeva from the river, shooting the swift baldpate, or listening to young barristers trying to wrestle defeats back into wins in the Court of Appeal. He looked Manley in the eye: "There is positive evidence that Mrs V.C. Alexander did not write the letter, and that at the time the letter was written, she had left the island. With regard to the second point, it appears that the fact that the appellant went to the General Post Office and asked for a letter addressed to 'Unknown' is sufficient under the circumstances to justify the conclusion that he had written the letter. The appeal is therefore dismissed." Justices DeFreitas and Brown concurred.

Bust of Norman in 1924 by Edna Manley

12

Cutting the Cotta

The cotta – a circular pad usually made of plantain leaves or cloth and which is placed under a load carried on the head – was formerly used as a token of divorce. In early times, when a man and woman separated, the cotta would sometimes be cut in two and each person would take a half as a symbol of their separation.

Pop Story Gi' Mi'
Olive Senior

The first divorce in Jamaica was granted in 1739 when Edward Manning, member of the House of Assembly for Kingston, petitioned the House to dissolve his marriage since at that time there were no ecclesiastical or spiritual courts or other jurisdiction in the island which could do so. The Assembly not only granted the divorce but kicked out another member who had been named co-respondent. Until 1938, when amendments were made to the Divorce Law to include desertion, cruelty and unsoundness of mind, adultery was the only ground for divorce in Jamaica. Over the years, Manley found the emotion and cruelty involved in the majority of divorce cases "interminable and dreadful".[1] There were moments of levity, however, which would draw one of his enigmatic smiles. Such was the case of the petitioner who said his wife was unfaithful. "She called me a 'countryman' and a 'chief'," he told the court.[2]

"And you thought that was degrading?" asked H.M. Radcliffe, representing the respondent.

"Yes, it was," the piqued husband replied. "She said that countrymen were chiefs but Kingston men were generals." Everyone in court laughed. Manley, who was representing the petitioner got to his feet and addressed his client: "I understand that in 1919 you advertised in the *Gleaner* that your wife had left you and that you were not responsible for any debts?"

"Yes, sir, Mr Manley. And the very next day she inserted an advertisement in the *Gleaner* saying that she owed no debts and was quite independent of my means."

"Aha!" Manley barked. "A declaration of independence."

The divorce petition of Herbert Headlam, asking for the dissolution of his marriage with his wife, Evelyn, on the ground of adultery was heard in the Supreme Court before His Honour, Mr Justice Anthony DeFreitas on 6 December 1923. Mr George Guy was named as co-respondent.

The Headlams had been married in June 1919. Continuing to answer questions posed by Manley on the nature of their relationship, Herbert Headlam recalled that one night in October 1919, his wife went out and didn't return until ten minutes to eleven. "She said she'd been visiting a Sergeant Major Burke," he recounted testily. "Another time I found her down by the wharf hugging and kissing up Clarence Wallen when he was leaving for America."

Following a dispute over her visit to Burke and the incident with Wallen, Headlam said his wife left him and went to live with her mother. The following May, she gave birth to a girl child; the child was very fair.

Radcliffe objected. "Do you say it is evidence Mr Manley?" asked DeFreitas. Manley replied in the affirmative. "In view of the fact that he alleges that it was not his child," Manley added. Radcliffe contended that evidence could not be given of adultery with some person unknown unless the leave of the court was obtained to dispense with the citing of such a respondent. Manley asked the court leave to make the application. In answer to Radcliffe's submission that it was "too late now," DeFreitas deferred the application until the afternoon. Continuing, Headlam told the court that after the child's birth, his wife came back to live with him. One night, he came home to find her with a bottle of rum and some camphor. "She was drinking the stuff!" Headlam exclaimed. "The next day, she was so ill, she couldn't leave her bed, she just lay there swearing she would never have a child for me." Following this episode, Headlam said his wife left him again and went to her mother's place. He asked her to come back but she didn't return until some four months later. Soon, they were having disputes again over the company she kept and her staying out late at nights. Asked by Manley if he could cite some examples, Headlam said that he was a cabinet-maker, and in May 1922, he exhibited some of his furniture at the Fancy Fair held at the Race Course. He took his wife with him and at 2.00 a.m. when he'd had enough and wanted to go home, his wife refused to join him. He left her dancing and the next time he saw her she was "jumping through the window" at 6.00 a.m.

"She left me again", Headlam recounted, "the following month with a letter telling me she was off. Immediately after, she applied for maintenance, and on the suggestion of the judge at the Half-Way Tree Court, I agreed to give her ten shillings a week to support herself and her child."

Pausing every now and then to wipe his face, Headlam recalled that on 4 December 1922 he went to a dance in Jones Pen where he saw his wife dancing with the co-respondent, George Guy. "When the dance finished, she went outside with Guy and sat in his lap. He was rubbing her face and kissing her all over." Headlam pulled a slip of paper from his pocket and consulted it before continuing his story. "Three weeks later", he said, "on 28 December, I was walking down Admiral Pen Road with my friend, Thomas Jarrett. I saw my wife together with George Guy coming up the road. Jarrett and myself followed them to Mulberry Lane — that's where my wife was living with her mother," Headlam confirmed. "I saw Guy and my wife go in the house. I tried to get in by the back gate but a dog was chained up nearby. The front gate was locked and guarded by another dog. I stayed there until 12.20 p.m. but Guy never left the house."

Referring to the slip of paper once more, Headlam noted that on 12 January, he met Guy and his wife coming up Septimus Street. "They didn't recognize me", he confided, "because I'd disguised myself in some old clothing." So earnest was Headlam in recounting his marital woes that he ignored the outbreak of chuckles and plodded on, regardless, with his narrative. "I saw them go into Guy's house at about 10.30 p.m. I tried to get through the gate but it was locked. About forty minutes later, Guy and my wife came out and I accused her of adultery. I told her I'd been watching her and now I'd caught her. About two or three days after that, I met Guy and my wife again, walking this time with a man called Messam. My wife told Messam to give me a good beating", Headlam mumbled dolefully, "and he did."

The court adjourned for lunch. On the resumption Manley said that he would not apply for leave to cite an unknown co-respondent. Radcliffe then cross-examined the petitioner on the quarrel between himself and his wife over her behaviour with Clarence Wallen when she had gone to the wharf to see him off.

"Don't you think that was a bit narrow-minded?" asked Radcliffe.

"No," Headlam replied. "I objected to her being friends with Wallen."

"Now, I see," said DeFreitas.

"She even told me Wallen was a better man than me," Headlam said.

"To show how narrow-minded you are, didn't you know that Wallen's wife was going away too?" asked Radcliffe.

"No."

"Wasn't Mrs Wallen a friend of your wife?"

"Yes," Headlam admitted.

Thomas Jarrett, giving evidence on behalf of the petitioner, said he had accompanied Headlam to Jones Pen and saw when Mrs Headlam sat in Guy's lap: "He stroked her face and they kissed several times."

The co-respondent, George Guy, was then given the opportunity to cross-examine the witness himself. "You said you saw myself and Mrs Headlam kissing?"

"Yes."

"Hugging and kissing?"

"Yes."

"Describe what went on to this court."

"Oh, no", DeFreitas intervened, "that's unnecessary. If there was kissing and hugging, we can imagine how it was done."

Continuing, George Guy asked the witness, "Do you think a man would be so mad as to hug and kiss a girl before others? How long were you out with Headlam watching?"

"Until 3 o'clock in the morning."

"And did you go to work that day?"

"Yes."

"You were out so late and yet you went to work?" Guy quizzed.

"He's probably a supporter of daylight saving time," DeFreitas mused.

Manley called Nathaniel Thomas, a shoemaker, to give evidence on Headlam's behalf. He testified that he saw Mrs Headlam and George Guy go into the house in Septimus Street. When they came out, Headlam accused his wife of infidelity. Mr Radcliffe, cross-examining Thomas, asked: "Were you disguised?"

"Yes, sir. I turned up the collar of my coat."

When the laughter subsided, Radcliffe moved for a dismissal saying that satisfactory proof of misconduct had not been given. The court had been asked to act on inferences and the evidence did not support them. Following Manley's submission that there was ample evidence to support the petition, DeFreitas said he would like to hear Mrs Headlam's evidence.

Evelyn Headlam took the stand and calmly disclosed that she had left her husband in October 1919 because he quarrelled about her visit to Major Burke. Who was Burke? He was her cousin. As for Clarence Wallen, she had known him for some time; their families were all friends. Describing her relationship with her husband now, Mrs Headlam said that he had a bad temper and was a jealous man. Asked about the time he said he found her drinking rum and camphor; that was untrue. At times, she would visit her mother and when she returned she would find the house locked up. In December 1922, she met the co-respondent, George Guy at a dance in Jones Pen. She danced with him once. It was untrue that she sat in Guy's lap and was kissing him. In January she was walking along Septimus Street with a girlfriend and a young man named Messam in addition to George Guy. Unfortunately, Messam was now dead and the girl had gone away. On that occasion, she met her husband and another man. Her husband turned on his flashlight and began to tear up her clothing. He then drew a stick and hit Guy saying, "You're the man I hear is playing with my wife."

Manley, cross-examining: "Do you think you owe any duty to your husband now?"

"No."

"Were you justified in leaving your husband?"

"Yes, he was cruel to me."

"Your husband supported you?"

"Yes, he was all right so far as the money part was concerned but he was disagreeable and miserable otherwise."

In summing up the evidence, DeFreitas concluded that the facts did not support the petitioner's allegation of misconduct and dismissed the petition with costs against the petitioner.

Although the majority of the divorce cases handled by Manley in the 1920s involved alleged misconduct on the part of the wife, there were exceptions, such as one suit which Manley described as "so simple" that "it is hardly necessary for me to say much".[3] And he let the petitioner take the stand to explain how she had gone to the country and returned to find her husband in bed with her sister. "There was a violent quarrel", she told the court, "and my husband kicked and beat me. Then he packed his bags and left. I haven't heard from him since."

Manley called witnesses who testified to seeing the beleaguered wife being "kicked from her front door into the street by her husband". Another witness, an acquaintance of the husband, confirmed that he was now living with another woman with whom he had three children, the eldest child being ten years old. "When I went to visit him", the witness deponed, "he told me that the children were his." The respondent did not appear in court, neither was he represented by counsel. The judge lost no time in granting a *decree nisi* to the petitioner and costs against the respondent.

Overall, the divorce rate in Jamaica at the turn of the century was low. The highest figure for the late nineteenth century was six in 1897. Between 1905 and 1907 there was an increase to between fifteen and seventeen per annum.[4] Unfortunately, divorce statistics for 1923/4 are not available. According to the evidence emanating from the divorce cases handled by Manley in the 1920s, however, the "unfaithful wife" emerges as one who did not work outside the home and domestic help not only left her with time on her hands but made a significant contribution to her downfall. The witness box became a confessional for domestics who could recite reams about assignations "after hours" when husbands were off on business. There were "rollicks in the hammock", the "creaking floorboards", the inevitable "crumpled sheets" and no end of cigar stubs, ashes and matchsticks to be swept from the bedroom floor. There was many a chauffeur too who just "happened to look back" to see the lady of the house and a "friend" locked in a fervent embrace while he was taking them for a drive.[5] Other chauffeurs, such as Stanley Lingwood, went far beyond the call of duty, and were themselves the apex in the eternal triangle. One morning, when the cook, Estella Evans, took Lingwood his breakfast, she found her mistress, Mrs Ellis, in his bed.

"As you quite sure it was Mrs Ellis in the bed?" Manley asked when the case came to court.

"Oh, yes, sir. She sat up and drank the tea."

Estella Evans captured the scene in the Divorce Court before His Honour, Mr Justice Anthony DeFreitas on 21 January 1924 when William Nathaniel Ellis, a butcher from Annotto Bay, accused his wife of adultery with his driver, Stanley Lingwood.[6] Manley appeared for the petitioner. J.A.G. Smith represented the respondent, Emma Eugenia Ellis, who denied the allegation.

Taking the stand, Ellis said he lived at a place called Crab Hill. One afternoon he returned home unexpectedly. He called to his wife; there was no reply. About two chains from the main house was an outbuilding where his driver, Stanley Lingwood, lived. Ellis ran up the steps and banged on the door. It flew open and there was his wife, lying on Lingwood's bed; the man himself jumped through the window.

"I hear about your doings; I catch you now," the irate husband declared.

"You say me and Stanley living? Yes, him a better man than you," the wife retorted.

Continuing to answer questions posed by Manley, Ellis said his wife had told him she didn't want any old man. He was 47 years old. His wife was ten years younger. He had employed Lingwood to drive his motor car at a salary of 25 shillings per week and board and lodging. After the incident related above, he fired Lingwood.

As Smith began his cross-examination, Ellis fainted in the box, and had to be given a chair. On the resumption, Ellis said that when he hired Lingwood, he told his wife that he should be fed. For the first week they had meals together in his house. After that Lingwood had his meals in his room.

"Didn't you tell your wife that you wanted to divorce her in order to get a straight-haired girl?" asked Smith.

"No, sir. I don't bother with that."

"Is it not true to say that Lingwood drove you out to Water Valley to buy cattle on the day the incident is supposed to have taken place?"

"No. Lingwood didn't drive me at all that day. I drive myself in the buggy to Water Valley."

Re-examined by Manley, Ellis told the court that he had received an anonymous letter about his wife's goings on. And he held up a scrap of paper. His wife had the other portion, he said. On taking it out to show her, she had snatched it away.

Smith was on his feet: "I object, Your Honour, to the introduction of a scrap of paper and secondary evidence as to its contents." The objection was upheld.

Rachel White, examined by Manley, said she went to work as a domestic with Mrs Ellis. She observed that when Mr Ellis went to market on Saturdays and Wednesdays, Mrs Ellis went to Lingwood's house when there was nothing there for her to do. Mrs Ellis made undergarments and told her she was going to make Lingwood try them on. She later saw Lingwood with one of the garments and she said to him, "Can you stand damages?" Lingwood replied, "Ah, Rachel! After the woman won't leave me." Lingwood then gave her a sixpence.

Charles James was in the box. He was a butcher and worked with Ellis. He had seen familiarity between Mrs Ellis and Lingwood on more than one occasion. For example, the time he pulled coconuts, "and them drink till them stomach full. Miss Ellis say she can't walk, Lingwood must carry her, and she place her hands on him shoulder. But Lingwood say she too heavy and must walk".

William Anderson, a schoolboy, said he was Ellis's nephew and lived in the outbuilding with Lingwood. One Saturday he and Mrs Ellis were inside when Lingwood came in and took off his clothes. He asked

Mrs Ellis to mend a garment as he was going to St Thomas. Lingwood also asked Mrs Ellis for a kiss. Mrs Ellis mended the garment and after she was finished, she kissed Lingwood. He said he was going to St Thomas and not coming back until Monday. Mrs Ellis said she would save something nice for when he came back. The following Saturday his uncle sent him to look for Lingwood. He went to his room and found the door shut. He pushed the door and Mrs Ellis jumped off the bed and asked him what he wanted. He saw Lingwood lying on the bed and told him that Mr Ellis wanted him.

At the close of Anderson's evidence, Manley announced that that was the end of the case for the petitioner. Smith moved that the petition be dismissed: "There is no proof of adultery, the facts do not support any inference of misconduct being drawn. I submit that the story which the witnesses for the petitioner have given is an improbable one, and cannot be believed." Smith analysed the evidence and pointed out the improbabilities as to the allegations of misconduct being carried out during daylight.

Manley argued that the petitioner's case was a strong one: "It is not extraordinary that the alleged acts of misconduct took place in daylight. The fact is that these acts occurred in the daytime, when the petitioner was away, and the acts of misconduct were committed in a manner consistent with the action of a woman who is much older than the co-respondent. The fact is that the respondent was reckless in her conduct, and did not care how she acted. Either the witnesses for the petitioner saw what they swore they saw, or they have committed wilful perjury."

The judge would not discuss the evidence, he said, as he did not want to interfere in any way with the freedom of action of the parties in the future. But as far as he was concerned, the evidence of the petitioner's witnesses could not be relied on; there must be a verdict against the petitioner. The petition was dismissed with costs.

13

THE SPALDING MURDER TRIAL   *Part 1*

The Bowden Hill Tragedy

*My head is full of the murder case. It has been a very
dramatic affair, & is not yet over. I think I'm beaten. The
black dress has pursued me like a nightmare . . .*

Norman Manley, in a letter to his wife Edna,
18 September 1924

In September 1924, Manley was assigned by the Crown to defend one
Luther Spalding, accused of murdering his paramour, Miriam Ross.
She had been reported missing from 31 May that year. Her body was
discovered one month later buried in Spalding's banana field. According
to Spalding, Miriam said she was leaving him, and took off with one of
his war medals. He went after her, and they had a scuffle. When Miriam
cried for help, Luther's sister, Esther, flung a clothes iron at him, but it
caught Miriam and killed her. Together, Luther and Esther had buried
Miriam in the field.

With Leslie Clerk for company, Manley had ridden on horseback
to the scene of the crime in Stony Hill, full of enthusiasm but as the case
progressed the more pessimistic he became.

The trial opened on 17 September 1924 at the Home Circuit Court in the Public Buildings which also housed the Supreme Court on King Street in Kingston. Both the Attorney-General, F.C. Wells-Durrant, and his Acting Assistant, John St John Yates, appeared

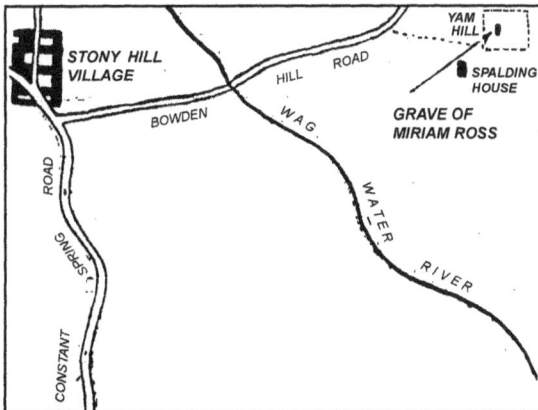

Bowden Hill: Sketch showing principal areas mentioned in the case.

for the Crown. Sir E. St John Branch, Chief Justice, presided.[1]

The case had attracted quite a large number of spectators, and but for the rain, the spacious hall of justice might have been more packed. Manley had taken advantage of the weather and gone for a night gallop at Knutsford.[2] A ride against driving rain, he thought, was the best ride of all. But even that had not left him feeling overly optimistic: either Luther or Esther was lying; the one building up an artfully devised case against the other.

The prisoner, Luther Spalding, was escorted to the dock just as the Court was about to assemble. The following jury was empanelled after one challenge by Manley: Messrs. Caleb Scott (foreman), Hubert S. Campbell, Walter Breakenridge, Leonard Solomon, William Isaacs, Reginald S. Creswell, Frank Nunes, Leonard Brammer, Claudius Priestley, W. Anderson, Duncan McCorkell and Frank Thwaites.

Dressed in what the newspapers described as a white 'bag' suit, without a collar, Spalding stood tensely in the dock, squeezing his fingers one into the other as the first witness, his sister, Esther Spalding, gave evidence. Judge, jury and spectators looked on with fascination.

"I am a cultivator," Esther told the court. "The accused is my brother. He lived with Miriam Ross at my mother's home at Bowden Hill. My brother and Miriam used to quarrel. On the 31st of May, Miriam and I went to Kingston. She carried some clothes, two table drawers and a puppy. Earlier, Miriam say to me: 'In case I go to my bed and don't wake in the morning, be sure Luther kill me,' for he threatened to kill her. I parted from Miriam at Cross Roads and never saw her again until I saw the body on the 30th of June. I started to go home on the 31st of May from Kingston after dark. I slept at Edith Richard's yard at Stony Hill. Next morning, I went to my yard, reaching there a little before 5 o'clock. I didn't see Miriam and Luther quarrelling that day. I never come out my house with a clothes iron, and throw it at Luther and it catch Miriam. On the 30th of June I saw a dead body in my brother's field. It was Miriam; I know it from the size, the clothes, and hair which was red."

As Manley stood to cross-examine someone at the back of the court laughed audibly. "Who is that wretched person who finds mirth here during so serious a charge?" Chief Justice Branch snapped. "Have him removed if you find him."

After this interruption, the courtroom fell silent as Manley turned to face the witness.

"Miss Spalding, were you ever arrested in connection with this matter?"

"No, sir. But I was taken to Half-Way Tree."

"How long were you there?"

"Four days."

"Why did they keep you there?"

"Because my brother said I'd hidden Miriam."

"Did the police ask you many questions?"

"Yes, sir."

"After that the police came up and searched the field?"

"Yes."

"I put it to you, Miss Spalding, that you told the police that they should search the field?"

"No."

"Do you know why the police searched the field?"

"Because Miriam couldn't be found."

"Were you in the field at the time of search."

"I was in my yard, sir."

"You knew Miriam Ross was leaving the accused?"

"Yes."

"Miriam had a lot of clothes?"

"I don't know, sir. I never look in her trunk."

"But she had plenty of clothes didn't she?"

"Yes."

"You have some of her clothes now?"

"No, sir."

"Look at that black dress. Isn't it yours?"

"No, sir."

"Didn't you put it in the grave because it had blood on it?"

"No, sir."

"Did you see Miriam and Luther having a struggle near your house?"

"No, sir."

"And didn't you fling an iron at Luther which missed and hit Miriam?"

"No, sir."

"I put it to you, that you and Luther buried Miriam."

"No, sir. I never knew Miriam dead."

"And you told the police to search the field so as to get yourself out of it?"

"I say, no, sir."

Manley sat down.

Nathaniel Garron, interrogated by the Attorney-General, F.C.

Wells-Durrant, told the court that he was at Esther Spalding's house on the night of 31 May. Her house was about a chain and a half from where the prisoner lived with Miriam Ross. Esther wasn't there — she'd gone to town. "At about 8 o'clock, I heard Miriam's voice in Luther's yard. About 10.30 I heard a stumbling, like someone fighting. Later, I passed the house and called out to Luther, but got no answer. There was no light in the house. A few days later I see Luther and tell him that I pass the house that night and call about four times. He said he didn't hear."

F.C.Wells-Durrant, KC Attorney–General of Jamaica, 1921–31

Cross-examined by Manley, the witness said he called out a little louder than he was now speaking in court. It was about midnight. The noise he had heard earlier? It was a stumbling; not a noise. Like someone fighting, like a stamping of feet.

Acting Corporal Percival Fuller was on the stand. After Miriam was reported missing, he had searched for her for some time. Then, "On the 30th of June I went with Sergeant Morris to the premises of the accused. We searched the house, and under it, and then we went into the field. We had a rod, and when we pushed it in a particular place, it went down easier than at any other spot. There was also an offensive smell and flies began to gather. I fetched Luther Spalding and took him to the field where he was cautioned by Sergeant Morris. The sergeant asked him whose field it was and Spalding said it was his. We started to remove the earth. After going two and a half feet, we came upon clothing and the upper portion of a human body. I left and reported the matter to the District Medical Officer, Dr Johnston. I returned with the doctor and by his instructions the earth was further removed and the body taken out. I could not recognize the body, it was badly decomposed. The arms and feet were tied. The mother of the deceased was brought to the spot, and identified the body as that of her daughter."

The court adjourned for lunch. On the resumption, Fuller resumed his stand in the witness box and was cross-examined by Manley.

"Who reported that Miriam Ross was missing?"

"Her father, sir. I went with him to the house and made enquiries."

"Who accompanied you on the final search?"

"The district constable, myself and about four or five civilians."

"Is that usual — to take civilians with you in a search?"

"It's the first case of its kind I've had to deal with. I can't say whether it was usual or not."

"You were told to look for signs of a person buried?"

"Yes."

"When did the idea of such a search occur to you?"

"Sometime after the 27th of June."

Claudine Spalding, examined by Mr Yates, told the court: "The prisoner is my brother. Him come to me on the 12th of June and say the sergeant want me to make a statement. I say, what for? Him say I must tell the sergeant I see Miriam. I say, why? I don't see Miriam. Him say, don't say so, for plenty people see her, and they want to say him kill Miriam. I don't go. On the 24th I see Luther again, and him say I must see Sergeant Morris. I went next morning and tell him I see Miriam at Constant Spring on the 3rd of June."

"Was that true?"

"No, sir. The last time I see Miriam was April."

Claudine Spalding was cross-examined by Manley who asked: "When did you first know that Miriam was missing?"

"When Luther come to me on the 12th."

"Did Esther Spalding tell you she thought your brother knew something about it?"

"No, sir."

"Didn't Esther tell you she thought Luther had killed Miriam?"

"No. Luther the first person who tell me that people say him kill Miriam."

"Did you tell Esther you had seen Miriam?"

"No, sir."

"Did you, of your own accord, go to the police and tell them that it was not true you had seen Miriam?"

"Yes, sir."

Yates called Cecelia Rowley to the stand. She deponed: "Luther Spalding come to my yard at Stony Hill and tell me that people say him kill Miriam Ross, and him going to get a barrister and put on it. Him ask me to say that I see Miriam in June; me say me don't want anything to do with it. Then him come with two detectives and say, this is the woman who see Miriam in June in the grass yard. They ask me if that true, and me say yes. But it wasn't true."

Cross-examined by Manley, Cecelia Rowley couldn't say why Luther should have sought her out to swear that she had seen Miriam. Claudine had told her Miriam was missing; she didn't believe Miriam was dead. She was told by Luther to say she saw Miriam in Grey's grass yard buying a load.

Henrietta Ross, Miriam's mother, told the court that she last saw her daughter on 30 May. Miriam had brought some clothes to her yard. She left at about 3 o'clock for Bowden Hill. She went to Luther's yard the first week in June and asked him for Miriam. He was sweeping his house and ignored her. Later he went under a mango tree and laughed at her saying she should go and bring a policeman as her husband had done. She subsequently identified Miriam's body. Yes, she knew the black dress, it was Miriam's. She'd bought the cloth for the dress and made one for herself and one for Miriam.

Answering questions posed by Manley on the black dress, Henrietta Ross explained: "The dress is old. I saw it in the grave. I call it calico black. It's common cloth. Lots of people wear it . . . . No, sir, it had no name on it."

A small boy, Joseph Dalton, said he was Luther Spalding's nephew and lived with his grandmother, Elizabeth Spalding, in the same house as Miriam Ross and Luther. On the Saturday night Miriam came in and started to curse Luther. His grandmother put her finger to her mouth and told him to go to sleep. Next morning he saw Luther with a sheet: "It have plenty blood on it. Him go to the river and wash it. There was blood on the wall — Luther wash it off with white lime."

Manley asked: "What colour was the marks on the sheet?"

"Red, sir."

"Did you hear Luther complain of bugs biting him in his sleep at nights?"

"Yes, sir. Him pour dark stuff on the bed to stop the bugs biting him."

"When was that?"

"The Friday night."

At this stage it was decided that the hearing should be adjourned until the following morning. The jury were conveyed to the South Camp Road Hotel under the charge of Staff Sergeant Major Murphy for the night. When the trial resumed the following morning, the courtroom was uncomfortably packed with spectators.

Dr Thomas Henry Johnston, DMO for Stony Hill, told the court that he was present on 30 June when the body of Miriam Ross was exhumed. There was a cord tied to the arms and waist, and another about the knee. He could not give an opinion as to how many days the body had been buried, but it had been for some time. There was a dislocation on the right elbow joint, and a dislocation of the right arm pit. He could not say if it had taken place before or after death.

In answer to Manley's question now in cross-examination, the doctor said he had completed his examination of the body on the spot. He had not attempted to examine the internal organs, decomposition had gone too far. He couldn't make out any definite lines of the stomach.

"Did you examine the skull for fracture?"

"Had there been a fracture of the skull, the opening of the skull would have shown it. I examined the inner and outer layer of the skull and there were no traces of fracture."

"How did you examine the skull?"

"With my fingers."

"Do you consider that a thorough enough method of detecting a fracture," Manley asked the doctor.

"I made a careful examination of the skull; there was no fracture."

"Could there have been an internal fracture?"

"It's possible."

"Could that have been detected from outside?"

"Some fractures cannot be detected from outside the skull."

"How does one detect such a fracture, Doctor?"

"By sawing and examining the inside of the skull."

"But that was not done in this case?"

"No."

Dr Ludlow Moody, the Government Pathologist, said he had received two parcels in July from Sergeant Ewart. One contained a shirt and a stone, the other some plasterings and chips of wood. He examined them for the detection of blood. None of them gave the reaction for bloodstains.

Cross-examined by Manley, Dr Moody said of all the items he received, the chip of wood had the best stain but he could get no reaction for blood. Asked to elaborate on the features of the human skull, paying particular attention to the temple, Dr Moody commented: "There is a cavity in the temple and a muscle known as the temporal muscle. A blow to the temple can be a most effective cause of death because resistance there is less than elsewhere. The force of a blow at that spot is more easily transmitted to the other side of the skull. You might find the fracture on either side."

"Is it possible to have a fracture in the skull which manual manipulation or feeling with the fingers would disclose."

"Yes, it's possible."

"Suppose, doctor, you have a case in which the skull is practically bare?"

"In that case, a slight fracture might be overlooked."

Virginia Ballantine, an elderly dressmaker was on the stand. She remembered making two black dresses, one for Miriam, the other for her mother. She recognized the skirt now shown to her as the one she made for Miriam. She knew it by the hem of the skirt, by the length and by the waist. It was her style of work — see how the pleats on the waist were fixed, she said.

Sergeant Alexander Morris, questioned by Yates, the Crown prosecutor, said that when the body was exhumed, the black dress was found in a bundle, but not on the body. On two occasions Luther Spalding came to the police station and reported that Miriam had been seen. The day after the body was dug up, he drove Spalding and his mother, by car, to Half-Way Tree. Detective Sergeant Ewart accompanied them. Both were charged with the murder of Miriam Ross. Neither Ewart nor himself asked them any questions. But when Elizabeth Spalding started to cry Sergeant Morris quoted Luther as saying:

"What you crying for? If you die, you die innocent. *Me do it.*"

Manley was on his feet: "From the time you left Stony Hill, did the accused speak to you?"

"No."

"Who drove the car?"

"Kenneth Jones."

"Was it his car?"

"Yes, sir."

"So you hired it?"

"Yes."

"Any other person besides Ewart and the two accused in the car?"

"No."

"Where did Ewart sit?"

"In front. The prisoners and myself sat in the back."

"You knew the mother of the accused?"

"Yes.

"Isn't she rather hard of hearing?"

"Slightly."

"Where did the accused make the remark you spoke of?"

"At the deep turn below Red Gal Ring."

"You were going fast, Sergeant?"

"No, sir."

"I suppose the car was making some noise coming down the hill?"

"A little noise, sir. But not so much."

"You told Sergeant Ewart what was said?"

"No. He turned round and looked at me. I asked him if he heard what was said. Then I took out my pocket book and wrote it down."

"Did you repeat the words to Ewart?"

"No."

"Did the prisoner say anything more?"

"Yes, but nothing in relation to the offence."

"Don't you think it extraordinary that the man who had kept his tongue still all the time should have made that confession?"

"No."

"I put it to you that the prisoner said: 'If you die, you die innocently. *Is not we do it*'?"

"No, sir."

Luther Spalding shuffled about the witness box, obviously distraught. On the suggestion of the chief justice, he was given a chair.

Manley, proceeding carefully and concisely, continued his cross-examination of the witness: "You will agree with me that with the rumours going about, if Spalding did not come to the police and make reports, suspicion would be all the more stronger on him?"

"Yes."

"You suggested he go to Half-Way Tree to help the police?"

"Yes."

"Don't you think if he had murdered the girl, he would not have gone to assist the police?"

"I thought he did it to keep off suspicion."

"But away from your official mind, don't you think the position would be awkward?"

"Yes."

"Who gave you instructions to search Spalding's place?"

"I received orders from Half-Way Tree to make a general search."

"Why did you take civilians with you?"

"Only to help in the search."

"How was the body tied?"

"With string."

"What kind of string."

"It looked like string, but it might have been cloth."

"It wasn't banana trash?"

"No."

The prosecution called Sergeant Ewart to the stand. "Did you hear what the prisoner said to his mother when she started crying?" asked Yates. "Yes, sir. The prisoner said: 'What you crying for? If you die, you die innocently. *Me kill her*'. Sergeant Morris asked me if I heard. I said, 'yes'." Ewart described how he had subsequently gone to the prisoner's house. He noticed splashes of recent whitewash on the wall and what appeared to be bloodstains at the foot of the doorway and on some stones nearby. Then he found a stained shirt. He took these items, along with some plastering from the wall and chippings off the posts, to Dr Moody for analysis.

"Did Dr Moody find traces of blood on any of the items that you sent to him for testing?" enquired Manley in his cross-examination.

"No, sir."

"Were you at the scene before the body was taken out."

"Yes."

"Where was the black dress?"

"On the body."

"You know Sergeant, it has been stated that the black dress was in a corner?"

"It was in the hole."

"Did you mean to convey that the girl was wearing the black dress?"

"No."

"Did you make a note of what the prisoner said in the car?"

"No, sir."

Charles Hall, examined by Yates, said he was a prisoner awaiting trial on a charge of stealing a mule. On 31 July he was a prisoner in the Half-Way Tree lock up. The prisoner Spalding was put in the same cell and they had a talk. Spalding told him he was charged for the murder of a woman named Mirry, but he didn't kill her. His sister, Esther, had flung a clothes iron at him but it caught Mirry and killed her. Esther said they must bury her, and they did. He was sorry to have to bury Mirry . in his field, but the earth was soft."

Manley had one question for Hall: "Did Luther Spalding tell you to inform the police about this conversation?"

"No, sir. Me tell them, about a month after."

The case for the Crown was closed.

Manley opened for the defence and called Luther Spalding to the stand. Spalding approached the witness box. He was in his mid-thirties, a short, fairly thick set man, with sharp, dark features, a receding chin and quick eyes which darted back and forth as he told the court he was a cultivator and had served in the army for two years. He had lived with Miriam Ross for five years at Bowden Hill. She had left him once before, for about three months, and asked him to take her back. They got on pretty well together. On 26 May they had a row. He went to Hermitage to get work but did not succeed. On his return he discovered that Miriam had removed some of her things to his sister's house. He asked her about it and she said that Esther had told her he was going with another woman, and she was leaving. She told him he would have to pay her for the work she had done in the house.

On 29 May they went to bed as usual, but he couldn't sleep on account of the bugs, so he sprinkled the sheet with Jeyes. The whitewashing on the wall was done by Miriam to get rid of the bugs. On the night of Saturday, 31 May, Miriam came home from town and, without speaking to his mother, or himself, went into his room. Soon after, she started to use bad language over some missing rice — his mother advised him not to sleep in the room with her. About 8.45 p.m. Miriam gave him some fish and bread. He heard when Garron passed and called to him three times, but he didn't answer because he was eating. He heard a donkey bray at the time. It was a donkey that whenever it brayed, the village knew it was 9 o'clock. Miriam went to bed about 10.30. He slept in the hall on a chair. He was awakened in the morning by a stir in the room. It was about 5 o'clock. Miriam left the house with a basket and went down a track leading to Esther's house, put the basket under a tree and returned to the house. She went in the room for a minute or two, and came out with a paper parcel, then went over to Esther's place and called out that she was leaving.

"I went in the room to see if my things were correct," the prisoner stated. "One of my two war medals was missing. I looked out and saw Mirry going down the road by the big number eleven tree. I follow her and catch her near the Wag Water River. I say: 'Now, Mirry, remember, I don't prevent you from taking away your things, but don't take my medal'. She tell me: 'Luther, is five years we together, the medal is my servant wages'.

"I told her she could take anything else, but I wanted the medal."

According to Spalding, Mirry refused to give it up, turned back and headed for Esther's yard. He held on to her hand, she collared him and called out 'Esther! Esther! Luther out here fighting me. Run come here.' Esther came out with an old clothes iron, and shouted, 'What you hold the girl for? Let her go.' The iron was thrown at him, but he ducked and it caught Mirry. She fell. Esther came up and said, 'You see you make Mirry get a blow that don't belong to her.' Then Esther looked at Mirry and said she was dead. She was bleeding from her nose and Esther took her apron and wrapped it around Mirry's head. She brought two hoes and said they should bury her in the field where it was soft.

"I say: 'Esther, why you don't bury her in your land?' She said her land was facing the road and it was hard, but as I had land dug up ready to plant, it would be easier to dig. Esther ask me to help in taking up Mirry, but I say, 'No. Is you lick her down, you must take her up'. She lift up the body, the two feet dragging on the ground and carry it to a spot where she put it down. I dug the hole. Esther brought Mirry's bundle of clothes and threw them in the grave. Then she take off a black frock she using as an apron, and throw that in the hole too."

Spalding said he was grieved at Miriam's death: "I turn to her and say: 'Miriam, Miriam, may God cause you to reveal this secret death to your mother in Kingston.' And Mirry groan and her foot kick out."

He became frightened and fell down beside her with his arm over her breast. Esther told him to get up. He was crying. She tied Miriam's legs and hands with banana string and put the body in the hole. They both covered up the grave and went to Esther's house where she gave him a big gill of rum. Her children begged a little rum and she gave each of them a little. After this the children got merry and knocked the tea off the fire. Esther borrowed his belt and flogged the children, then gave him ten shillings and begged him to keep quiet. He went straight home and saw his mother. He never told anyone what happened, but he began to hear rumours about himself a week afterwards. People were saying that Miriam was missing, and he killed her. Sergeant Morris sent him to Half-Way Tree to assist the police in looking for Miriam. Claudine Spalding and Cecilia Rowley told him they had seen Miriam, and he mentioned this to the police.

"And what did you say to your mother coming down in the car?" Manley enquired.

"I say: 'You crying. If we get our dead, we get it innocently. *Is not me do it*'."

"Did Sergeant Morris make a note of it."

"Yes, sir. But not until about a quarter mile away. He call to Sergeant Ewart and tell him that I say something, and that's what he termed it to be."

The court adjourned for the day. The jury were taken back to the South Camp Road Hotel for the night. On the resumption of the court the following morning, Luther Spalding was fiercely cross-examined by the Attorney-General, F.C. Wells-Durrant, an able and forceful speaker:

"I think you told us yesterday that you served two years in the army?"

"Yes. In the contingent."

"Where did you serve?"

"In France and Belgium."

"And you got two war medals."

"Yes, sir."

"Where are they?"

"The police have them at Half-Way Tree."

"So you took one away from Miriam?"

"Yes."

"After she was killed?"

"Yes, sir."

"You told us you slept on the chair the Saturday night?"

'Yes, sir."

"Is that the only night you slept in a chair?"

"One other night, sir."

"Would it be true if your mother said you slept the whole of that week on a chair?"

"No, sir."

Manley was on his feet. "I object, Your Honour. His mother has not been called."

"I may have to call her after this," the attorney-general retaliated.

"She ought to have been called," said the chief justice.

The attorney-general continued his cross-examination: "How many nights did you sleep on a chair?"

"Two nights, sir."

"Why did you not sleep on the bed?"

"The soft bedding had been removed to Esther's house."

"Were you on good terms with your sister, Esther?"

"No, sir."

"Why was the bedding removed to Esther's house?"

"Because Miriam was going away."

"It was not removed on account of bugs?"

"No, sir."

"Did you put the lime wash on the wall?"

"No. Miriam did."

"Did you put Jeyes' fluid on the sheet and mattress."

"Yes."

"When the little boy says he saw you washing a blood stained sheet, he is not telling the truth?"

"No, sir."

"What reason would that little boy have for making such a statement?"

"I think he must have been taught by someone."

"Who do you think taught the boy?"

"Someone in the family."

"Do you consider that Esther taught the boy?"

"I do, sir."

"Then you thought that Esther taught him to make that untrue statement to get you in trouble?"

"Yes, sir."

"You said yesterday that Miriam left the house at 5 o'clock?"

"Yes."

"How long after did you leave?"

"About a quarter of an hour after."

"When did you overtake her?"

"When she was a little over a quarter of a mile away from the house."

Manley jumped up: "I might say she came back to the house after she first started," he intervened. "The attorney-general is forgetting that."

"Was it a quarter of an hour after she left the second time that you overtook her?"

"No, sir. It was a quarter of an hour from the first time she left."

"When you followed her down to the Wag Water River, did you see Esther at all?"

"No. I walked by a different track."

"Are there two separate tracks leading to Esther's house from yours?"

"Yes."

"What happened between 5.15 and 6 o'clock when you saw Miriam?"

"I was trying to get the medal from Miriam."

"For three quarters of an hour?"

"Yes, sir, there was a little argument."

"You were talking for three-quarters of an hour?"

"Yes."

"You say she turned back to get protection?"

"Yes."

"And from whom was she going to get protection?"

"My sister, Esther Spalding."

"Where was the medal then?"

"In her hand."

"What were you doing?"

"I held her left hand and she grabbed me by the throat and yelled for Esther."

"Is it a sloping track from Esther's house?"

"No. It's a level road."

"How far away was Esther when she flung the iron?"

"About four yards."

"How it didn't strike you?"

"I bent down my head."

"How did Miriam fall?"

"On the left side."

"Did you let go her left hand?"

"Yes."

"What became of the medal then?"

"It flash into my hand."

"Was there much blood on the track?"

"A quantity."

"Then you said Esther took an apron and chucked it around Miriam's neck?"

"Yes, to prevent the blood from draining on the track."

"You didn't touch the body at all."

"No."

"You never went to the house to bring anything in case she might only have been unconscious?"

"No."

"You just stood there doing nothing."

"Yes."

"While Esther rushed off to her yard?"

"Yes."

"How long was she away?"

"About two minutes. She went for a pudding pan to take the dirt out the hole."

"And Esther dragged the body to the spot where you dug the grave?"

"Yes."

"How long did it take you to dig the grave?"

"About ten minutes."

"A two and a half foot grave with a pudding pan in ten minutes?"

"Yes."

"Did you lay your hands on Miriam's breast?"

"Yes."

"And you heard Miriam groan?"

"Yes."

"So she couldn't have been dead! Are you sure she groaned?"

"Yes."

"And you buried her without knowing for sure she was dead?"

"I don't know, sir."

"What about the black dress?"

"It belong to Miriam. Esther had it wearing as an apron that morning."

"And you say that Esther gave you some rum?"

"Yes, sir."

"And then she gave you a ten shilling note?"

"Yes."

"What for?"

"For not revealing the secret."

"From your own sister you took ten shillings?"

"Yes."

"That is the sort of man you are? And you say you fought for your country in France?"

"Yes."

"You say you got home at 10 o'clock?"

"Yes."

"That was the first time you saw your mother that day?"

'Yes."

"Did you tell her anything?"

"No."

"And you induced Claudine to go and tell the police she saw Miriam?"

"No."

"Then your sister is lying?"

"Yes."

"Your own sister? Why would she come and tell a lie against you?"

"I never instructed her to go to the police and say what she did."

"Why should she have gone unless someone instructed her?"

"I don't know."

"Did you go to Cecilia Rowley's yard and instruct her to say that she saw Miriam at the grass yard?"

"No."

"Why then should she come and give this false evidence against you?"

"I don't know, sir."

"You say you never made the statement attributed to you by the two sergeants?"

"No."

"So the sergeants have concocted a falsehood to take away your life?"

"Yes."

"When did the apron get the blood?"

"When Esther had Miriam's head resting on her."

"Now Mr Garron said he heard a stumbling in your room when he passed. Is that true?"

"Yes. Miriam was packing up the tables."

"Esther gave evidence at the Half-Way Tree Court?"

"Yes."

"Why didn't you say then that Esther killed Miriam and that you only assisted in burying her?"

"My mind gone, sir. I was not collective."

"But don't you realize how important it was for you to have talked about it then?"

"I was not collective, sir."

As Spalding returned to the dock, the attorney-general rose and announced: "I propose to call Elizabeth Spalding, the prisoner's mother. I do not want it said that the Crown was afraid to call the witness."

"Your Honour", replied Manley, "it is not fair at this stage, seeing that the Crown took a statement some time ago from this witness."

"I will call the witness," roared the chief justice.

Elizabeth Spalding, an older version of her daughter, went into the witness box.

The chief justice had just one question: "When you started to cry in the motor car", he asked kindly, "what did your son say to you?"

"Him say: 'What you crying for? If you die, you die innocently. *We all do it*'."

At that, Branch adjourned the court for lunch.

Manley was in no mood to eat. He still worked up a fever of nerves before a closing address and he was up next. A brisk walk always helped to release the mental stress and he headed downtown, dodging the buggies and horse hackneys lurching and sorting their way over the glistening tram lines until he came to the sea. When the court resumed, his face had the burnished lustre from the Jamaican sun as he turned to address the jury:

"The Crown have tried working on the theory that the death

occurred in the house of the accused; that they discovered blood stains on the wall, and that this discovery led them to enquiries into certain fresh marks on the wall. There are only two people at the time who could possibly have been involved in the matter: the mother and the son. No one suspects that the little boy, Joseph Dalton, killed Miriam Ross. To clinch the matter, the prosecution has introduced evidence of a confession made in a motor car. Let me say this", said Manley, raising his voice, "it is an extraordinary thing in this country, that whenever the links of evidence are not closely connected, the police always appear with a confession. The Crown's case is that the woman was killed during the night, and that she was buried that same night. I ask the jury to carefully consider that story, because the Crown's case stands or falls upon that sequence of events. If you have any reasonable doubt that the killing occurred in the room during the night, and that from the time the woman went to bed, she was never seen again alive by anybody, except the accused, unless you are so satisfied, I would without a shadow of doubt acquit . . . . The prisoner's account of what happened is absolutely and utterly inconsistent with the story of the Crown . . . . The first gap in the Crown's case is that there is no evidence before you as to the cause of death. In murder you have to set up two elements: that the person is dead, and that the person was killed by the act of another person. The examination of the body was absolutely inadequate. In the first place, the body should have been taken away to where a proper postmortem could have been carried out; where the parts of the body could have been sent to the public analyst for examination. The body was merely looked at. You heard me ask the doctor whether he had examined the skull for fracture. He replied that he had done it with his fingers. The doctor had to admit that many fractures were undetected from the outside, but could only be determined by sawing the skull and examining the inside for internal fractures. In the name of common sense, I ask you through what part of the skull did the doctor put his finger? I submit that no proper examination of the body was ever made and the medical evidence, such as it is, must leave you entirely in doubt."

Proceeding to deal with the stain and the whitewashing, Manley said that the boy's evidence on that score was totally unreliable. Then there was another feature: motive. "Have the Crown suggested to you at all", he asked the gentlemen of the jury, "any motive why that man, standing in the dock, should kill Miriam Ross? There is no suggestion. Let's look at the facts: the parties were not getting on very well, and Miriam planned to leave him. If he wanted to get rid of her, she was already going. The more we examine the Crown's case, the more incredible it becomes."

Manley next dealt with Esther, the prisoner's sister, and the question of the deceased's clothing. "Why", he asked, "were there articles in the grave other than those she was wearing?"

Regarding the "confession", Manley suggested that the prisoner had never opened his mouth during the time he was in custody. "It is beyond human understanding, that in front of two detectives, he would shout a confession to his deaf mother. Then the prisoner is put into a cell with somebody else — to get him to talk. And what does he say? He didn't do it. As to the morals of that practice, I have my own views about that." In conclusion, Manley submitted that, "If Spalding had not gone assisting in the search, people would have gone about asking the question: Why are you not helping us to find the woman? Or it would be said, if he went with them, he must deceive them. I cannot imagine in this world a more difficult and awkward position to be in . . . The prosecution have got to prove their case beyond a reasonable doubt. I am not suggesting that there is any doubt at all, but the balance of probability is entirely in favour of the accused. The Crown have failed to establish their case because the element they have chosen to establish has not been established at all."

Replying for the Crown, the attorney-general said the prisoner had had the benefit of a very able counsel, so that everything that could be said in the case for him, had been said but, "There is no doubt at all that the woman was killed between the evening of the 31st of May and the 30th of June. Was the woman murdered, or was she accidentally killed by Esther, when the iron was thrown, striking her on the temple? You have been told that bad feelings existed between Luther and Miriam, and that, I submit, was the motive for the crime . . . . A very curious thing, is that the prisoner never mentioned a word about his sister having struck the fatal blow when he was before the resident magistrate. It is true that he told the prisoner, Charles Hall, about it soon after he had gone to jail, but why did he not bring it out at the examination if it was true? My learned friend has told you that it is the custom of the police to make up confessions to fit in where the evidence is scanty. Do you believe that two men like Sergeants Ewart and Morris could swear to such a falsehood? For what purpose? I certainly don't think the two men would go out of their way to lie. I submit that on the evidence, it is open to you to find that the prisoner murdered Miriam Ross. It is not for the Crown to try and prop up their case. Our duty is to simply place the facts before you fairly and impartially and leave you to say which side you believe."

The chief justice at last summed up. He dealt at length with what he termed the full and graphic story from the prisoner, Luther Spalding: "Everyone is sorry that this graphic story was not given to the resident magistrate in order that it might have been examined in the light of medical evidence. I will express no opinion as to whether a dead body can groan some time after death, but if the prisoner's story is true, Esther Spalding must be a creature of extraordinary courage to have carried out such a cold-blooded act. She must be a woman of great resourcefulness to have gone through all the prisoner has described. Another feature in the case is the black dress which was strenuously claimed as being that of Esther and not Miriam, even after Mrs Ballantine, who had made the dress, had sworn that she made it for Miriam. Then it came out from the prisoner in the box, that the dress was Miriam's; he tried to explain that Esther was wearing it around her waist as an apron. You will have to consider the question of the confession, and whether you believe the two police sergeants, and the prisoner's explanation that the sergeant did not write down the words immediately . . . If you believe that Esther aimed the blow at the prisoner but it caught Miriam, then you will acquit the prisoner. But if you believe that the prisoner was the man who did it, you will find him guilty."

At 4.20 p.m. the jury slowly filed out. How long would they be away? What would be their verdict? Manley and the prosecuting counsels filed out after the judge had left the court. Most spectators turned to the 'cage' or dock to look at the prisoner. He was looking at the scenery outside. Trams were rushing by and the tinkle of the omnibus bell could be heard. A fresh breeze cooled the atmosphere.

The courtroom clock showed 5.00 p.m., then 5.15, 5.30, 5.45. It was nearly 6.00 p.m. when suddenly, there was a rush, a few minutes later, silence. The jury had returned. Spalding stood up to hear his fate. He put his head forward and visibly leaned on the rail. Everybody's eyes turned to the first of the twelve men. One among them had smiled slightly when they filed into the room. Another's features were slightly relaxed. Those of the rest were set; one or two looked at the man whose life they held in their hands. Those experienced in studying juries' expressions as they file into court with a verdict, say that when they decide to acquit a man, they look at him, but when the dreaded result weighs on their minds, they avoid looking at anything but the ground. They had looked at Luther Spalding.

A long discussion, which seemed to last an hour, but only occupied three or four minutes, was held between judge and jury . . . The jury, it turned out, could not possibly agree.

Luther Spalding was remanded until the next Sessions.

The Hon. Hector Josephs, KC (1871–1936). A Jamaica
Scholar, he attended Trinity Hall, Cambridge in 1891, to
become First Prizeman in Law the following year and Law
Tripos 1893/4. He was called to the Bar, Lincoln's Inn in 1896
and returned home to appear in all the prominent cases. He
took silk in 1911 and was the first black to be appointed a
colonial attorney–general (of British Guiana) in 1925

14

THE SPALDING MURDER TRIAL *Part 2*

Message from the Grave

Neither the learned and experienced KC, the Hon. Hector
Josephs, representing the Crown, nor his younger, but none
the less able, adversary on the defence, Mr Norman Manley,
missed any point that was material to the issue. If there
was a tendency to the emotional or to that warmth that
sometimes appears to the disinterested bystander as
unnecessary, it did not come from the calm, calculated
director of the case for the Crown. If it did arise from the
learned counsel for the defence, he himself asked the Court to
forgive any warmth that might have been manifested
as the outcome of a strong feeling in the matter.

The Gleaner
2 April 1925

After the jury had failed to agree at the first trial held in September, the body of the unfortunate Miriam Ross was exhumed and a postmortem carried out by Dr Ludlow Moody, the Government Pathologist. The result was conclusive: there was a fracture of the skull to the right side of the head. The request for the exhumation was as much from the prisoner, Luther Spalding, as from the Crown.

Spalding entered the dock for the second time on 31 March 1925, looking extremely well and showing no signs of deterioration during his eight month period of incarceration. He faced the densely packed spectators with ease.

At the Bar, representing the Crown once more, was the Attorney-General, the Hon. F.C. Wells-Durrant, this time assisted by the learned and experienced Hon. Hector Josephs, KC. Manley, for the second time, was assigned by the Crown to defend Spalding.[1] After the din of formalities had ceased, the empanelling of the jury got underway. The first juror, Mr R.E. Taylor, a merchant, asked to be excused on the ground that he did not believe in capital punishment. "Were you born in Jamaica?" asked the Acting Chief Justice, Anthony DeFreitas. The juror assured him in the dialogue which followed, that he was born and bred in Jamaica, and it was by study that he had come to the conviction against capital punishment. "I don't think you are fit to be a juror, Mr Taylor," commented DeFreitas, as he discharged the gentleman. The other jurors empanelled were: Edwin Enwright (foreman), Louis Ballantine, J.H. Vendryes, James Hill Cox, Eric Arnold Gadpaille, Waverley E. Pinto, Chas. J. Gillies, A. Martinez, H.C. Hitchins, Sigismund Allen and Jaspar Leopold Campbell.[2]

Hector Josephs opened the case for the Crown and in slow, perfect sequence, detailed the cruel murder of Miriam Ross at Bowden Hill in June the previous year. He called Esther Spalding as his first witness and Manley subjected her to a gruelling cross-examination:

"I put it to you, that yours were the hands that threw the iron?"

"No, sir."

"That it was you who suggested her burial?"

"No, sir."

"That it was your pan that dug the grave?"

"No, sir."

"That it was you who flung the black dress in the grave because it had blood on it?"

"No, sir."

"Blood had got on it while you were carrying the body, hadn't it?"

"No, sir."

"You still say you knew nothing of the death of Miriam Ross until you saw the body dug up?"

"Yes, sir."

"Was it you who told the police where the body was?"

"No, sir."

"They had you at Half-Way Tree for three days?"

"Yes. And they roughed me up too."

"You see a black dress in court ?"

"Yes. It belong to Miriam."

"Isn't it true that Miriam gave you that dress and you used to wear it as an apron when you did dirty work at home?"

"No, sir."

"You have clothes iron at your yard?"

"Yes, sir."

"Why didn't you go and look for Miriam on the Sunday morning?"

"Miriam usually come to my yard on a Sunday."

"Didn't you tell me the last time Miriam must have been tired and that was why you didn't go to see her?"

"I don't remember." Manley slumped in his seat. Esther Spalding had become a formidable courtroom opponent. By the end of the day, the most outstanding feature was the evidence given by Luther Spalding's nephew, Joseph Dalton, who said he didn't know his age, and was so tiny the judge had him placed on the platform beside him. Though small, the boy answered sharply, especially when being tested by the registrar, as to whether he realized the value of the oath he was about to take.

"If you don't tell the truth, what will happen to you?"

"I go to hell."

Questioned by Josephs, who had to leave the sacred precincts of the inner bar to question the witness on the platform, Joseph Dalton related once more how Miriam had gone to town the Saturday morning, and returned home the same night. She was grumbling about some missing rice and his grandmother told Luther not to answer her, but to take his book and read. The young boy then threw out some information not offered in the first trial. Luther, he said, had taken out a bottle of rum and given some to his mother. She told him to "throw water in it," but Luther told her it wasn't strong, and she drank it. Luther then poured some in a cup and told him to drink it. He didn't want it, but Luther insisted . . . "and it turn my eyes round, and around, and around".

What happened next? He and his grandmother went to lie down and left Luther sitting in a chair in the hall. Mirry was in her room still grumbling to herself. Next morning, he woke up, said his prayers and went outside. Luther was white-liming the wall in Mirry's room. There was blood on the wall and "plenty blood on the sheet". Luther ran out with the sheet and washed it in the river. He saw him return with the sheet and spread it on the wire: "It look nice then, sir, no blood on it."

Had he seen Miriam that morning? No. The next time he saw Mirry was when they dug her up.

As Josephs returned to his seat, Manley left the outer bar, and approached the boy seated on the platform: "Do you remember giving evidence at the last trial, and before the resident magistrate at Half-Way Tree?" he asked him.

"Yes, sir."

"Don't you remember saying that you saw Miriam come out of the room the Sunday morning."

"No, sir."

Manley said he would have to put in the deposition. The judge read over the boy's deposition at the preliminary examination when he said he had seen Miriam come out of her room on the Sunday morning.

"As a matter of fact", said Manley, "didn't Miriam Ross give you a bit of bread for your tea that morning?"

"No, sir."

"You don't remember telling the resident magistrate that she did?"

"No, sir."

"Were you at the house when the police came up and dug pieces out of the wall?"

"Yes, sir."

"That was where you said looked as if it had blood?"

"I don't know if it was blood."

"Did you ever see Luther put Jeyes on the sheet to kill fleas or bugs?"

"No."

"What was the first thing you saw Luther doing when you got up that morning?"

"Whitewashing the wall."

"Did you go into his room?"

"I went to the doorway."

"Did you speak to Luther that morning?"

"No, sir."

"You don't remember telling the court last time that you saw Luther put something dark and wet on the sheet on the Saturday?" asked the judge.

"I think I said so, sir."

"To be accurate," said Manley, "it was on the Friday night that you said you saw it?"

"Yes, sir. Luther say insect biting him and him sprinkle something on the sheet."

On the second day of the trial, the courtroom was packed to its utmost capacity and the police had a job keeping out spectators desirous of entering. Dr Johnston entered the box and described the condition of the body after it was taken from the grave in Spalding's banana field: "The hands and arms were lashed to the side with a cord and around the legs below the knees. I examined the cord and found it was not string. The body was not properly clothed. Except for the garments thrown over the body, it was nude. The body was very much decomposed. I examined it and found no fracture to the skull."

Manley cross-examined: "Are you aware, that evidence was given that the woman was fully clothed?"

"I was present when the body was taken out of the grave."

"You are not prepared to say whether the woman was nude or no?"

"There were clothes in proximity to the body."

"Are you aware of the importance of this case?"

"Yes."

Sergeant George Morris was the next person to testify. Cross-examined by Manley, he confirmed that he was present when the body was found in Luther Spalding's field. According to Morris there was one garment on the body. A piece of banana leaf tied the two feet and another piece tied the arms. There was another piece around the shoulders, and a cloth around the neck. Beside the clothing on the body there were other clothes in the hole which he took charge of.

Manley asked: "Who do you say was the person who found the spot?"

"Mr Dalmedge."

"Did you say that at the last trial?"

"I don't remember."

"Do you remember saying before the resident magistrate: 'I then dug up a spot I had previously found'?"

"Yes."

"You didn't mention Dalmedge in the September trial?"

"No."

"What occurred to you that you should have mentioned it this morning?"

"Nothing special."

"You gave evidence at the trial in September last?"

"Yes."

"Is it the same on the important points as it is today?"

"No, sir."

"Were you lying on the last occasion?"

"No, sir, but I wasn't asked certain things."

"You heard the prisoner being asked questions about the banana string on the last occasion?"

"Yes, sir."

"And you told me then that it was string and string only."

"It was banana string."

"Don't quibble. Did you, or did you not, say it was string."

"I did."

"You knew then that the suggestion was that the girl was killed in the house?"

"Yes."

"And that it was more likely to be string if in the house?"

"Yes."

"And if in the field, banana string was more likely?"

"Yes."

"Why then did you lie?"

"I didn't lie. I didn't take particular notice whether it was string or banana string."

"You now say it was banana leaf bone that tied the feet?"

"Yes, sir."

"You definitely swore at the last trial that it was ordinary string?"

"Yes, sir."

"Now you want to bring in string by saying the shoulders were tied with string?"

"Yes, sir; it was."

"But you never mentioned it at the last trial?"

"I was only asked how the body was found."

"You remember saying before the magistrate that the hands were tied to the body with a piece of string, and the feet were tied?"

"Yes."

"I put it to you that it is an invention of yours today to put around the shoulders a string to cover up the lie."

"No, sir. I produce the string today. The hole was reopened on the 13th of October and some articles of clothing left in it were taken out, including the string."

"That is just what by insinuation, you are being charged with corruptly producing today," the judge interrupted.

"Did you intend to mislead the jury then?" questioned Manley.

"No, sir."

"You say now you found a cloth around the head?"

"Yes, sir."

"Why did you omit the last time to tell the court that there was a cloth around the head?"

"I wasn't asked, sir."

"Who asked you today?"

"I was allowed to speak freer today than at the last trial."

"As a sergeant presenting the case, you would have great latitude at the preliminary examination. What did you say then about the cloth on the head?"

"I don't remember."

"You haven't told me yet why you tried to mislead the court on the last occasion?"

"I didn't try to mislead."

"Although this man is on trial for his life, you thought, as a sergeant, your word would go down, and you swore about that string?"

"No, sir."

"You wanted to get a feather in your cap by swearing away a man's life!"

"Oh! My friend!" exclaimed Hector Josephs.

"No, Mr Manley", rebuked the judge, "that is a little too much."

Manley scenting danger, switched tactics: "As Your Honour pleases. I ask the Court's forgiveness for any warmth that might have been manifested, as the outcome of a strong feeling on the matter."

In that genteel manner which the scriptures say turneth away wrath, the acting chief justice poured oil on the seemingly troubled waters. He counselled Manley not to "bang the sergeant so hard," and attributed the outburst to the counsel's youth. Manley gripped the stand in front of him and proceeded, a little more calmly now: "Were you in a hurry coming down from Stony Hill in the car, Sergeant Morris?"

"No, sir."

"Did you find it difficult to write down what you said the prisoner stated?"

"No, sir. I wrote it in my pocket book."

"Did you show it to the prisoner?"

"No, sir."

"Don't you know your Police Handbook requires you to?" the judge intervened.

"No, sir."

"Don't you know that the rule says that the statement should be shown to the prisoner and that he should sign it?" asked Manley.

The sergeant hesitated.

"I'm waiting, Sergeant Morris . . . shouldn't a statement be shown to the prisoner and should he not sign it?"

"Yes, sir."

"You know the prisoner's version is different as to the words?"

"Yes."

"Now, you might have been mistaken?"

"No, sir. I wrote it down."

"Was the road very rough?"

"No, sir."

"Do you think it possible the prisoner said to his mother: 'If we die, we die innocently.' And yet he goes on to say that he did it?"

"Yes, sir."

"You don't think it strange, Sergeant Morris?"

"Not then, sir."

"Not then? What about today? Do you think it possible the prisoner said to his mother, 'If we die, we die innocently, *not we do it*'?"

"No, sir."

"There is no grave to be dug up to discover the truth of that?"

"No, sir."

"You are clear that the body of the woman was clothed?"

"Yes."

"Was a black dress found in the hole?"

"Yes, in a corner."

"One lot of clothes was bundled up near the body?"

"Yes, sir."

"But the black dress was separate?"

"Yes."

"You heard Sergeant Ewart say at the last trial that the black dress was on the body?"

"Yes, sir."

"And after I challenged him, he changed his statement?"

"Yes."

Manley sat down.

Detective Sergeant Ewart, the next witness to be examined by Hector Josephs, said that when he first saw the body in Spalding's field, the arms and legs were tied with banana string.

Manley fastened on the sergeant's answer like a hawk.

"It's funny you said nothing at the last trial about banana string."

"No. I think I said string."

"Don't you recollect at the last trial, the attorney-general laid stress on the point about whether it was real string or banana string?"

"I don't recollect, sir."

"Don't you know that the theory then, was that the woman was killed in the house?"

"Yes."

"That was part of your great detective work. And didn't I ask you what kind of a string it was?"

"I don't remember."

"Do you remember the question about the black dress?"

"Yes."

"You remember you said at the last trial, the black dress was on the body?"

"Yes; I left out the word 'top'."

"Did you write down what the prisoner said in the car?"

"No."

"Don't you think it would have been more honest if you had done so?"

"It didn't strike me then."

"Is it possible the prisoner said: 'If we die, we die innocent; *not we do it*'?"

"No, sir."

"You couldn't have made a mistake?"

"No, sir."

"Doesn't it strike you as strange," Manley continued, "that the prisoner should have said, 'If we die,' when he was admitting his mother knew nothing of it, and that it was he who did it?"

"It didn't strike me then."

"But still you say it is not possible the prisoner said: '*not we do it*'?"

"No, sir."

After Manley's attack on the police witnesses, Hector Josephs called Dr Ludlow Moody to the stand. That was Manley's cue.

"Might Dr Moody produce the skull?" he asked the judge.

"Yes."

To an awesome hush, Moody produced the skull of the unfortunate Miriam Ross. With the judge's consent, he left the witness

Dr Moody describes the fractured skull to the jury

box and pointed out the fracture to the jury. One by one, they viewed the gruesome relict as the doctor explained that the fracture must have been caused by contact with a direct blow or fall. It required a considerable amount of violence; the victim would have fallen like a log.

Answering questions posed by Hector Josephs as to the physical effects of such a blow, Moody explained: "The appearance in the first stage is like death. Then there would be signs of recovery, and haemorrhage inside and outside the skull would take place. Complications would follow, which would cause death. The blow itself might have caused sudden death."

"Was recovery possible?"

"Recovery might have been possible."

Manley was on his feet:

"Would an ordinary clothes iron flung at the head, be likely to cause such a fracture, Doctor?"

"Yes."

"If such a missile struck the head, would the fracture indicate the way in which the blow was struck?"

"Yes," said Moody, explaining that, in this case, the fracture was perpendicular.

Long before 10 o'clock in the morning on the last day of the trial, standing room in the courthouse was not available, and the precincts of the court were crowded throughout the day. The acting chief justice took his seat at 10 o'clock sharp and Manley opened briefly for the defence:

"This is the second time the prisoner is on trial and yet I am still completely in the dark as to what theory the Crown is putting forward in this case. The story of the defence today, is the same as it was before. In the last trial, it was a vital issue as to whether there was a fracture of the skull or not. Dr Johnston said there was no fracture. Now you have it that Dr Johnston was wrong: there was a fracture. There is no change in the prisoner's story; everything found by the police this time absolutely corroborates the prisoner's version of what took place. The whole truth was not told the last time, and the accusation that the prisoner had invented his story is now disproved. As the attorney-general told you in the opening, the request for the exhumation of the body was as much from the prisoner as from the Crown. Luther Spalding was confronted with Dr Johnston's statement, that there was no fracture. Spalding couldn't say there was a fracture, but he told you what he saw, and that would certainly account for a fracture. The defence submits that Esther Spalding was responsible for the death of

Miriam Ross . . ." There was an impressive pause in Manley's delivery before he concluded: "It is no easy task for a man on trial, for the second time, for his life, to stand here, and tell his story clearly. I ask the jury to bear with him."

Luther Spalding took the stand and repeated his version of the sad affair: "It was 5 o'clock in the morning when Mirry left. I heard the Reformatory bugle blow . . . . Mirry went outside and came back. She went in the room and came out again with a paper parcel . . . . she gave the boy Joseph a piece of bread . . . . It was Esther who flung the iron and hit Mirry . . . . It was Esther who got a piece of banana string and tie down Mirry's arms and legs. It was Esther who took the body and put it in the hole and threw the rest of Mirry's clothes in the grave. Esther was wearing an old black dress as an apron, she threw that in the hole too. It was not true that I took any sheet to the river that morning . . . . the week before Miriam left I put some Jeyes' fluid on my bed. Miriam also used some white lime on the wall to wipe out the marks of insects . . . . when my mother started cry in the car, I said: 'You crying! If we die, we die innocently; *is not we do it*'."

The calm, calculated counsel for the Crown, Hector Josephs rose slowly to cross-examine:

"Which hand did Esther use to throw the iron?"

"The right hand."

"And you ducked your head to dodge the blow?"

"Yes."

"Why didn't you pull Miriam down too?"

"Self thought was in me then, sir."

"How did you know Esther was going to throw the iron at you?"

"She gave me a caution, sir."

"When Miriam fell on the ground, didn't it strike you that you might have got assistance and helped her?"

"I was frightened."

"For what? If it was an accident, why were you frightened?"

"My mind was not prepared to see such an accident."

"When she moved her leg, didn't you think she was alive?"

"I thought she had just given up the ghost."

"And you, who had been a soldier, got frightened, so easily?"

"I was frightened, sir."

"Why didn't you call out to the neighbours?"

"I didn't think they would believe it was not me who killed her."

"When next did you speak of it?"

"To a prisoner in the lock-up at Half-Way Tree."

Manley next called Dr O.D.F. Robertson, who testified as to the fracture of the skull and the possibility of its having occurred in the manner suggested by the defence. Such a fracture was quite consistent, he said, with a blow from a clothes iron flung at a distance of ten yards. It was not consistent with a blow from a person holding a stick. Cross-examined by Josephs, the doctor didn't think the fracture could have been caused by a man holding a blunt instrument in his hand. Of course, much depended on the force of the blow.

At this stage, 3.45 p.m., the court adjourned for half an hour to enable the jury to go and have tea before the closing addresses started.

On the resumption of the court, Manley faced the jury:

"The duty of the Crown is to prove their case. It is for them to establish the guilt of the prisoner. Whatever your own suspicions or personal feelings might be, forget them. In the interest of justice, you must deal with the evidence, and the evidence alone. And what is the evidence? Here is a man in whose field was buried a woman. That did not connect him with the deed, but to obtain that evidence they brought the boy from the house who said that he saw Luther Spalding putting fresh whitewash on the wall. If that was to cover any blood marks, the blood would still remain. But what happened? The whitelime was scraped off and tested, but no blood was found. Then came the story of the bloody sheet; that was tested and no blood was found on it. Then there was the fractured skull. The prisoner couldn't tell if the skull had been fractured, but he knew of the blow to the head, and he spoke of it. It was disputed, but the exhumation of the body proved his story was correct. Then came the clothing found in the grave. It was clear that the body was clothed, though the doctor said he thought the body was naked. It is a great pity that a man should stand on trial for his life with such slipshod evidence when we have a doctor, an inspector of police and two sergeants present. They had eight months in which to repair their case, which I submit had been shattered, but again they have failed. Dr Moody has said that the articles submitted to him contained no blood stains. That does away with any suggestion that Miriam Ross was killed in the house. The Crown never even opened to the evidence of the little boy, which shows what reliance they place on it. We come next to the question of the string. There are no words too strong to denounce Sergeant Morris. He stood in the box and deliberately swore to what was untrue, on just the little points of corroboration for which the case for the prisoner was crying out . . . All Luther Spalding did is consistent with his story, and I invite you to accept it, assuming it is true that he was foolish enough to assist Esther in the burial, but who would have believed him if he had said it was Esther? She would say it was a lie; he would have been arrested and ended up in the same position as he is today: right there in the dock.

"Up to now, the Crown has given nothing that can positively show how the crime was committed and I have yet to hear the motive. The only positive evidence in this case is that submitted by the prisoner. He told my learned friend that he was not sorry Miriam was leaving him, because he had another woman. Why then should he have gone and murdered that woman? Does he look like a homicidal maniac? Go on, look at him . . . I think not.

"The next point I ask you to consider is the evidence of Esther Spalding. She was the great friend of Miriam Ross, and yet on the Sunday morning she never went to look for her, although they lived within hailing distance and saw each other every day. Of course, she didn't go looking for her. She knew Miriam wasn't there; she was dead. And what did Esther tell you? She thought Miriam was tired. Do you believe that?

"As far as the alleged conversation between the prisoner and his mother in the motor car is concerned, I ask you, what reliance can you place on that? It is absurd.

"There is more than a doubt in this case; it is riddled with doubt. Wherever there is abundant evidence of guilt, there is never confusion; but where a case is weak, there is always confusion. I ask you to weigh the evidence with care, and give the prisoner the benefit of the doubt."

At 6.15 p.m. Hector Josephs started his reply for the Crown. He said he had to agree with some of the remarks of his learned friend with regard to the cursory performance of certain duties when the body was discovered. But that was different from wilful perversion. It should be remembered that one very often became wise after the event. Perhaps they had not done their very best, but,"In weighing the evidences of those men, I would ask you not to think that they were wilfully trying to mislead. I also admit, that had the medical officer carried out his duties as he ought, he would have arrived at the probable cause of death. It is regrettable. Today, however, you have the evidence, and on that you will decide. You have heard the evidence of the prisoner, and [looking at Manley] the brilliant advocacy of the learned counsel whom he was fortunate in having to defend him. It is for you to determine whether you believe the prisoner killed Miriam Ross or not."

Josephs then proceeded on a masterly analysis of the evidence. He laid emphasis on the fact that the prisoner gave his mother and her grandson some rum that Saturday night, which meant that they would be hard sleepers. That statement was not denied. Then there was the evidence of the little boy. Was he mistaken as to everything? He was a bright, alert lad. He next dealt with the prisoner's story of how Esther flung the iron, lifted up the body, and dragged it to the grave because the prisoner told her it was her burden, and she would have to bear it.

"Do you think that Esther, in giving her evidence, gave the impression that she knew of her brother's deeds, or that she was the party who flung the iron? I submit not. You have seen the prisoner in the witness box, you have seen his demeanour. Do you believe him? It is for you to say."

At 7.20 p.m. the judge began his charge to the jury. He explained that it was murder or nothing; there was no alternative. They must be satisfied that the prisoner was the person who committed the act; that he was the person who flung a hard missile that struck Miriam Ross. As regards motive, he pointed out that it was not necessary to show motive, though it sometimes helped. He also dealt with the evidence of Sergeants Ewart and Morris as to the confession in the car. He asked them to be cautious in relying on Ewart's memory. He didn't write down what was said, and he may have made a mistake. Sergeant Morris, he would say, was a bad witness, who had to admit that he had gone back on what he had said at the first trial. The judge suggested that Sergeant Morris had fraudulently introduced the string. Everyone else spoke of banana string, while he falsely swore to a bit of string. He hoped that Sergeant Morris would not have any more criminal cases, unless he was made an inspector — when he would have no cause to investigate a case.

The jury retired to consider their verdict at 8.10 p.m. and returned to court half an hour later. Luther Spalding stood up, and in perfect silence, the registrar asked the foreman of the jury if they were agreed on their verdict.

"No, sir. We cannot agree."

Manley's pencil snapped. The prisoner's jaw dropped; a hum of disbelief hovered over the court.

"Do you wish me to offer you any guidance, gentlemen?" asked the judge.

"We stand ten to two, sir," replied the foreman.

"Is there no point I can help you on, that would lead you to agree?"

"Not possible," piped one of the jurors.

The judge tactfully suggested that they retire again and let their foreman know any point of difficulty on which he could assist them.

The jury filed out once more and returned eleven minutes later.

"Have you agreed on your verdict, gentlemen?"

"No, sir . . . We cannot possibly agree."

The case was put down for trial at the next circuit. Luther Spalding was remanded in custody.

Several courses were now open to the Crown. When the trial came up for the third time, they could either prosecute or they might decide not to offer any evidence when the case was called. In that event Spalding would be acquitted and the Crown prevented from making use of any new facts in connection with the case in order to try Spalding again. Another option was for the Crown to enter a plea which would leave it open to the authorities to prosecute should information come into their possession which would warrant a new trial.[3]

Three weeks later, on 24 April, the terror of the gallows that had gnawed at Spalding's vitals for many a month was suddenly removed by the stroke of the attorney-general's pen. The Crown ordered a *nolle prosequi* to be entered. Luther Spalding was a free man; the Crown had decided to relinquish its suit against him. Twice the jury had indicated that the case against Spalding was not perfectly clear and British justice demanded that the accused always be given the benefit of the doubt.

When Luther Spalding left the irksome confines of the St Catherine District Prison, the next morning's *Gleaner* noted that he had been defended on both occasions by Mr Norman Manley "with great force and ability".[4]

"Well", said Manley's friend, Leslie Clerk, putting down the newspaper, "you've made front page news. By the way, has any one ever been tried three times on a capital charge?"

"As far as I know", Manley replied, "only once, in Ireland."

"And what was the result?"

"He was convicted."

Marcus Garvey

15

"RE GARVEY: I am of the Opinion . . ."

Before many years roll by, I hope we will have a real and active President of the Republic of Africa, whose affairs will be administered from New York, the United States of Africa, instead of New York, the United States of America.[1]

Marcus Garvey
From speech of acceptance on being re-elected
Provisional President of Africa
UNIA Convention, New York, 28 August 1922

In 1916, Marcus Garvey left Jamaica for the USA to undertake fundraising for his fledgling organization, the Universal Negro Improvement Association (UNIA) which he had founded in Jamaica in 1914. What was planned as a five-month speaking tour turned into an eleven-year stay, during which time the UNIA grew into the largest Pan-African movement ever. Garvey had become one of the most stirring orators of his time, arousing the black world as no one before. From the first United States branch of the UNIA formed in New York in 1916, Garvey was to build an enormous mass movement that would number millions of supporters in North America, the Caribbean and Latin American countries. "If Europe is for the Europeans, then Africa is for the black peoples of the world,"[2] he proclaimed during the first spectacular UNIA conference held at Madison Square Gardens in August 1920, when he was elected Provisional President of Africa.

Through the UNIA, Garvey pursued his plan to secure black independence by establishing black business enterprises. The most significant was the steamship company known as the Black Star Shipping Line which, however small in comparison, was an attempt to invade the white monopoly of world commerce.

In its first year, the Black Star Line was able to raise US$610,000 through stock sales and subscriptions, and acquire three steamers. Yet the project failed; by 1922 the ships were lost, the corporation had collapsed and Garvey was charged with using the mails to defraud in stock operations of the Black Star Line.

Garvey was brought to trial before Judge Mack of the Federal District Court in May 1923. On the 22nd of that month, Garvey dismissed his counsel, W. McDougald, and he himself stood forth to smash the Federal Prosecution. Pacing majestically before the jury, now twirling his ornate moustache, now stroking his stubby beard, a gold-rimmed monocle swinging upon his ample breast, Garvey created sensation after sensation in the courtroom with his cross-examination of Leo Healey, Assistant District Attorney-General, and former counsel for the North American Steamship Line.

"Mr Healey", began Garvey impressively, "do you know Marcus Garvey?"

"Indeed I do."

"What, Mr Healey, is your opinion of him?"

"Why, Mr Garvey, I was greatly impressed with Mr Garvey's personality, his speech, his noble bearing; greatly, I assure you."

"Do you believe he is serious?"

"I certainly do not!"[3]

The outcome of the trial evoked a tornado of wrath among Garvey supporters. On 21 June 1923, Garvey was found guilty and sentenced to serve five years in the Atlanta penitentiary and fined $1,000. His appeal failed and, on 8 February 1925, Garvey began his prison sentence. But his spirit remained indomitable. Although his sentence was commuted in late December 1927, Garvey was deported to Jamaica as a convicted alien felon. Garvey spent his time revitalizing the UNIA in Jamaica and making plans for its sixth international conference in Kingston. Meanwhile, Norman Manley one day picked up his pen and began to write an Opinion:

Re Garvey, I have reached the conclusion criminal proceedings for Bigamy ought not to be instituted in this matter.[4]

Garvey's private life was no less spectacular than his public pursuits. He had married two women with the same name, from the same country, who were bosom friends, wife No. 2 having been bridesmaid to wife No. 1.

Born in Port Antonio, Jamaica, in 1897, wife No. 1, Amy Ashwood, had married Garvey on 25 December 1919 at Liberty Hall, the Harlem meeting place of the UNIA. The newlyweds left for Canada where Garvey set about promoting the Black Star Line. It was to be a working honeymoon and, as such, Garvey's private secretary, Amy Jacques, joined them. Less than three months later, the marriage was on

Amy Ashwood

the rocks with Garvey accusing his wife of infidelity and dishonesty among various other things. Amy Ashwood, for her part, said that she had disagreed with some of her husband's ideas.

"I worked with Garvey for six years," she later told a *Gleaner* reporter.[5] "I started with him here in Jamaica in 1914, and continued in the United States. I saw where he was wrong. Garvey's idea of an African kingdom was a geographical blunder. There are too many tribes, each differing from the other in customs, that it is quite impossible to form them into a single people. What is more, they want no Afro-Americans or West Indians as rulers over them. They want no kings, or dukes or earls created over here, sent there to them. Mr Garvey never did a worse thing for his movement than when he began to create peers, for all that he succeeded in doing was to bring his whole scheme into ridicule, and what was good in his plans naturally suffered with what was bad."

"Didn't you advise him?" enquired the reporter.

"Of course I advised him. But he wouldn't listen. Success had turned his head. He thought everybody wrong who didn't agree with him."

The interviewer enquired whether this difference of viewpoint between her husband and herself had anything to do with their domestic breach.

"Yes," Amy replied, "but I would like to be quite fair to Mr Garvey. He has done one thing. He has awakened the race consciousness of the Negro, and created the desire in him to raise his status. Which is where I will come in, for I know that the only possible means of raising his status is education."

Beginning in 1920, Amy Ashwood brought a series of legal actions for divorce and alimony against Garvey in New York. The first, on 1 August 1920, was discontinued in April 1921 by Justice Finch of the Supreme Court, who had appointed a referee to examine the books of the Black Star Line and other allied interests for the purpose of determining the respective amounts to award the plaintiff as alimony and counsel fees.

In August 1921, Amy Ashwood left the United States, first for Montreal, then London, to continue her sociological work. In 1922, she started divorce proceedings in New York through the

Amy Jacques

Seventh Avenue law firm of Marshall and Garrett, who were given power of attorney by the American consul general in London to represent her.[6]

Meanwhile, unknown to her, Garvey had established a fictitious legal residence in the state of Missouri where he obtained a divorce and subsequently married Amy Jacques in Baltimore in July 1922. When asked by a reporter for *The World* if he would shed some light on his domestic status, Garvey said, "I am legally divorced. I have nothing else to say".[7]

Amy Ashwood challenged the legitimacy of the divorce and in 1926 picked up the cudgel again, only to find herself holding the wrong end of the stick. On 8 April that year, detectives raided her apartment in New York and said that they found her in bed with a male friend, Joseph Frazer. Garvey, who was by this time in prison in Atlanta, cross-charged Amy Ashwood with adultery and named Frazer as co-respondent. The case, which was heard in the Heights Court on

28 April, was said to have been the most amusing to be tried in that court for some time. During the hearing H.S. Boulin, head of Boulin's National Detective Agency, was summoned by Ashwood and Frazer and charged with disorderly conduct arising out of the raid. The merciless cross-examination by Mr Kohn, of Kohn and Nagler, the West 44th Street attorneys for Marcus Garvey and Boulin, however, shattered Ashwood and Frazer's story that at the time of the raid, they were engaged in writing a book. Both complainants admitted that they were undressed and asleep at the time the raiding party dropped in, so the court did not quite understand where the book part came in. The hour was 3 a.m. Mr Frazer explained that he was a Pullman porter, but was assisting Amy Ashwood with her book as a sideline. According to Frazer, he became tired by his literary efforts and when Ashwood complained of not feeling well, he decided to stay overnight and act as a "substitute nurse". At this point, everyone in court laughed aloud, and the judge rapped for order and threatened to clear the court. The most embarrassing moment for Frazer, however, came when attorney Kohn asked him to give the names of any other married women he had assisted in a literary way while undressed and in bed. Frazer promptly responded with the name of a Boston woman![8]

The New York County Supreme Court subsequently heard the combined case of Amy Ashwood's 1922 suit against Garvey and his countersuit against her. Both Ashwood and Garvey were found guilty of adultery and the suit ended in a stalemate, with no verdict one way or the other on the validity of Garvey's second marriage.[9] Amy Ashwood, however, did not let the matter rest. When asked by a journalist whether Garvey's deportation to Jamaica in December 1927 would cause any change in the status of their relationship, she promptly declared: "My fight will have to be staged in the courts of Jamaica now. After all, that will be the best place to settle our differences. As soon as my lawyers notify me, I shall proceed to Jamaica and meet him face to face. I am his legitimate wife — he has never obtained a divorce from me."[10]

In November 1928, the British consul general in New York reported to the Governor of Jamaica, Edward Stubbs, that Amy Ashwood had renewed her British passport and was travelling to Jamaica for the stated aim of instituting "an action against Marcus Garvey as she contends that he is a bigamist and that she is his lawful wife".[11] As far as Jamaica was concerned, her contention with Marcus Garvey would go no further. "The law in Jamaica with regard to bigamy is framed on the provisions which exist in England", Manley continued his Opinion, "and after providing that the offence is committed wherever the second marriage takes place contains a provision similar to the proviso in English Law exempting from the operation of the law all persons save British subjects.

"Apparently the Law in New South Wales which was expounded in *MacCleod* v. *The Attorney-General for New South Wales* 1891 A.C. does not contain a proviso restricting it to British Subjects and the question arises whether the existence of this proviso would lead to a different result from that arrived at in the MacCleod case. Now in the MacCleod case, the Privy Council held that the word *Whoever* in the statute must be restricted to mean persons within the jurisdiction of the court. They also held that the word *Wheresoever* which refers to the second marriage must be restricted to places within the colony. It is of the first importance to notice that both words were restricted as above mentioned, because if the court had thought that the jurisdiction to punish was exercisable wherever the offence was committed, provided that the person charged was amenable to the jurisdiction of the court, it would have been sufficient for them to have restricted the meaning of the word *Whoever* without restricting the meaning of the word *Wheresoever* and to have held that it was a sufficient restriction of the meaning of the word *Whoever* to limit it to residents in the colony or to British subjects.

"I think the true conclusion to be derived from a comparison of the MacCleod case with the Earl Russell case is that the Imperial Parliament can properly legislate for British subjects in any place in the world whatever, but a Colonial Legislature can only legislate for the peace and order and good government of the colony unless in terms authorized by the Imperial Parliament to do more. Section 36 of the Order in Council of May 1884 pursuant to the Imperial Statute 29. Vic. Ch. 12 provides that the Council in Jamaica may make laws for the peace, order and good government of the island. Consistently with that, No. 19 of the instructions to the governor made in July 1887 requires him not to assent to any law whereby the rights of subjects not residing in Jamaica are affected.

"In view of these considerations it seems clear that it is *ultra vires* for the Legislature of the colony to provide for the punishment of offences committed by British subjects out of this island.

"With regard to the question of instituting proceedings in divorce, I cannot advise without being more fully instructed on the facts. At the moment I can only say that the question of domicile will require careful consideration as well as the question of the delays which have occurred since the parties separated.

It does not however appear likely that the proceedings in New York will in any way operate as a bar to the proceedings in Jamaica."

Both Amy Ashwood and Amy Jacques went on to achieve fame in their different ways. Amy Ashwood became an outstanding member of the Pan-Africanist movement; Amy Jacques, the guardian of her husband's flame and, later, a respected author and lecturer in her own right.

Chief Justice, Sir Arthur Fiennes Barrett-Lennard, presided over the trial

The victim – Stedman Case, the 24-year-old chauffeur who was stabbed to death by Louise Walker

16

THE LOUISE WALKER MURDER TRIAL

Louise Walker

Murder between Intimates

Mr Manley must be congratulated as a barrister on the persistent and brilliant fight he has made for the liberty as well as the life of Louise Walker . . . In this instance we must remember that he was employed by the Crown itself to defend the woman, and the fees attached to such a function are fixed. In a private case his remuneration would probably have been three or four times as much as the Government has paid him. But if his remuneration had been ten times as much he could not have worked harder, more conscientiously, more brilliantly . . .

The Gleaner
6 October 1926

L ouise Walker was on trial for her life. She was accused of murdering her lover, Stedman Case, with a knife which had cut right through the jugular vein under his right ear.

Norman Manley had been assigned by the Crown to defend the slightly built twenty-one-year-old, who came into court dressed in pink, with a pink hat drawn well down over her eyes. If she looked, as one court reporter noted, "somewhat pale under her brown complexion," she was composed, if not particularly vocal. When asked to plead to the charge, Louise Walker, in a voice barely above a whisper, replied, "Guilty, with explanation," which the court registered as a plea of *Not Guilty*. Her "explanation" was self-defence; Stedman Case, she said, had threatened her with a revolver. The only problem was, the revolver was nowhere to be found.

The Chief Justice, Sir Arthur Fiennes Barrett-Lennard, presided over the trial which signalled the opening of the Home Circuit Court in

149

Kingston on 27 September 1926.[1] Four large fans rotated vigorously above the spectators and reporters who packed the courtroom. The Attorney-General, F.C. Wells-Durrant, represented the Crown. A jury of twelve men was empanelled to include Messrs Frank Kinkead, Victor Williams, L.J. Fogarty, Allan D. Roberts, W. Peynado, Maxwell Earle, Horatio Hollar, Chas. D. Rowe, Theodore Scotland, Donald M. DaCosta, Cyril E. Sherman and Isaac J. Livingston. When the chief justice pointed out that no foreman had been nominated, Manley quietly but firmly explained that it was the custom in Jamaica that the juror placed as No. 1 was accepted as foreman, in this instance, Mr Frank Kinkead.

In his opening address, the attorney-general told the court that Louise Walker was charged with the murder, on 6 June 1926, of a man named Stedman Case, a chauffeur employed to Mr E.V. Clarke, a well-known solicitor. The Crown submitted that the crime was motivated by jealousy, a result of Case's tangled love life. According to the attorney-general, Case was living in concubinage with a woman, Ethel Lipman, who had three children for him. He was also intimate with the accused, Louise Walker, and the evidence would show that she threatened to kill Case so that neither woman could have him.

Curiously enough, all the chief witnesses for the prosecution were women. The attorney-general called one of them, Lucille Ramsay, a young girl of thirteen, to the witness stand. She told the court that she lived at Luke Lane and remembered Sunday morning, 6 June, vividly:

"I was going along North Street. When I got to No. 3, I saw a motor car standing a little below the corner of Hanover Street. I was walking towards the car and saw a man sitting in the car."

"Did you see anyone near the car?" asked the attorney-general.

"Yes, the prisoner, Louise Walker."

"How was the man sitting?"

"His back was turned to the woman."

"What did you see the woman do?"

"I saw the woman take a knife out of her bosom and go down with a force on the man's neck."

"Was the man's back still turned towards her."

"Yes."

"What did the man do after this?"

"He jumped out the car."

Lucille Ramsay said she was an eye-witness to the murder

"How far were you from the car?"

"About four feet."

"Where did the man go?"

"He ran into No. 3 North Street."

"What did the woman do?"

"Ran in after him."

"Did you see if she still had the knife?"

"No."

"Did you see if the man had anything in his hand?"

"I didn't see anything."

"The man passed quite close to you?"

"Yes."

"So much so that blood smeared your dress?"

"Yes."

"What happened to the woman?"

"A man held her and she fell down on the step pretending a faint."

"Did you know either the man or the woman before?"

"No."

"Did you see any revolver?"

"No, sir."

Manley started his cross-examination of Lucille Ramsay quietly, but as he warmed to his argument he frequently made gestures with his hands to illustrate a point.

"Was the car close up to the sidewalk?"

"Yes."

"And it was pointing down to the sea?"

"Yes."

"And the man was sitting in the left side of the car at the driving wheel?"

"Yes."

"And the woman was to the right?"

"Yes."

"What side did the man get out?"

"On the right side."

"Are you quite sure of this?"

"Yes."

"What part of the car was the woman at that time?"

"On the right, towards the front."

"The woman was standing on the road when she struck the blow?"

"Yes."

"Was anyone else approaching?"

"Yes, a man was coming along a few yards in front. He was going in the direction of East Street."

"Can you describe the man?"

"No."

"Were you walking down the middle of Hanover Street?"

"Yes."

"As Stedman Case ran past you, his left side was towards you?"

"Yes."

"Then how did you come to get the bloodstains on your dress? The wound was to the right side of Stedman Case's neck, you know."

"It did stain my dress."

"What has become of the dress?"

"I washed it out."

David Louis Ward, a clerk in the Jamaica Government Railway was sworn in. "On the morning in question", he said, "while walking along North Street, I saw a man running across followed by a woman. I saw a car standing in Hanover Street. There were bloodstains on the right front fender and on the ground. I heard someone screaming and I saw the accused, the same woman I saw run in the yard, being brought out."

Cross-examined by Manley, the witness couldn't remember seeing anyone else walking along the street.

As Manley took his seat, Edward Vincent Clarke was called to the stand and took the oath. "I am a solicitor of the Supreme Court of Jamaica", he told the attorney-general, "and reside at 3 North Street."

Clarke confirmed that Case had been working for him as a general-servant-cum-chauffeur for five years. Around 9 o'clock that Sunday morning, Case had come to him, as usual, for instructions. "About ten minutes later", Clarke recalled, "I heard a great commotion and Case ran on to the verandah where I was sitting. His face and clothes were covered with blood."

"Did you see anyone else?"

"Close behind him was the accused, Louise Walker. She had a knife in her hand. I went after her and got hold of her."

"Was that on the verandah?"

"No, in the garden. I caught hold of her and took the knife from her."

"Is that the knife?"

The witness was shown an ordinary bone-handled table knife, worn down to a point, with stains on the blade and handle.

"Yes, that's the knife."

"What did you do with it?"

"I put it in my pocket and afterwards gave it to a policeman."

"When you caught hold of Louise Walker, did she resist?"

"After a little force she gave up the knife. She was hysterical."

"Where did you take her?"

"I took her to the back of the house and handed her over to Mr McLarty. I told him to hold on to her while I went after Case. I saw him make a few staggering steps and then fall. I ran to Dr Grabham's house which is close by and returned with him."

"Case was then dead?"

"The doctor told me so."

"The accused did not say anything to you?"

"I don't recollect her saying anything."

Cross-examined by Manley, Clarke said his car was an old Dodge car.

"About what year?" Manley enquired.

"1922."

"Left-hand drive?"

"Yes."

"It would have the gear lever and brake on the right of the driver?"

"Yes."

"Is the front seat wide or narrow?"

"It holds two comfortably."

"The car was drawn up on the left of the road?"

"Yes. Close to the sidewalk, on a downward slope."

"The sidewalk there is rather high?"

"Yes, it is."

"Did you examine the front seat and front part of the car for bloodstains?"

"Yes. There were no bloodstains inside the car but there were some on the front fender and a few drops on the curve of the right fender."

"Were there any blood marks on the wheel?"

"There were a few drops on the tyre of the right front wheel and a considerable amount on the street."

"This car of yours, were you prepared to sell it?"

"I'd been offering it for sale."

"And would you have taken between £50 and £60 for it?"

"I was asking £60."

"And would have taken £50?"

"Very possibly."

"It could have been used to run as a taxi?"

"Yes."

Dr Lawson Gifford was next called by Henry Milne Radcliffe for the prosecution as the attorney-general had to leave the court to attend a Privy Council meeting. The chief justice asked the doctor to be as simple as possible in his use of medical terminology. "I always am," the doctor replied testily. Asked by Radcliffe to give the results of the postmortem performed on the body of Stedman Case, Gifford described how an incised wound to the right side of the neck had split the fleshy part of the ear.

"What was the direction?" Radcliffe enquired.

"It was downwards, forwards and inwards, towards the throat; the back of the throat. On its course, it made an oblique incision in the wall of the internal carotic artery and punctured the jugular vein."

"How long was the wound?"

"About one inch."

"Would a knife like this do it?" asked Radcliffe, showing the witness the knife.

"Yes. It was more like a thrust."

"How much of the blade was embedded?"

"I should say about three inches."

"If the knife produced had caused the wound, would it require a considerable amount of force?"

"Yes. I base that on the fact that the cartilage was cut."

"From the direction of the wound can you give any idea where the person using the knife was standing?"

"The stroke made was slightly behind, and perhaps slightly to the right, but I couldn't be certain of that."

Cross-examined by Manley, the doctor confirmed that the direction of the knife was "forwards, downwards and inwards".

"You traced it right through?" Manley quizzed.

"Yes."

'How far forward did the knife go?"

"I cannot say. It might have been half-an-inch or an inch."

"We will say that then."

"It would be about that."

"There is another distance, the external inwards?"

"I would not say more than half-an-inch."

"The downward direction would be about two inches?"

"Yes."

"On those figures, Doctor, the principal movement was undoubtedly downwards?"

"It might be."

"If someone stood in front of you", suggested Manley, "could you indicate with the knife the direction of the wound?"

"It is impossible to account for the vagaries of knife wounds."

"The point of the knife tends to turn backwards?"

"If you hold it that way, yes, but if you hold it the other way, it will turn forwards. The wound indicated that the cutting edge of the knife was lowest."

"It's difficult to place the position of the proper striking?"

"It would be very difficult to predict the position of the person inflicting the wound in relation to the person receiving the wound."

"And a good deal on the way in which the knife was held?" Manley submitted.

"Yes."

At this point, the foreman of the jury, Mr Frank Kinkead, requested that the jury would like to know if a person standing on the right side of the motor car could inflict such a wound on a person sitting on the left side of the car.

"If they stood on the running board they might," the doctor replied.

The chief justice questioned whether the wound could have been inflicted by a person standing parallel with the deceased.

"Yes," the doctor confirmed.

"Or in front slightly?"

"I don't think so," Gifford concluded.

The court adjourned for the day and the jurors were driven to the South Camp Road Hotel for the night. The chief justice instructed that they could, if they wished, walk in the grounds of the hotel, but leaving the premises was out of the question. When the court resumed the following day, David Gayle, a detective, was sworn in. He said that he had searched the body of Stedman Case and found no revolver on it. He had also searched the premises of 3 North Street on the day of the killing and did not find any revolver. He searched down to the gate and in the street. Later, that same day, around 4 o'clock in the afternoon, he returned with a search party and searched at the corner of North and Hanover Streets and the neighbourhood, also the premises of Mr Clarke once again, but found no revolver. The following day he went to the house of Ethel Lipman at 54 Luke Lane with Detective Corporal Allen. "We searched her room", he said, "but found no revolver."

Cross-examined by Manley, the detective stated that he had considerable experience in these matters, "I know how to search a room," he said in answer to Manley's insinuation that his search might not have been as thorough as he intended. "If the revolver had been in that room", Detective Gayle insisted, "I would have found it. I went there specifically to search for the revolver. I went through every article in Ethel Lipman's room where a revolver could possibly be hidden."

Mr Radcliffe called David Samuel Stewart, another detective, to the stand.

"Were you present when the accused was brought to the office?"

"Yes."

"Did you hear her say anything?"

"Yes. While sitting on the bench she said, 'I stabbed him because he took out a revolver at me'."

Manley rose to cross-examine. "Was the accused alone on the bench?" he enquired.

"Yes."

"Were you the nearest person to her."

"I was sitting near her."

"Was anyone nearer than you?"

"I don't remember."

"Was she speaking to anyone?"

Sybil Case (left) the victim's sister, accompanies Ethel Lipman (right) to the courthouse

"No, she wasn't speaking to anyone."

All eyes were on the stand when Ethel Lipman was called to give evidence. Conservatively dressed in black with a white open collar and white cuffs, she carried a vanity bag and had a handkerchief neatly tucked under a jade bangle on her left arm.

Answering questions posed by the attorney-general who had returned to court, Ethel Lipman said she was twenty-five years old and a domestic servant who lived at 54 Luke Lane. Yes, she knew Stedman Case, he was the chauffeur for lawyer Clarke: "He lived at Luke Lane with me, lived with me for seven years. I have three children for him." At this point, Lipman slipped the handkerchief from under the bangle to wipe away her tears. The attorney-general gave her time to compose herself before asking her what she knew about Louise Walker.

"On 24 May, I saw her on Luke Lane. Stedman's sister, Jane, was with me. Louise came up to me and said: 'Why you won't leave Stedman? If it's his ring you want, you won't get it. I'll kill him and then both of us lose him'."

"Did Stedman Case own a revolver?" asked the attorney-general.

"Yes. He kept it in a grip at my house. He took it away on the Saturday, the day before he was killed. He returned to my house at midday and slept there that night. He left about 8 o'clock the Sunday morning. That was the last time I saw him alive."

Ethel Lipman started to cry again but continued to give her evidence clearly and consistently even under severe cross-examination by Norman Manley:

"Did you expect Stedman Case to marry you?"

"Yes, sir."

"Did he fix a time to marry you?"

"He promised to marry me about a year ago."

"You knew Louise Walker?"

"Yes."

"When did you first meet her?"

"One evening she came in at the gate, looked at me and then went out. I didn't know who she was then."

"When did you get to know?"

"Some months after when I saw her and Stedman walking in the street."

"Did she ever speak to you?"

"She threw words at me in passing."

"You know Jane Case well?"

"Yes. She's one of Stedman's sisters."

"You knew that Jane was living with Louise Walker at one time?"

"Yes, sir."

"So you must have known that Louise and Stedman were on very friendly terms."

"Yes, sir."

"And you didn't like it?"

"No."

"Did you have a quarrel with Louise Walker?"

"Yes."

"You were angry when you found out about herself and Stedman?"

"Yes."

"Did she ever come on friendly terms to your yard?"

"No, sir."

"Didn't she come once when you were sick to help you?"

"No."

"Whereabouts did you meet Louise on 24 May?"

"At Luke Lane and West Queen Street corner."

"What were you doing there?"

"Jane Case and myself went out to buy cloth."

"I suggest that Jane Case was never there that morning."

"Yes, she was."

"And that it was you who accosted Louise."

"No, sir."

"Didn't you tell her you were going to Constant Spring to work obeah for her?"

"No, never," replied Ethel Lipman as she started sniffling.

"What sort of revolver did Stedman have?"

"I don't know."

"How long before the killing did you see him with this revolver?"

"About a week before."

"Did you ask him what he was going to do with it?"

"He told me it was for when he was travelling around."

"He used to keep it in a suitcase?"

"Yes."

"Was it in the suitcase on the day before the incident?"

"No. He said he wanted cartridges for it because he was going to the country."

"Did he get the cartridges?"

"No, he said he couldn't get them."

"You have no idea what happened to the revolver?"

"No, sir."

"Is that the truth?"

"Yes."

"The whole truth?"

"Yes, sir."

"You're quite sure?"

"Yes."

"Suppose you'd found the revolver in Mr Clarke's garden that morning when you went to see what had happened to Case. What would you have done with it?"

"Given it to Mr Clarke."

"You're quite sure about that?"

"Yes, sir."

Manley stared at the witness for a few moments then grasped the stand in front of him with both hands and leaned forward. "Miss Lipman, are you prepared to swear on your oath that you haven't got the revolver?"

The witness hesitated and the chief justice intervened: "Have you got the revolver?"

"Yes," Ethel Lipman sobbed.

"Why did you say you hadn't seen the revolver after Saturday, 5 June?" Manley mercilessly shot back.

"I only found it a few days ago."

"Where?"

"In Stedman's clothes."

"You must have examined his clothes earlier?" Manley queried. "Didn't you go through his belongings after he was dead?"

"No, sir."

"Can you remember what day it was that you found the revolver?"

"A day last week, sir. I can't remember if it was early in the week."

"And you say that you are telling the truth?"

"Yes."

"You heard that Louise Walker made the allegation that Stedman had threatened to shoot her?"

"Yes."

"As far back as 30 June, you heard that suggestion at the preliminary enquiry?"

"Yes."

"And you took no steps then to look for the revolver?"

"Yes, I did, but I didn't look in that particular suit."

"What sort of suit was it?"

"His drudging suit."

"You washed Stedman's clothes for him?"

"Yes."

"You had no idea why he should put the revolver in the suit?"

"No."

"Have you got the suit still?"

"Yes, sir, at home."

"Why did you say you that you hadn't seen the revolver since 5 June?"

Ethel Lipman shuffled uncomfortably in the box. "I intended to tell that I found it."

"And when, may I ask, did you intend to tell?" Manley challenged, a note of sarcasm creeping into his voice. "You also said at first that you didn't have the revolver."

Ethel Lipman lowered her head: "I have it, sir."

Manley sat down with relief. The revolver was the heart and soul of the matter.

The attorney-general, meanwhile, called Jane Case, sister of the deceased, to give her version of what took place on 24 May:

"Ethel and myself were going down Luke Lane and met Louise off Beckford Street. Louise said to Ethel, 'Why you don't leave my man?' I turned to Louise and said, 'She has children for him and you have none, why don't you leave him?' Louise then said, 'If I don't get Stedman's ring you won't get it. I'll kill him'."

"Anything else?"

"Louise said, 'If I don't revenge you, I'm not a Kingstonian'."

Cross-examined by Manley, Jane Case said that she didn't know that her brother owned a revolver.

"Did you tell Ethel Lipman that your brother and Louise Walker were on intimate terms?" Manley enquired.

"Yes. Ethel often come to my place."

"How did Ethel and Louise get on?"

"At first they used to talk, but afterwards they quarrelled."

"What time was it on 24 May that you met Walker along with Lipman?"

"About 11 o'clock."

"You didn't hear Ethel tell Louise she was going to Constant Spring to get an obeahman to kill her?"

"No. If I wasn't there they might have quarrelled but I told Ethel to say nothing."

"Was your brother going to marry Ethel?"

"I don't know, but he had children by her, and I suppose he might."

"There was reason to hope?"

"Yes."

"Did you hear that your brother was about to buy a taxi?"

"No."

The court adjourned for lunch. On the resumption, Elizabeth Case took the witness stand. Examined by the attorney-general, she confirmed that she was the mother of Stedman Case and knew both Louise Walker and Ethel Lipman. Asked about the events of 5 June, the day before the incident, Elizabeth Case replied:

"I went to Louise Walker's yard. It was about 8 o'clock in the evening and my son was there. While we were there, someone called out. Louise went outside, Stedman followed and I went out after. There was a woman at the gate; I didn't know her. I said goodnight and left for home. My son said he would soon catch me up. I didn't see him again till the Sunday morning when I went to Mr Clarke's yard and saw him lying dead."

Cross-examined by Manley, Mrs Case said that she had known Louise Walker for about a year.

"Were you and Louise on friendly terms?"

"Yes, since she knew my son."

"Did your daughter, Jane, bring any story to you about Louise and your son?"

"Yes, she heard Louise say she was going to kill Stedman."

"You went to Louise and told her that you had heard that she was going to kill Stedman?"

"Yes."

"Did you see your son again that night?"

"No."

"Did you see Louise in Luke Lane later that night and take her back home to Beeston Street?"

"No."

"You're quite sure of that?"

"Yes."

Elsie Veira was the next witness to be sworn. Questioned by the attorney-general, she told the court that Louise Walker used to live in a room next to her at 24 Beeston Street. Stedman came often to see Louise and sometimes slept there. What happened on Saturday night, 5 June? "Stedman and his mother were in Louise's room," Elsie Veira recalled. "I heard a rapping at the gate and went outside and saw Louise talking to another woman. I went back inside. Later, I went out and saw Louise and Stedman in Beeston Street. When they reached me, I heard Louise say, 'Yes, Stedman, if it wasn't for something, Nellie wouldn't have come to the house tonight'. Stedman and Louise went to the other side of the street and I went home to bed. Later, I heard Louise crying. I went to her and she said that Stedman's mother saved him that night. I went back to sleep. Next morning, the Sunday, Louise got up, dressed, and gave me a key and a grip and said that if I heard anything happened I was to go to Sutton Street and give up the key to the

Elizabeth Case, mother of the deceased

landlord and deliver the grip to her mother. I said, 'Louise, you not going to work?' She told me she was going to waylay Stedman at Mr Clarke's gate and serious things were going to happen. She then left the yard with a little biscuit bag in her hand. Later, that same Sunday morning I heard about the killing and I gave the grip to the police."

Cross-examined by Manley, Elsie Veira said that Louise was a "very quiet person" around the house.

"Do you know who the person Nellie is?" asked Manley.

"Yes."

"Nellie Bray, isn't it?"

"Yes, sir, that's correct."

"Did you gather that Louise was complaining about a friendship between Nellie and Stedman?"

"Yes."

"It was Nellie Bray who came to the house that Saturday night?"

"Yes."

"When she rapped on the gate, who went out first?"

"Louise."

"You didn't see the mother again that night?"

"No."

"Did you ask Louise what was the meaning of her strange conduct that Sunday morning?" Manley asked.

"No."

"Did Louise say anything about money?"

"No."

The attorney-general said that that concluded the case for the Crown and the court adjourned for the day. When the court resumed next morning, Manley applied to the chief justice for the revolver to be produced. He said he would have made this application the previous day but he thought that the prosecution would have produced the revolver. The attorney-general observed that if Manley had mentioned the revolver on the previous day, he would have had it there, but he didn't think there was any obligation on his part to produce it. At this point, the chief justice intervened and instructed the Inspector of Police to send for the revolver. Sergeant Major Humphries later went into the box and said that he'd found the revolver in the pocket of a man's jacket in Ethel Lipman's room at 54 Luke Lane.

Manley, meanwhile, faced the jury and outlined his defence. "This is a case which has attracted a great deal of attention", he said, "not only in Kingston but throughout the whole island of Jamaica. That is unfortunate, for it leads to discussion which in turn leads to opinion and that leads to judgment. You probably thought there was no defence. Your friends also, no doubt, said there was no defence. I am sure, gentlemen of the jury, that you will forget what you've heard, what you've thought and also forget what judgments you arrived at. The girl, for girl she is", said Manley as he pointed to the prisoner in the dock, "was not represented at the preliminary hearing before the magistrate. She is a poor girl, and the Law does not provide for her to get any assistance before she comes to this court. Her defence has not then been outlined with the clarity with which it will now be put before you." Manley's eyes beneath the heavy eyebrows, roved with cold scrutiny over the all-male jury. "After her arrest, Louise Walker spoke once, and only once, and you have all heard what she said: she stabbed Case because he drew a revolver at her. And she made this statement while sitting by herself in the detective office, and not in answer to any question or any suggestion, but quite voluntarily, and on her own account. That, gentlemen, is the defence.

"The theory of the Crown is that this was a crime motivated by jealousy. They have brought evidence to show that there were violent quarrels between the accused, Louise Walker, and another woman with whom the deceased had been living for many years. They have brought evidence to show that Louise Walker threatened to do violence to Stedman Case if the other did not give him up. You have been asked to believe that the strain became more than she could endure. There are crimes committed in the name of jealousy", Manley admitted, "but if you stop to reflect, you will find that there is more likelihood of a man killing for jealousy than a woman. You will find very few cases of a woman killing a man for jealousy, but there are many cases of men killing women for the same cause. It is also a fact, that in this country, women of Louise Walker's class are not particular in demanding that they should have their men exclusively unto themselves. They forgive a great deal. If you go into the facts of this case, you will find that this woman continued to live on terms of the greatest intimacy with this man, even though she knew that he had another woman and probably more than one."

Manley then brought some new facts into play. "You will shortly hear from Louise Walker herself", he told the jury, "that she worked in a place kept by Chinese in Barry Street, where she was employed as a cook. She was paid twelve shillings per week, but she also was employed as a general servant and she received many tips. Over a period of time, she had saved £20, and that she lent to Stedman Case. Why? Because he wished to buy a motor car to run as a taxi. He told her that he wanted to buy Mr Clarke's car and that he could get it for £50. When Case didn't purchase the car, Louise Walker demanded her money which no doubt the deceased had spent long before in trying to support the various establishments he kept up. They had a violent quarrel in the street about it on that Saturday night."

Manley then called Louise Walker to the witness box. "Tell us now what happened," Manley encouraged the young woman, who was still dressed from head to toe in pink.

"I told Stedman I'd made up my mind to leave him because he was only fooling me. I asked him for my money. He didn't give it to me."

"What did he do?"

"He threw me to the ground. I got up and then he took out a revolver and said, 'If you hold me, I'll shoot you'."

"What did you do?"

"I said I wanted my money. I told him if he didn't give it to me I would go to Mr Clarke and make a complaint."

"Did he say anything to that?"

"He said if I went to Mr Clarke he would shoot me."

"Did you know before this that he had a revolver?"

"No. I never saw him with a revolver before."

"What did it look like?"

"It was black and about nine inches long."

"Would you know a revolver that looked like that one?"

"Yes."

"Was it like this?" asked the chief justice holding up a cheap-looking nickel-plated gun.

"Yes."

"After you told Stedman that you were going to Mr Clarke, and he said that if you did, he would shoot you, what did you do?"queried Manley.

"I went home."

"Until you got home, did you see Stedman's mother at all?"

"No."

"Is it true that you said to Elsie Veira that it was Stedman's mother who saved him that night because she brought you home?"

"No."

"What happened next?"

"I went to bed."

"What time did you get up next morning?"

"About 6.30."

"Did you intend to go anywhere?"

"To see Stedman and if I couldn't get no satisfaction, to go to Mr Clarke."

"Did you see Elsie that morning?"

"Yes."

"Did you have a conversation?"

"No. She asked me if I'd drunk my tea and I shook my head."

"Did you give her your key?"

"No. She kept my key."

"Why?"

"So she could get in. She got home before me."

"Did you tell her to take your things to your mother?"

"No."

"Did you tell her that you were going to waylay Stedman and something serious was going to happen?"

"I had no talk with her."

"You've seen a knife in court."

"Yes."

"Is it yours?"

"Yes."

"Did you take it with you?"

"Yes."

"Why?"

"Because Stedman threatened me. I took the knife to protect myself."

Louise Walker went on to describe what happened when she reached North Street that morning. "I saw Stedman but he passed as if he didn't see me. I called to him."

"What did he say?"

"He said, 'Don't call me, you common woman'. Then he went on."

Louise Walker recalled that Case next came out of the Clarke residence driving the car with Mrs Clarke and the children inside. He returned after about ten minutes and parked the car in Hanover Street close to the sidewalk and facing the sea.

"Could anyone have passed between the sidewalk and the car?" Manley asked.

"No."

"Stedman went back to North Street?"

"Yes. He went in and came back out."

"Did you speak to him?"

"Yes. He walked towards the car and I went with him and we were talking."

"What about?"

"I said, 'Did you call me common?' He said, 'Yes'. I said, 'Why don't you tell Nellie these things?' He told me he didn't care a damn."

"Did you stop?"

"He stopped beside the front fender on the right of the car."

"Did you stop?"

"Yes."

"Did he ever get into the car?"

"No."

"Did you ask him for your money?"

"Yes. But he didn't answer. I said if he didn't give it to me I was going to Mr Clarke. He struck me with his hand and I fell down. I got up in a temper and said I was going to Mr Clarke."

"Then what happened?"

"Just as I was going to pass him, he put his hand in his pocket and started to take out the revolver and said if I tried to go to Mr Clarke he would shoot me."

"Did he take the revolver right out?"

"Yes."

"What happened then?"

"I got frightened and struck him with the knife."

"Take the knife and show the court how you held it."

Louise Walker was about to do so when the chief justice told a constable to take the knife away. "The witness should make the required demonstration with a pencil or ruler," he said, directing the jury that it was against all rules of procedure to allow any accused person to handle a lethal weapon whilst in the dock.

Manley accepted the rebuke and continued his questioning of Louise Walker after she had re-enacted the fatal blow with a pencil.

"When you struck did you mean to kill Stedman?"

"No."

"Did you mean to strike him?"

"Yes."

"Did you have it in your mind where you were going to strike him?"

"No."

"Was it solely because he drew out the revolver that you struck at him with the knife?"

"Yes."

"And when you struck did you see the blood spurt out?"

"Yes."

"What did you feel then?"

"Frightened."

"Did you realize that you had cut him badly?"

"Yes."

"He turned and ran up the road?"

"Yes."

"And you went after him?"

"Yes."

"Why?"

"I realized I'd hurt him. I wanted to catch him to see what happened. I never meant to hurt him seriously." Louise Walker had used a handkerchief to continually wipe her eyes whilst giving evidence, but now she openly sobbed. Manley paused so that she could collect herself before asking her if she remembered being handed over to Mr McLarty.

"Yes," came the reply.

"And you went to the gate with him."

"Yes."

"There were people at the gate?"

"Yes."

"What did they say?"

"They said Stedman was dead. I fainted."

"When were you next conscious?"

"I came to myself in the detective office."

"You said, 'I cut him because he took a revolver at me'?"

"I don't know. I never really came to myself until the next day."

The court adjourned. The next morning, the crowd trying to get into the courtroom was so great that the proceedings had to be adjourned in order to clear the doorways. Several minutes later the trial got under way with Louise Walker being cross-examined by the Attorney-General, F.C. Wells-Durrant.

"Am I correct in saying that Stedman was a slim, tall, good-looking young man?" he asked Louise Walker.

"Yes."

"Your height is about 5 feet 4 inches?"

"Yes."

"So Stedman was about 6 inches taller than you are?"

"Yes."

"What sort of dress were you wearing that morning?"

"A white dress."

"Is this the dress?" asked the attorney-general, showing the prisoner a white dress.

"Yes."

"What undergarments had you on?"

"A slip and a merino."

"Tight fitting?"

"Yes."

"On what day did you lend Stedman Case this £20?"

"In March this year."

"Did he give you a receipt?"

"No."

"There was no one present when you lent him the money?"

"No."

"Did you tell Elsie that you were going to waylay Stedman at Mr Clarke's gate and serious things were going to happen?"

"No."

"Why should Elsie say those things?"

Manley was on his feet, "I object!"

The chief justice said that the attorney-general could ask the witness if she knew of any motive.

"Can you give us any motive why Elsie should say those things?" the attorney-general asked.

"She's engaged to one of Stedman's friends."

"When did you first hear about Nellie Bray?"

"I took lunch at the soap factory and I saw Stedman kissing her under a tree."

"He explained it to your satisfaction?"

"I let him know I was angry. He followed me and we made it up."

"When next did you see Nellie Bray?"

"Not until Saturday 5 June."

"On that night she came to the yard gate?"

"Yes."

"You were angry when you found her there?"

"Yes."

"You spoke to her?"

"I asked her who she wanted and she said, 'Stedman'. I called him."

"What happened when Stedman came?"

"They were whispering and I couldn't hear. I walked off and when I came back Stedman was still standing at the gate. I said, 'Stedman, if it wasn't something, Nellie wouldn't come here'."

"What happened then?"

"He sucked his teeth and walked away."

"Where did he go?"

"To the west side of Beeston Street."

"Where did you start to quarrel again?"

"When we were walking along the street."

"You asked him for your money and he wouldn't give it to you and he chucked you on the ground?"

"Yes."

"There were people in the street?"

"I only saw a policeman." A ripple of mirth passed over the courtroom.

"When he threw you down, you saw a policeman?"

"No, after."

"When he chucked you down, there was no one in the street?"

"No."

"You got up, and as you did, he drew his revolver out of his pocket?"

"Yes."

"And you said that if he did not give you the money, you would go to Mr Clarke?"

"Yes."

"And he said that if you went to Clarke, he would shoot you?"

"Yes."

"Let's talk about what happened on the following morning. Did you wrap up the knife before you went out?"

"Yes, it was in a piece of thin paper."

"Tissue paper?"

"No, a piece of brown paper."

"Where did you put it?"

"I had it in my hand."

"Why did you wrap it up in paper?"

"Because I was taking it out."

"Was it to prevent Stedman seeing it was a knife?"

"I wasn't hiding it from him."

"Is it not true that you had it in your bosom?"

"No, my dress was slack."

"Do you know Lucille Ramsay?"

"I know her face but I've never spoken to her."

"When she says that you took the knife out of your bosom, it isn't true?"

"No."

"I understand that the stabbing did not take place in the car?"

"No."

"It took place outside the car?"

"Yes."

"Beside the front wheel?"

"Yes."

"You were face to face?"

"Yes."

"Stedman put his hand in his pocket and started to draw out the revolver?"

"Yes."

"Just as he was drawing it out you stabbed him?"

"Yes."

"Did you tear the paper from the knife?"

"It dropped off."

"You still held the knife?"

"When he pitched me, the paper dropped off."

"Show us again how you stabbed him."

Louise Walker demonstrated with a pencil.

"Stedman was six inches taller than you."

"Yes."

"You must have raised your hand?"

"As I struck, he moved his head."

"You were still facing him?"

"I tried to pass him."

"But you were facing him when he tried to draw the revolver?"

"Yes."

"And you must have been facing him when you stabbed him?"

"Yes."

"And he ran and you ran after him?"

"Yes."

"How were you holding the knife when you ran after him?"

"I don't know. I ran after him to see what happened."

"Why didn't you throw away the knife?"

"I was frightened. I didn't know what I was doing."

Manley next called Stephen Fyffe who said that he worked as an assistant to Hwee Sam who had a wholesale provision store at 108 Barry Street. The witness incorrectly pronounced the name as Hugh and was promptly corrected by the chief justice, "No, no. Hwee not Hugh."

Fyffe said he'd known Louise Walker for about ten months. She cooked, kept the office and ran errands and did odd jobs for the lodgers who lived above the store.

"So besides her wage, Louise Walker had the opportunity of earning extra money?" Manley asked Fyffe.

"Yes."

"What sort of girl was she about the place?"

"I don't think you can do that, Mr Manley," the chief justice intervened.

"Are you ruling that I cannot bring evidence as to her quiet and gentle character?" Manley asked the judge.

"The general rule is that it is admitted that there is nothing against the accused. Mr Attorney-General, do you object?"

"I was going to object when Your Honour interrupted," replied Wells-Durrant.

"There has been a suggestion that the girl was of a quarrelsome disposition. I was going to show that it was contrary to the general disposition of the accused by all who knew her," Manley responded.

The attorney-general moved that as public prosecutor, he was loath to take objection to anything that might assist the accused, but he could not really see that this evidence was admissible. He was not conscious of any attack being made on the girl.

"I think it would be creating an evil precedent if we deviated from the rule of evidence," the chief justice concluded. "The character of the accused should not be drawn in."

Manley turned back to the witness and asked him if he remembered having a conversation with Louise Walker about her personal affairs.

"Yes," the witness replied. "She said, 'Mr Fyffe, I'm living with a man who has plenty of girls and I want to leave him to go away'. I said, 'Then why you look so sad? There are plenty of other men in Kingston'. She said, 'It's not the men, it's the money'. I asked, 'What money?'"

"What did she reply?"

"She said she lent the man money."

The attorney-general leapt up. "I must object."

Manley redirected his line of questioning. "On Saturday, 5 June, Louise Walker was at work?"

"Yes."

"She went about it in the usual way?"

"Yes."

"Did she seem her normal self?"

"Quite normal."

"Can you give me some idea of when this conversation took place?"

"About midday."

"I mean what month?"

"Just a few days before this awful thing happened."

Manley said that this closed the case for the defence. He removed his wig and ran his hand through his hair before making his final address to the jury.

"When a person is killed and it is admitted that another person is responsible for the killing, and you have all the facts before you, the circumstances will lead to one of three possible verdicts. First, if you believe in the unvarnished tale of the prosecution, your verdict will be one of murder. On the story told by the defence, there are two verdicts open to you. The first is manslaughter. If you believe that Louise Walker struck the blow in fear or anger, then your verdict will be one of manslaughter, that is, if you do not believe that she was in danger. If a person threatens someone with a revolver, it is the law that they are entitled to protect themselves. They cannot wait until the weapon is fired. If you come to the conclusion that Louise Walker was speaking the truth when she said that she was threatened with the revolver on the night of 5 June, and on the following morning the threat was repeated, and the revolver was drawn or attempted to be drawn by Case, and that she struck him with the knife because of that, then your verdict will be one of not guilty.

"The Crown has suggested that it was as a result of jealousy between Ethel Lipman and Louise Walker that the accused eventually decided to take the man's life. But you have heard Louise Walker say that she had made up her mind to leave this man but wanted to get her money back so that she could go in peace. The appearance of Nellie Bray on that Saturday night prompted Louise Walker to make her final decision to leave Stedman Case. Louise Walker told you about it with real candour. She didn't try to keep anything back. I ask you to accept her story that on 5 June she made up her mind to leave Stedman Case, but she wanted a satisfactory understanding about the money. She was sure that he still had this money because she had given it to him to put towards £50 to buy a car, and this he had not done."

Manley next went on to examine the relations between Louise Walker and Ethel Lipman. "There are a good many women who do not mind sharing a man and that is why it is rare for a woman to kill a man. She will fight for him but she won't kill him. With regard to the statements made that Louise Walker said that she was going to kill Stedman, you will appreciate that it was an attempt to poison the mother's mind against her, for no doubt it was believed that the person of whom the mother approved would be the wife of the man."

Manley next referred to the night of 5 June. "We know that Louise Walker was angry. She asked Stedman for her money and as he did not have it, he no doubt tried to frighten her off. It's how people of his class behave. He knocked her down and told her to keep her mouth shut. When she got up, determined to get her money, he took out a revolver, and said he would shoot her if she held on to him. She then said that she would go to Mr Clarke. It was natural that the man would not want her to go to his employer if he had spent the money. He then told her that if she did that, he would shoot her. The next morning, Louise Walker got up to go and see Case. You have heard the witness, Elsie Veira, say that when Louise came home, she said that Stedman's mother had saved him that night, for she had brought her home. But you know that Stedman's mother did not take her home; she said so. And if you don't believe that statement, I ask you not to believe the statements that Elsie Veira testified that Louise made the following morning: that she was going to waylay Stedman and serious things were going to happen. Remember, Elsie was a friend of Stedman's and was engaged to a friend of his. You know that people come into court and say things that are not in the remotest way relative to the facts. I ask you to carefully consider those statements. Then we come to the events after Louise set out that morning. I know the girl took a knife with her. She has told you her reason for taking the knife that day, it was because she had been threatened. The girl might not have intended to use the knife, she might have thought that if she showed it, it would be enough. She took this knife with the intention of protecting herself. I ask you to imagine what took place during that meeting with Case. The act could not have been done in the way in which it was described by the young girl, Lucille Ramsay. The man would not have sat still in the car and done nothing to protect himself. I submit you will have great difficulty in accepting her evidence. As soon as the knife was drawn from the wound, the blood would have pumped out. You have heard that there was no blood on the car except on the front wheel. There was none at all in the car. The blood on the front of the car is consistent with the story told by the accused. If the blow had been struck when the man was sitting inside the car there would have been blood all over the inside of the car. I do not suggest that the girl came into court to tell what she had not seen, but I submit that she told us what she believed she saw. You then heard how Louise Walker had run after Stedman Case. Isn't it human nature to go after someone you're close to when you've hurt them, to see the extent of the injury and to apologize? That's what Louise Walker did. When she heard that the man was dead, she fainted. You have heard the story of the eye-witness, and also the story of Louise Walker, and you will have to decide. The revolver, however, is at the core of this case. I don't know what conclusion the Crown is going to come to with regard to this. They have to give some explanation of it. The Crown should bring witnesses to show where it was on the Monday, after the crime had been committed. It must have been given to the person who now has it by someone who picked it up. Ethel Lipman told you that she did not see the revolver until one day last week. No one except herself and perhaps one other person will ever know how it came into her possession. I submit, that if Stedman Case drew the revolver and the girl struck because she was afraid, any human being is entitled to that measure of protection. You don't have to wait until the weapon is levelled at you. She would have struck him blindly, not knowing where she struck. You have to be sure in your minds that you are not making a mistake in giving your verdict. I ask you to consider carefully every point."

The court adjourned for lunch. On the resumption, the attorney-general addressed the jury. He asked them to get clearly into their minds the facts that were beyond dispute. "It is quite clear that on Sunday morning, 6 June, Stedman Case was killed by being stabbed with a table knife. It is also quite clear that the person who stabbed him was the accused woman, Louise Walker. It then boils down for you to decide whether Stedman Case was wounded under justifiable circumstances or not. My learned friend has said, very properly, that there is one central factor in the case, and that is the revolver. Whether Case had the revolver on the morning of 6 June, is a matter for you to consider. The evidence on that point is very conflicting. One witness of the occurrence said that there was no revolver, and the only other evidence that there was a revolver, is the evidence of the accused herself. The incident took place about 9 o'clock on a Sunday morning in a public street in the vicinity of Mr Clarke's house. You have heard that the police searched diligently on the spot and on the man's person but found no revolver. You have therefore only the evidence of the accused woman herself that the revolver was there. The only other evidence about the revolver was from the witness, Ethel Lipman, who said that last week she found it in the pocket of a jacket owned by the deceased. You will have to ask yourselves how this revolver, if it was in the possession of Stedman Case on the morning of 6 June, got into the possession of this woman. There are only two possible ways that I can see. Either the police failed in their search or Ethel Lipman went to the scene, found the revolver and took it home, not saying anything about it until she was in the witness box. Why, you might ask, should she do that? She might not have said anything in the witness box. It would have been easy for her to say nothing at all about it. I think it is a fair assumption that the revolver was not there on that Sunday morning. If the revolver was there, does it justify the accused committing the act she herself confessed that she committed? If the revolver was not there, there is only one possible verdict you can come to on the facts, and that is murder. There does not seem any justification for the act in the absence of the revolver. You will remember that the girl left the house with a knife wrapped up in a piece of paper, and that she carried that knife in her hand. When she was asked if she took the paper off before she stabbed Stedman Case, she said that it dropped off. It is rather difficult to see how the paper could have dropped off without the knife falling out of her hand. The paper fell off when the deceased pushed her on the ground. She held the open knife in her hand and approached him. It may be that Case drew the revolver to defend himself. If, indeed, he saw the woman coming towards him in a threatening manner, he would be quite justified in doing so. You have to consider carefully the facts with regard to this revolver. It is a fact that Louise Walker and Stedman Case could not have been facing each other. Dr Gifford has said that it would have to be done by a person standing at the side or behind. You will have to take that point into consideration. You have been told a great deal about the attributes of the female sex with regard to their relations with men and other members of their sex of whom they are jealous. So far as their relations with men are concerned, I do not profess to be able to speak of it with the positiveness of my learned friend. I find it remarkable that the accused could go to visit Ethel Lipman when she was sick and look after her children and yet become so virtuously indignant when she hears about Nellie Bray. It does not seem to me quite natural. You have heard the story of the accused, and you are asked to come to the conclusion that Ethel Lipman, Jane Case and Elsie Veira all came to this court and deliberately told falsehoods. I suggest that you will hesitate to believe that when you come to consider the facts. Can you as conscientious men, anxious to do your duty, say that this girl cut the man in self-defence? I venture to ask you to consider the facts very carefully."

The chief justice, in summing up to the jury, remarked on the evidence given by the prisoner herself and emphasized that "to totally discharge her from the indictment, would misconform to Law". For this direction, he gave two reasons. First, the prisoner told them that Case had threatened her with a revolver on the night of 5 June. She told them, secondly, that consequently to this, she went on 6 June to waylay him to demand her money, and armed herself with a knife. That conduct was not reasonable, and the circumstances which led to the killing of Case as deponed by the prisoner herself, was manslaughter and not justifiable homicide. The chief justice explained that manslaughter was a crime between murder and excusable or justifiable homicide. Sometimes it was on the borderline of murder, and in England, it was occasionally punished with all the severity of murder itself. On the other hand, it might be on the borderline between murder and justifiable homicide. In that event it was dealt with in the manner suitable. The jury had to consider whether Louise Walker killed Case deliberately on the morning of 6 June or whether she killed him in the way she herself described. "You are not called upon to find in your verdict exactly where she stood when she dealt the blow," the chief justice concluded. "What you have to ask yourselves is whether the prisoner stabbed a man who was defenceless and not prepared, or, alternatively did she slay a brutal fellow who had taken her money and then when she asked for it, retaliated with savage violence?"

The jury retired to consider their verdict at 3.50 p.m. Louise Walker remained in the dock while the crowded courtroom buzzed with comment and speculation as to the outcome. As the minutes ticked slowly by, Louise Walker appeared increasingly uneasy. She played nervously with her handkerchief, twisting and turning it in her hands. Suddenly, she got up from her chair and dropped in a huddled heap on the floor, her face hidden in her arms. After an absence of fifty minutes the jury returned and Louise Walker was asked to stand up for the verdict. The foreman, Mr Frank Kinkead, was grim, "Your Honour", he said, addressing the chief justice, "we cannot agree."

The chief justice asked if there was any difficulty which he could deal with or any point which needed simplifying. Frank Kinkead asked for an explanation of manslaughter. The chief justice replied that if they had any reasonable doubt as to the clearness of the prosecution's story, they could convict on the lesser offence of manslaughter which was an unlawful slaying.

The jury retired again at 4.49 p.m. Louise Walker, who throughout the trial had maintained a composure that showed considerable self-control, became hysterical just before the jury returned half an hour later and had to be soothed by a sub-inspector and two constables. When she finally quietened down, the chief justice asked the foreman of the jury if they had reached a verdict. This time, Frank Kinkead without any hesitation announced: "Your Honour, we find the prisoner, Louise Walker, guilty of manslaughter."

Manley was on his feet in a trice. He had an application to make, he said, but the chief justice advised him to save it until 10.30 a.m. the following day. Louise Walker was remanded in custody to await sentence.

When the Circuit Court resumed the next morning, Manley asked that before sentence was passed on Louise Walker, he would like to make an application under Law 25 of 1872 which directed that if there was doubt surrounding the whole of the case for the Crown, it could be retried before a Full Court. Manley said that they had no Court of Criminal Appeal[2] and it was the only course open to him. The chief justice said he gave his directions on old authorities; he would look into it. Manley asked if the chief justice would accept a written application. Sir Barrett-Lennard said he had no objection, Manley could search the old authorities and he would think it over.

Addressing the prisoner now, the chief justice said that he had intended to be ready to deal with her case, but the matter had given him a great deal of trouble and anxiety because he was anxious that the sentence should be the right one, and he was a little dubious as to what was right. He was going to give up the luncheon interval to consider it further and sentence would be passed at 2 o'clock.

The crowd outside and in the courtroom during the early stages of the proceedings was nothing like as large as on previous days, but as the day wore on, and it became evident that a verdict would be arrived at that day, the crowd had grown steadily larger until there were several hundred waiting outside the court, and the room itself was packed. The Hon. J.A.G. Smith looked in for an hour during the summing up. Mr Radcliffe was also present for a time, as was the Solicitor-General, Mr Baggett Grey, and Mr MacMillan in addition to several other well-known solicitors, to say nothing of a regular host of solicitors' clerks. Several strangers were also present, including two American women who had been following the trial throughout.

When the court resumed, Louise Walker stood quite still while the chief justice addressed her, but she seemed to be thinking of other things and not paying much attention to what was being said. There was a hushed expectancy amongst the dense crowd packed behind the barrier at the back of the courtroom and all were straining and standing on tiptoe to look at the Bench.

"Louise Walker", began the chief justice, "I have been considering your case with a great measure of attention, and though bound to accept the verdict of manslaughter, I regard it beyond question, a type of manslaughter which is on the very borderline of murder itself. The sentence you will receive is the sentence which was passed some years ago in England on a young woman who behaved not exactly as you behaved but whose conduct was roughly like yours. She received a sentence of seven years penal servitude and such will be the sentence passed on you, but by good conduct you will earn a very appreciable remission and directions will be given in according with usages known hitherto to me that the sentence be brought up for consideration at the end of three years."

When the chief justice pronounced the sentence there was a gasp from the rear of the courtroom and voices were raised in discussion pro and con the verdict. Over the past few days, the public did not cease to ask why Louise Walker had carefully wrapped up a knife and taken it with her to the fatal interview. To protect herself? But if she really believed that her life was threatened, why did she so deliberately jeopardize it? The man did not seek her with a revolver; she sought him with a knife. And he was killed. As for the revolver. Was Ethel Lipman early on the scene? Did she remove the revolver and take it home? Or did someone pick it up and give it to her?

During the sentencing Louise Walker stood perfectly still in the box looking at the wall above the chief justice's head and at the end seemed oblivious to her fate. A police officer touched her on the shoulder and she turned round and followed him out the courtroom and down the steps.

Three days later, at a sitting of the Home Circuit Court, before the chief justice, Manley advanced further arguments in support of his application that the case be slated for the Full Court.[3] Manley said that he did not propose to go over the ground he had previously covered re old authorities, but so far as those cases went, it laid down the doctrine that the party seeking to justify itself by self-defence must be free from original fault. No man can justify self-defence when the incident was started by himself. Unlawful conduct of any sort which led up to the killing robbed them of justification. A threat by a person to prevent another from committing an offence would not deprive him of the right to claim self-defence. Manley submitted that in this case, the accused was not guilty of any unreasonable conduct. There was no evidence of any intention to use force, but that when a sudden assault was made, force was used to repel it. Manley asked the chief justice to consider the point which he believed important.

The chief justice replied that he had had the opportunity of considering the matter before and after Manley's charge. Additionally, Mr Justice Brown had been good enough to afford him the advantage of his opinion and both of them agreed that the sentence should stand. The chief justice said that his view then, and now, was that when a person said he would kill if molested by another, it was unreasonable that such an act was with the avowed purpose of protecting life and limb. Society was originally organized for the express purpose of depriving persons from personally venting their spleen. "In my opinion", the chief justice concluded, "there is no evidence to support the application on the ground of self-defence and I am unable to accede to the request."

The following day, an editorial appeared in the *Gleaner* praising Manley for his defence of Louise Walker.[4] "All that an able advocate could do he has done", the paper said, "and we for one, as we survey the case, are decidedly of the opinion that the stars in their courses fought for Louise Walker when the government appointed such a lawyer as Mr Manley to appear on her behalf. The charge was one of murder, the jury brought in a verdict for manslaughter; the chief justice expressed the view that this woman's crime was, if manslaughter, on the borderline of murder, and yet he sentenced her to only seven years imprisonment and informed her that if she conducted herself properly in prison she would be brought before the court three years hence for a revision of her sentence . . . In our opinion, Louise Walker has been very lucky to escape with her life."

Headquarters House on the corner of Duke and Beeston Streets, Kingston, where Manley appeared before a 1925 Commission of Enquiry on behalf of the Mayor and the KSAC. Now the head office of the Jamaica National Heritage Trust, Headquarters House was once the meeting place of Jamaica's legislature. It was here in 1955 that Manley was sworn in as chief minister

17

KSAC under Fire

In Mr N.W. Manley, we have a man and a lawyer of whom this country has every reason to be proud. He owes his position to his own unaided exertions; what he has obtained he has toiled for; his character has matched his intelligence, and both have been informed by a degree of modesty rarely found amongst the young men of any profession.

The Gleaner
10 November 1925

In October 1925, Manley found himself performing in a different arena: Headquarters House on Duke Street, Kingston. A commission had been appointed to enquire into the conduct and management of the Kingston and St Andrew Corporation, following a public outcry over the street improvement programme. Owners of properties which fronted and flanked the areas set aside for improvement were outraged to hear that they would have to contribute to the cost of reconstruction, and when a heap of stones for the project disappeared from Port Royal Street, they cried foul. The Press took up their case. Questions were raised whether contracts had been given to any members of the governing council. Added to this, the continuing arguments between the engineers for the project as to whether or not the high level intercepting sewer should be a gravity sewer or a pressure one, had seriously held up the completion of the work and the KSAC had come under fire from both the Press and public at large.

The Mayor, the Hon. Altamont E. DaCosta, and the corporation's councillors themselves were at loggerheads over various aspects of the project, but when the government called for a commission of enquiry, they unanimously voted for legal representation. Manley was subsequently briefed by Mr S.B. Cargill of the firm Cargill, Cargill and Dunn, to appear before the commission on behalf of the mayor and the corporation.[1] It was a long-drawn-out enquiry which began on 12 October 1926 and came to an end twenty-nine days later when Alderman Dr E.E. Penso gave evidence. He contended that the improvement works should have been the responsibility of the Public Works Department which had the organization and the equipment to carry them out. Penso said that he was still strongly in favour of handing over the remaining portion of the work to the Public Works Department, but objected to the proposal that the director of Public Works should exercise supervision and control while the responsibility for the work should still rest with the corporation.

On the last day of the hearing, Manley cogently summed up the position of the KSAC in the matter. He asked the commission to confine its attention to essentials and ignore trivial matters which had not been fully investigated. "I strongly urge you, in the preparation of your report", Manley implored commission members, "to confine yourselves to determining the broader issues, the main one of which is street reconstruction, and not waste time with minor matters, such as the charges made against employees which have not been fully investigated, and criticisms of the councillors, as this will only tend to increase the adverse criticism by members of the public and the Press of the corporation, and probably end in its dissolution and the disenfranchising of the Corporate Area."

Manley submitted that the members of the commission had all the evidence before them and so their findings would be based on fact. "If, in the course of your investigation, you find cause for blame, then I ask you to apportion the blame where it is due, be it the council of the corporation, the staff of the corporation, the commissioner or the government itself."

Manley contended that the government had shirked its responsibility in the matter of street reconstruction by taking advantage of a loophole provided in one of its own laws which was badly drawn, and had thrown the burden of street improvement on the corporation which it should not have been made to bear. He urged the commision to put forward some acceptable scheme to carry on the work immediately, as the reconstruction programme was almost at a standstill. This meant money was being wasted and the longer this went on, the greater would be the waste.

Four days later, the regular fortnightly meeting of the council of the KSAC was held.[2] Among those present were His Worship, the Mayor, the Hon. Altamont E. DaCosta, and Councillor Augustus Bain Alves. During the meeting, a letter from Messrs. Cargill, Cargill and Dunn was read. It enclosed their statement of account for £80, the amount due for legal representation. "Great Scott! Where's the money to come?" Bain Alves blurted out. Alderman Farreir said, "There was a lot of talk about it when the matter came up. Now who's going to pay?" "The councillor who moved the motion and carried it will have to pay," Bain Alves responded amid laughter. "I brought out that point as to whether there was any provision for us to retain counsel for that purpose when Mr Manley was here and there was none, so you've got to ask the government's sanction."

Councillor H.G.T. Drew said no one thought the bill would have been so much. It was necessary for them to have the best legal assistance at the enquiry owing to the misrepresentations which had been made to the government. He felt sure that government would sanction the expenditure.

The commission's lengthy report was published on 3 December, advising that the work should remain in the hands of the KSAC. The commissioners found that no contracts had been given to any members of the council, nor had any contracts been given to middlemen. As to the provisions of Law 36 of 1923, whereby the owners of properties which fronted and flanked on the improved areas were required to contribute to the cost of reconstruction, the commission suggested that the government repeal that portion of the law and the cost of the work be met by the general funds for the Corporate Area. Additionally, the commission made nineteen recommendations to assist the KSAC in becoming more efficient, the first of which was the appointment of a chief accountant.

Meanwhile, the *Gleaner* published a lengthy editorial on the enquiry and Manley's representation of the KSAC. "We are of the opinion that the commission had no sort of intention of stressing petty matters or of emphasizing little carelessnesses and neglects for the purpose of humiliating the mayor and the corporation," it read. "But of course, Mr Manley in making this appeal was doing his duty, and here we come to the subject upon which we propose to say a few words today. We wish to write about a young man whose ideal of duty is high, and whose endeavour to live up to that ideal is winning for him the approbation of every man and woman in this colony . . . N.W. Manley will win the attention of his audience, whether it be an audience of learned judges, of politicians, of government officers or of the working public; he will always command attention, for what he has to say is worth hearing, and it is the man with something to say who secures an enduring regard. Such a man might win to the highest position open to a West Indian barrister, if he aimed at it. The chief justiceship of one of these colonies is not an impossible goal to him; it is indeed a very probable goal if his ambitions should lead him to aspire to it."[3]

Little did the *Gleaner,* or Manley himself, know that in Headquarters House, thirty years later, Manley would make another masterly speech, this time on his appointment as chief minister, not chief justice. But all that lay ahead. For the moment, arsons, murders, seductions, and other frailties of human nature would continue to call for Manley's attention.

NOTES

PREFACE

1 The Manley Papers.

2 Wayne Brown, *Edna Manley, The Private Years: 1900–1938* (London: André Deutsch, 1975).

3 Sir Philip Sherlock, *Norman Manley – A Biography (London: Macmillan, 1980)*, p. 65.

4 The Hon. Vivian Blake, Memorial Lecture, p. 32.

5 See, for example, trial notes: *Hawthorne* v. *Barclay*, National Library of Jamaica.

6 The Manley Papers.

7 Manley, Unfinished Autobiography.

8 Michael Manley interview.

9 Manley, Diary, 17 October 1937.

10 The Manley Papers.

11 Rachel Manley, ed., *Edna Manley – The Diaries (*Kingston: West Indies Publishing Ltd, 1989).

12 Manley, Unfinished Autobiography.

13 *Gleaner*, 1 May 1929, p. 12.

14 *Gleaner*, 30 May 1923, p. 6.

15 18 April 1950.

16 *Gleaner*, 11 July 1951, p. 1.

17 Rachel Manley, *The Diaries*, p. 151.

SERIES INTRODUCTION

1 *Gleaner*, 3 February 1955, p. 1.

2 *Gleaner*, 15 August 1955, p. 11.

3 Manley, in a letter to his future wife, Edna, 14 October 1919.

4 Norman Manley, Unfinished Autobiography.

5 See Michele Johnson, "A Century of Murder in Jamaica 1880–1980", *Jamaica Journal* 3, no. 2 (May 1987).

6 Norman Manley, *Unfinished Autobiography*.

7 Ibid.

8 Miss Iris DeFreitas of British Guiana was the first woman to be admitted to practice at the Bar of any West Indian colony. She graduated from Aberystwyth College, University of Wales, and was admitted to the Bar of Barbados on 31 August 1929. In Jamaica, Gloria Cumper was called to the Bar, Middle Temple, 18 June 1947 and admitted to practice in Jamaica on 17 July 1948.

9 *Gleaner*, 10 November 1925, p. 8.

10 This is the highest professional honour that can be conferred on a practising barrister. The right to use the title 'King's Counsel', or 'Queen's Counsel', dependent on whether the reigning sovereign is male or female, to occupy a place in the inner Bar, and to wear a silk gown, is reserved for members of the profession of unimpeachable integrity and character, who have been in practice for at least ten years, and who have achieved distinction in the practice of the law.

11 Jamaica Law Debating Society Dinner. *Gleaner*, 6 December 1926, p. 3.

12 Vic Reid, *Horses of the Morning* (Kingston, Jamaica: Caribbean Authors Publishing Co., 1985), p. 49.

13 Ansell Hart, *Monthly Comments*, December 1968.

14 'Matters Under the Ken of the Man in the Street'. *Gleaner*, 19 January 1923, p. 13.

15 Sir Philip Sherlock, *Norman Manley – A Biography* (London: Macmillan, 1980), p. 66.

16 See the trial of Harold Kerr. *Gleaner*, 25 May 1923, p. 3.

17 The Manley Papers.

18 See note 10 above.

19 The Manley Papers.

20 *Gleaner*, 3 October 1932, p. 10.

21 Manley, Diary, 29 April 1937.

22 *Gleaner*, 6 February 1951, p. 7.

23 The Manley Papers.

24 Ibid.

25 Ibid.

26 *Gleaner*, 30 December 1946, p. 5.

27 *Gleaner*, 3 June 1931, p. 1.

28 *Gleaner*, 3 September 1969, p. 10.

29 Fletcher interview.

30 *Gleaner*, 17 September 1969, p. 8.

31 *Gleaner*, 25 May 1949, p. 13.

32 Fletcher interview.

33 Abendana, V.O. 'Personal Glimpses of Norman Manley'. *Gleaner*, 21 September 1969, p. 7.

34 Ibid.

35 *Gleaner*, 6 October 1926, p. 10.

36 The Alexander murder trial. The Manley Papers.

37 Manley, Diary, 26 April 1937.

38 *Rex v. Melville. Gleaner*, 1 May 1937, p. 1.

39 In a speech delivered to the members of the Philadelphia Bar Association. *Gleaner*, 23 June 1963, p. 1.

40 Ibid.

41 Abendana, op. cit.

42 Fletcher interview.

43 Manley, in a letter to his wife, 19 October 1923.

44 During a debate held by the Jewish Literary Society. *Gleaner*, 29 May 1937, p. 10.

45 Ibid.

46 *Gleaner*, 15 August 1955, p. 11.

47 *Lin Kin Chow v. Jones. Gleaner*, 29 March 1923, p. 13.

48 *Gleaner*, 12, 13 July 1928, p. 6 in both instances.

49 Manley, Unfinished Autobiography.

50 Manley, Unfinished Autobiography.

51 Manley, Diary, 17 October 1937.

52 Edna Manley, in a letter to Norman, 4 May 1937.

53 Manley, Unfinished Autobiography.

54 Manley, in a letter to his wife, 17 January 1924.

55 The Manley Papers.

56 Michael Manley interview.

57 *Gleaner*, 15 March 1959, p. 1. *Trinidad Chronicle*, 14 March 1959.

58 Posthumously on 15 September 1969.

59 Manley was buried on Sunday, 7 September 1969 at National Heroes Park.

60 Church Register, 30 May 1699. Marriage between Edward Tittle and Lucia Mollison.

61 After many years of discussion, the Federation of the West Indies was finally decided on at the London Conference held in 1956. It was established in 1958 and Manley, with his immense Caribbean-wide popularity, was expected to contest a seat and possibly become the first Prime Minister of the Federation. He decided to stay on in Jamaica. In 1960, the Jamaica Labour Party (JLP) declared against Federation as a matter of policy. The People's National Party leader, Norman Manley, who was also Premier at the time, decided to put the matter to the electorate in a referendum. The JLP slogan "Jamaica Yes, Federation No" won the day and Jamaica opted out of the three-year-old Federation of the West Indies in 1961 to go it alone into Independence.

62 McFarlane interview.

63 Ibid.

64 Ibid.

65 Manley, in reply to tributes paid him at a dinner held in his honour by the Bar Association of Jamaica. *Gleaner*, 15 August 1955, p. 11.

1 *FIRST TIME UP*

1 McFarlane interview. Manley did, however, present two papers to the Neo-Hellenist Society of which he was a member.

2 *Rex* v. *Samuels*. *Gleaner*, 26 September 1922, p. 6.

3 McFarlane interview.

4 Ibid.

5 For information on Leslie Clerk, see Rachel Manley, *The Diaries*, pp. 150–51.

6 From information kindly shared by Anna Maria Hendriks.

7 The dialogue between Manley and Clerk is based on information in McFarlane's interview.

8 Simon lectured to the Jamaica Law Debating Society at Wolmer's Boys' School on 19 September 1922. See *Gleaner*, 21 September 1922, p. 3.

9 Manley, Unfinished Autobiography.

10 *Smith* v. *Motor Car and Supplies*. *Gleaner*, 21 November 1922, p. 5. See also Stephens, *Supreme Court Decisions*, p. 416.

11 *Egerton Rickards v. Edwina McDonald. Gleaner*, 4, 5 December 1922, pp. 3
     and 6 respectively. See also Stephens, pp. 110–13.

2 A LITIGIOUS CHARMER

1 *Gleaner*, 21 January 1890, p. 2.

2 Marriage Settlement. T.A.S. Manley with Margaret Ann Shearer. LNS 60, f. 61.
   Island Record Office.

3 Ibid.

4 McFarlane interview.

5 Supreme Court Wills. Samuel Smith Manley. Will Book 13, f. 471. Island
   Record Office.

6 Rowlam, A.W. to Manley, J.W.S. Conveyance of land at Porus. LNS 80, f. 247.
   Island Record Office.

7 Information in Samuel Smith Manley's will.

8 LNS 65, f. 466. 13 December 1890. The Hon. C.J. Ward to T.A.S. Manley et al.
   and to Alex. Shearer, Esq. Conveyance of Belmont, St Catherine. Island
   Record Office.

9 For information on J.T. Palache see E.V. Clarke, *Jamaica Pie* (Kingston:
   Gleaner Co. 1943).

10 See judgment of the Lords of the Judicial Committee of the Privy Council on the
   Appeal of *Thomas Albert Samuel Manley v. John Thomson Palache*, delivered
   27 July 1895. Jamaica Archives.

11 Ibid.

12 *Gleaner*, 6 July 1893, p. 2.

13 Porus Methodist Church, Manchester. Register of Baptisms 1876–1911.
   Jamaica Archives.

14 *Manley v. Burke. Gleaner*, 20, 23, 25 January 1893, p. 2 in all instances.

15 Register of Births and Deaths, Old England District, Manchester. No. 1T,
   f. 50. Island Record Office.

16 McFarlane interview.

17 25 March 1899.

18 *Gleaner*, 11 April 1899, p. 2.

19 McFarlane interview.

20 Manley, Unfinished Autobiography.

21 Ibid.

22 Ibid.

23 McFarlane interview.

24 Ibid.

3 A CHINESE CONTROVERSY

1 Correspondence with Richard Ashenheim.

2 *Falmouth Post*, 11 August 1854.

3 *Falmouth Post*, 10 November 1854.

4 *Falmouth Post*, 26 January 1855.

5 Quoted in Howard Johnson, "The Anti-Chinese Riots of 1918". (Manuscript: West Indies Collection, UWI Library, 1979).

6 Ibid.

7 Clifton Neita, ed., *Who's Who in Jamaica* (Kingston: Who's Who Jamaica Ltd, 1951).

8 *Jamaica John Bull*, 23 August 1922.

9 *Rex* v. *Chin Chung, Ah Fat and Ah Bow. Gleaner*, 11, 12 January 1923, p. 6 in both instances.

4 AN EAST INDIAN AFFAIR

1 Lakshmi and Ajai Mansingh, "Indian Heritage in Jamaica". *Jamaica Journal* 10, nos. 2, 3 and 4 (1976).

2 Dr J.L. Varma, in a letter to the editor of the *Gleaner*, 13 September 1969, p. 12.

3 *Gleaner*, 17, 18 January 1923, p. 14 in both instances.

5 A SOAP OPERA

1 The Manley Papers.

2 *Dolphy* v. *Griffin. Gleaner*, 17 March 1923, p. 3.

3 *Gleaner*, 4 May 1923, p. 6.

6 THIS LAND IS MY LAND

1 *Lin Kin Chow* v. *Jones. Gleaner*, 29 March 1923, p. 13.

2 *Gleaner*, 15 May 1923, p. 13.

3 Michael Gilbert, *The Oxford Book of Legal Anecdotes* (Oxford: Oxford University Press, 1989), p. 279.

4 *Gleaner*, 19 April 1923, p. 13 and 4 May 1923, p. 11.

5 Rachel Manley, *The Diaries*, p. 153.

7 MONEY BY MENACES

1 *Gleaner*, 19 and 21 May 1923, p. 6 in both instances.

8 OF 'PANYA JAR' AND DROP PAN

1 Wayne Brown interview.

2 *Rex* v. *Jocelyn Davis. Gleaner*, 7, 8 June 1923, p. 8 in both instances.

3 Manley, Unfinished Autobiography.

4 *Harvey* v. *Johnson. Gleaner*, 18, 19 July 1923, p. 6 in both instances.

5 *Rex* v. *McCarthy, Wellington and McFarlane. Gleaner*, 3, 4 July 1923, p. 6 in both instances.

9 MOTOR MADNESS

1 Gilbert Griffith interview. See also Griffith's letter to the *Gleaner*, 28 August 1922, p. 8.

2 In a letter to the editor, the *Gleaner*, 9 August 1922.

3 *Vassall* v. *Owen. Gleaner*, 11 October 1923, p. 13.

4 *Sharp* v. *The West India Electric Company. Gleaner*, 2, 10 March 1923, p. 3 in both instances.

5 *Gleaner*, 6, 7 March 1924, p. 5 in both instances.

6 *Gleaner*, 25 March 1924, p. 13.

10 COMPELLING EVIDENCE

1 Paul Bogle, a successful small farmer and deacon of the Native Baptist Church of Stony Gut, St Thomas, was the leader of passive resistance to oppression and injustice in this parish. He was a supporter of George William Gordon, the son of a slave woman and a Scottish planter, who by his own efforts had become a prosperous businessman and member of the Assembly. Gordon was a champion of the poor and oppressed but his outspoken criticism created powerful enemies. On 11 October 1865, Bogle led a march of aggrieved

citizens to the Morant Bay courthouse. There was a violent clash with the armed volunteer force and in the process a number of citizens, including the custos were killed. The enraged mob set fire to the courthouse. Following the riot, rumour spread of a general conspiracy. The governor declared martial law and had George William Gordon arrested. He was tried and sentenced to death for treason, though there was no evidence of his involvement in the riot. On 23 October, Gordon was hanged from the centre arch of the burnt-out courthouse. Two days later, Bogle and his chief lieutenants suffered the same fate. The reprisals against the people of St Thomas and Portland were appalling. Over 430 men and women were either shot down or executed after court martial and over 1,000 homes were destroyed.

2 During a debate on the Secondary School System in Jamaica. *Gleaner*, 29 May 1937, p. 10.

3 In a letter to his wife, 19 October 1923.

4 Manley's cousin, the Rt Excellent Sir Alexander Bustamante, and the Rt Excellent Marcus Garvey are also buried in National Heroes Park.

5 See Thomas Harvey and W. Brewin, *Jamaica in 1866: A Narrative of a Tour through the Island* (London: A.W. Bennett, 1867).

6 *Rex v. Charles and Daniel Scott. Gleaner*, 5, 6 November 1923, p. 13 in both instances.

7 Manley would later invite Burke to be a founding director of Jamaica Welfare.

8 *Gleaner*, 28 December 1923, p. 1.

11 A RUM LETTER

1 Allister MacMillan, ed., *The Red Book of the West Indies* (London: W.H. & L. Collingridge, 1922), p. 74.

2 Ibid. p. 100.

3 *Rex v. Hanson. Gleaner*, 6 November 1923, p. 6.

12 CUTTING THE COTTA

1 Manley, Diary, 29 April 1950.

2 *Headlam v. Headlam.* Gleaner, 7, 10 December 1924, pp. 19 and 13 respectively.

3 *Hunt v. Hunt. Gleaner*, 9 March 1923, p. 15.

4 Patrick Bryan, *The Jamaican People 1880–1902* (London: Macmillan Caribbean, 1991), p. 102.

5 *Stephenson* v. *Stephenson. Gleaner*, 3 October 1923, p. 14.

6 *Ellis* v. *Ellis. Gleaner*, 22, 23 January 1924, p. 3 in both instances.

13 THE BOWDEN HILL TRAGEDY
The Spalding Murder Trial, Part 1

1 *Gleaner*, 18–20 September 1924, p. 3.

2 Knutsford Park was a race track until 1959 when the site was purchased by city businessman, Abe Issa and his associates, who came up with the idea of building a 'city within a city' which they named New Kingston.

14 MESSAGE FROM THE GRAVE
The Spalding Murder Trial, Part 2

1 *Gleaner*, 31 March, 1–3 April 1925, p. 3 et seq.

2 Only eleven jurors were mentioned in the court report.

3 *Gleaner*, 18 April 1925, p. 1.

4 *Gleaner*, 25 April 1925, p. 1.

15 "RE GARVEY: I AM OF THE OPINION . . ."

1 *Gleaner*, 6 September 1922, p. 13.

2 Amy Jacques Garvey, *Philosophy and Opinions of Marcus Garvey*, (New York: Atheneum, 1974), quoted from Preface.

3 *Gleaner*, 30 May 1923, p. 1.

4 Undated Opinion. The Manley Papers.

5 *Gleaner*, 25 September 1924, p. 7.

6 *Gleaner*, 6 September 1922, p. 13.

7 Ibid.

8 *Gleaner*, 4 May 1926, p. 14.

9 Robert Hill, *The Marcus Garvey and UNIA Papers*, (Berkeley: University of California Press, 1990), Vol. 7, pp. 289, 290, 583.

10 *Gleaner*, 22 December 1927, p. 3.

11 Robert Hill, *The Marcus Garvey and UNIA Papers*, Vol. 7, p. 583.

16 MURDER BETWEEN INTIMATES
The Louise Walker Murder Trial

1 *Gleaner*, 28–30 September 1926, p. 1 et seq; 1 October 1926, p. 1.

2 Until November 1935, Jamaica had no Court of Criminal Appeal. There were appeals from Petty Sessions to a single judge of the Supreme Court and from Resident Magistrates' Courts to the Full Court, i.e. three judges of the Supreme Court, sitting as a Court of Appeal. But there was no appellate jurisdiction in respect of criminal cases tried in the Circuit Courts.

3 *Gleaner*, 5 October 1926, p. 1.

4 *Gleaner*, 6 October 1926, p. 10.

17 KSAC UNDER FIRE

1 See the *Gleaner* from 13 October to 7 November 1925.

2 *Gleaner*, 11 November 1925, p. 3.

3 *Gleaner*, 10 November 1925, p. 8.

REFERENCES

PRIMARY SOURCES

ARCHIVAL MATERIAL

The Manley Papers, Legal Notes. Jamaica Archives, Spanish Town.

Manley, Norman. Diaries. MS 2035. National Library of Jamaica.

Manley, Norman. Unfinished Autobiography. MS 1771. National Library of Jamaica.

Manley, Norman. Trial Notes. MS 1774. National Library of Jamaica.

Manley, Norman. Unpublished transcripts of tape-recorded interviews with Basil McFarlane, 1968–9.

Manley, Norman and Edna. Personal Correspondence. Jamaica Archives, Spanish Town.

Births, Marriages and Burials. Registrar General's Department, Twickenham Park.

Wills and Deeds. Island Record Office, Twickenham Park.

CORRESPONDENCE AND INTERVIEWS

Ashenheim, Richard. Correspondence with Jackie Ranston, 8 March 1996.

Blake, Hon. Vivian. OJ, QC. Interview with Jackie Ranston, 6 January 1993.

Fletcher, Hon. Douglas, OJ, CBE. Interview with Jackie Ranston, 11 December 1989.

Griffith, Mr Gilbert, Bwthyn Rhosyn, Mandeville. Interview with Jackie Ranston, August 1971.

Hendriks, Anna Maria. Telephone interviews re her cousin-in-law, Leslie Clerk, with Jackie Ranston, February 1996.

Manley, Rt Hon. Michael. Tape-recorded interviews and correspondence with Jackie Ranston, 25 August 1989–11 July 1991.

Robinson, Hon. Leacroft, OJ, QC. Interviews with Jackie Ranston throughout February 1993.

Swithenbank, Mona. Unpublished transcript of tape-recorded interview conducted by Wayne Brown, 6 June 1972.

PRINTED PRIMARY SOURCES

NEWSPAPERS

The *Gleaner* 1892–1969.

Falmouth Post 1854–5.

Jamaica John Bull 1922.

Monthly Comments by Ansell Hart, 1968.

Planters' Punch 1924, 1937–8.

GOVERNMENT REPORTS

Blue Book, Island of Jamaica 1922–26.

Handbook of Jamaica 1922–30.

Jamaica, Departmental Reports 1922–30.

LAW REPORTS

Clark, A.J. 1936. *Supreme Court of Judicature of Jamaica. Judgments 1917–1932 with a Digest of the same.* Kingston. Government Printing Office.

Jamaica Law Notes. Vol. 1. Jan–Dec. 1924. Kingston.

Jamaica Law Reports 1935. Decisions of the Supreme Court 1933. Supreme Court of Jamaica. Kingston. Government Printing Office.

Laws of Jamaica 1873–1955.

Stephens, J.E.R. 1924. *Supreme Court Decisions of Jamaica and Privy Council Decisions from 1774–1923.* London: Crown Agents for the Colonies. 2 vols.

Supreme Court. c. 1922. *Judgments of the Supreme Court on Appeals from the Resident Magistrates' Courts.* Kingston.

SECONDARY SOURCES

Abinger, Edward. 1930. *Forty Years at the Bar.* London: Hutchinson.

Allen, D. 1980. "Crime and Treatment in Jamaica", in R. Brana-Shute and G Brana-Shute, eds. *Crime and Punishment in the Caribbean.* Centre for Latin American Studies, Gainesville: University of Florida.

Barnett, R.D., and P. Wright. 1997. *The Jews of Jamaica. Tombstone Inscriptions 1663–1880.* Jerusalem: Ben-Zvi Institute.

Blake, Vivian, OJ, QC. 1986. *The Pursuit of Excellence*. Norman Manley Memorial Lectures 1984 and 1986. London: The Norman Manley Memorial Lecture Committee.

Brown, Wayne. 1975. *Edna Manley, The Private Years: 1900–1938*. London: André Deutsch.

Bryan, Patrick. 1991. *The Jamaican People 1880–1902. Race, Class and Social Control*. London: Macmillan Caribbean.

Chevannes, Barry. 1989. "Drop Pan and Folk Consciousness". *Jamaica Journal* 22, no. 2 (May)

Clarke, Colin G. 1975. *Kingston, Jamaica: Urban Development and Social Change 1692–1962*. Berkeley: University of California Press.

Clarke, E.V. 1943. *Jamaica Pie*. Kingston: Gleaner Co.

Eisner, Gisela. 1961. *Jamaica, 1830–1930: A Study in Economic Growth*. Manchester: Manchester University Press.

Garvey, Amy Jacques, ed. 1974. *Philosophy and Opinions of Marcus Garvey*. New York: Atheneum.

Gilbert, M. 1989. *The Oxford Book of Legal Anecdotes*. Oxford: Oxford University Press.

Grant, Michael. 1975. *Cicero – Murder Trials*. London: Penguin Books.

Hall, Stuart. 1984. *Through the Passage of Time*. Norman Manley Memorial Lectures 1984 and 1986. London: The Norman Manley Memorial Lecture Committee.

Harvey, T., and W. Brewin. 1867. *Jamaica in 1866: A Narrative of a Tour through the Island*. London: A.W. Bennett.

Heuman, Gad. 1994. *The Killing Time. The Morant Bay Rebellion in Jamaica*. London: Macmillan Caribbean.

Hill, Robert. 1990. *The Marcus Garvey and UNIA Papers*. 7 vols. Berkeley: University of California Press.

Hill Stephen, ed. 1925. *Who's Who in Jamaica 1921–24*. Kingston: Gleaner Co.

Jamaica Journal 20, no. 3 (August–October 1987). Special issue to mark Marcus Garvey's centenary.

Jamaica Journal 25, no. 1 (October 1993). Special issue to mark Norman Manley's centenary.

Johnson, Howard. 1979. "The Anti-Chinese Riots of 1918". West Indies Collection. UWI Library.

Johnson, Michele. 1987. "A Century of Murder in Jamaica 1880–1980". *Jamaica Journal* 3, no. 2 (May).

MacMillan, A., ed. 1922. *The Red Book of the West Indies*. London: W.H. & L. Collingridge.

Manley, Rachel. 1996. *Drumblair – Memories of a Jamaican Childhood*. Kingston: Ian Randle Publications.

Manley, Rachel, ed. 1989. *Edna Manley – The Diaries*. Kingston: West Indies Publishing Ltd.

Mansingh, L., and A. 1976. "Indian Heritage in Jamaica". *Jamaica Journal* 10, nos. 2, 3 and 4.

Neita, Clifton, ed., 1951. *Who's Who in Jamaica*. Kingston: Who's Who Jamaica Ltd.

Neita, Clifton, ed. 1957. *Who's Who and Why in Jamaica*. Kingston: Gleaner Co.

Nettleford, R., ed. 1971. *Manley and the New Jamaica*. Kingston: Longman Caribbean.

Reid, V. 1985. *The Horses of the Morning*. Kingston: Caribbean Authors Publishing Co.

Roberts, G.D. 1964. *Law and Life*. London: W.H. Allen.

Scott, John. 1991. *Caught in Court. A Selection of Cases with Cricketing Connections*. London: André Deutsch.

Senior, Olive. 1977. *Pop Story Gi' Mi'*. Kingston: Ministry of Education.

Sherlock, Philip. 1980. *Norman Manley – A Biography*. London: Macmillan.

Simon, Lord. 1952. *Retrospect*. London: Hutchinson.

Smith, F.E. First Lord Birkenhead. 1959. *The Life of F.E. Smith by his Son*. London: Eyre and Spottiswoode.

Thomas, H.T. 1927. *The Story of a West Indian Policeman or 47 years in the Jamaica Constabulary*. Kingston: Gleaner Co.

Thoywell-Henry, L.A., ed. 1936. *Who's Who and Why 1934–5*. Kingston: Gleaner Co.

Thoywell-Henry, L.A., ed. 1946. *Who's Who and Why 1941–6*. Kingston: Gleaner Co.

Whetton, J. 1968. "A Perspective on Violence". *Jamaica Journal* 2, no. 1.

INDEX

Glasspole, Florizel, xxxiii
Gleaner: editorial on Norman Manley, xxvi, 183; and reporting of court cases, xiii
Gordon, George William, 80, 191-192
Grass yard, 27, 107
Gray, W. Baggett, 42, 177
Griffin, Thomas, 41
Griffith, H.W., 71
'Grow More Food' campaign, 16
Gunter, Godfrey G., 16, 47

Hanson, Scardeford, 92
Harvey v. Johnson, 67-69
Headlam v. Headlam, 96-99
Headlam, Evelyn, 96
Headlam, Herbert, 96
Headquarters House, 180
Henderson, Dr G.C., 72
Hill, Ken, xxxiii
Hindus: registration of marriage among, 33, 34
Hunt v. Hunt, 99-100

Immigrants: arrival of Chinese, 21, 22; in Jamaica, 33; language of in court, xxi
Innswood Estate, St Catherine, 91
Institute of Jamaica, xviii
Isaac Lin Kin Chow v. Alice Jones, 47-51

J. Wray and Nephew: sale of, 91
Jacquet, Sydney, 52-53
Jacquet v. Parish Board of Portland, 52-57
Jamaica Archives, xviii
Jamaica College, 4; Norman Manley at, 19
Jamaica Federation of Labour, 59
Jamaica Labour Party, xxxiv; on Federation, 187
Jamaica Law Debating Society: Manley's address to, 51-52
Jamaica Welfare Ltd.: Manley and formation of, xxxiv
Judah, Douglas: on Norman Manley, xxix-xxxi
Judges: Norman Manley and, xxx; selection of High Court, xxii
Jury Law: amendment of, xxxi
Jury system: Manley and, xxxii
Jones, Alice, 47
Josephs, Hector, xxvi-xxvii, 125

Kaffir pox: outbreak of, 52-53, 54
Kaffir Pox Hospital: establishment of, 53
Karsote Vaporub, xviii
King's Counsel, 185
Kingston and St Andrew Corporation (KSAC): enquiry into management of, 181-184
Knutsford Park, 104, 193

Pusey Hall Estate, 91

Queen's Counsel, 185
Queen's Hotel, 59

Radcliffe, Henry Milne, xxvi, 7, 42, 47, 177
Rajkumar, John, 34
Regardless, xxxvii
Rennie, Alfred Baillie, xxvii
Resident Magistrate's Court: land jurisdiction of, 11-12
Rex v. Cargill, 76-78
Rex v. Charles and Daniel Scott, 80-89
Rex v. Chin Chung, Ah Fat and Ah Bow, 21, 24-32
Rex v. Davis, 65-67
Rex v. Francis, 78
Rex v. Hanson, 91-93
Rex v. McCarthy, Wellington and McFarlane, 69-70
Rex v. Samuels, 1-4
Rex v. Spalding, ix, 103-123, 125-139
Rex v. Walker, 149-180
Rickards v. McDonald, 10-12
Rickards, Egerton, 10
Riots: against Chinese, 23
Rockfort, 72
Ross, Miriam: exhumed, 125; murder of, xxv, 103
Roxburgh, 13
Rum: export of, 91

Samuels, Joseph: murder trial of, 1-4
School system, secondary: Manley on, xxxii
Scott, Charles, 80
Scott, Daniel, 80
Sharp, F. Greenwich, 74
Sharp v. West India Electric Company, 74-75
Shearer, Alexander, 14
Shearer, Ellie, 17
Shearer, Elsie, 14
Shearer, Margaret Ann: marriage of, to T.A.S. Manley, 13. See also Manley, Margaret
Sherlock, Sir Philip, xiv
Simon, Sir John: on witness examination, 6
Simpson, H.A.L., 47
Slander: Manley in case of, 47-51
Smith, George, 7
Smith, J.A.G., xxvi, 9-10, 35, 177; first encounter with Norman Manley, 9, 12; in
    Rex v. Bugler, 9
Smith v. Motor Car and Supplies, 6-9
Social change: cases as indicators of, xxxiii
Solicitors: in early 20th century Jamaica, xxvi; relationship between barristers and, xxx

Lawyer Manley: Supreme Defence
Volume Two

Jackie Ranston

How does Garvey, the layman, shape up to Manley, the lawman, when Garvey defends himself in a suit of alleged libel? The paths of the two future fellow national heroes, Norman Manley and Marcus Garvey, cross several times and the pair nearly come to blows when Manley asks Garvey to "step outside" in *Supreme Defence*, the second volume in the series devoted to the legal life of the Rt Excellent Norman Manley, QC, MM.

Featuring selected cases from 1927 to 1934 *Supreme Defence* evolves around the days of the great King Street retail stores and a series of what Manley describes as "silly Syrian quarrels". But to the Issas, Hannas and Seagas, it was "business" and each would rush to retain Manley before the other had the opportunity to do so. A not-so-silly Syrian affair was what became known as the Alexander murder trial which put Manley on top of all the barristers then practising in Jamaica. Elias and Mary Alexander lived at Weblyn on the Constant Spring Road. One night Mary filled a wash basin with water, sat on the edge of the bed and washed her husband's feet before kissing him goodnight. Two hours later Elias Alexander had two bullet holes in his neck. The police reports noted that the house had been locked by the servants from the inside and showed no signs of forced entry; nothing was touched, nothing was stolen. Mary Alexander and her brother, Mansour Wheby, were arrested and charged with murder — Manley was retained to defend them. The following year Manley was made a King's Counsel. Congratulations were quick to follow with the *Gleaner* reporting that Manley "has had to run away from cases flocking on him; he is going to have a rest and a change in the country". Only Manley knew the real reason for his self-imposed exile . . .